Lives in the Balance

LIVES IN THE BALANCE

The Cold War and American

Politics, 1945-1991

Moti Nissani

Hollowbrook Publishing / Dowser Publishing Group
Wakefield, New Hampshire / Carson City, Nevada

Cover painting: *Enemies of the Mexican People* by Juan O'Gorman.

Distribution Information: Dowser Publishing Group, P. O. Box 3603, Carson City, NV 89702. Tel.: 1-800-336-9737.

Published in 1992 by Hollowbrook Publishing and the Dowser Publishing Group.

The following granted permission to quote previously published materials: Beacon Press: *The Media Monopoly* (1987; second edition), by Ben H. Bagdikian. Cold Spring Harbor Laboratory: *Quantification of Occupational Cancer* (1981), edited by R. Peto and M. Schneiderman. Harper & Row: *Brave New World Revisited* (1959) by Aldous Huxley. Houghton Mifflin Company: *Nuclear Hostages* (1983) by Bernard O'Keefe and *Cleaning Up America* (1976) by John R. Quarles, Jr. MacMillan Publishing Company: *War and Politics* (1973) by Bernard Brodie. Random House: *Russian Roulette* (1982) by Arthur Macy Cox. Swallow Turn Music, Warner Brothers, and Jackson Browne, *Lives in the Balance* copyright © 1986 by Jackson Browne.

Library of Congress Cataloging-in-Publication Data:

Nissani, Moti, 1947-
    Lives in the Balance: The Cold War and American Politics, 1945-1991
    p.   cm.
    Includes bibliography and an index.
      ISBN 0-89341-658-4 (cloth); ISBN 0-89341-659-2 (pbk).
    1. Nuclear Warfare, 1945-1991. 2. American Politics. 3. History.
    4. Reform strategies. I. Title.

UA10.N57 1991
355.0217′ dc20   90-27114
                                CIP

Printed in the United States of America

They sell us the President the same way
They sell us our clothes and our cars.
They sell us everything from youth to religion
The same time they sell us our wars.
I want to know who the men in the shadows are;
I want to hear somebody asking them why
They can be counted on to tell us who our enemies are
But they're never the ones to fight or to die.
And there are lives in the balance;
There are people under fire;
There are children at the cannons;
And there is blood on the wire.

Jackson Browne, 1986

CONTENTS

PREFACE

History tells us that freedom cannot be taken for granted: to remain free, a democratic society must be willing and able to defend itself. History also tells us that cold wars—especially when accompanied by conflicting ideologies, huge standing armies, and feverish arms races—have an alarming tendency of erupting, sooner or later, into full-scale wars. From 1945 through 1991, these two lessons from the past confronted the West with a seemingly hopeless dilemma: if it unilaterally laid down its arms, it faced the prospect of totalitarianism; if it did not, it faced the prospect of the arms race and nuclear war. Thousands of books and articles treat one or another aspect of this historical dilemma, but no published work known to me integrates *all* its aspects into a self-contained whole. This book attempts to close this surprising gap.

Such an integrated approach is rarely encountered, and for excellent reasons. Most historians are not in a position to carry out the extensive preparatory work which this approach requires. For the most part, interdisciplinary studies are forced to rely on secondary, and sometimes unreliable and outdated, sources of information. Because they compress many facts and ideas into a single volume, they require greater concentration on the reader's part. Because they are aimed at a large audience of specialists and laymen, they must eschew technical language, thereby inviting the scorn of those who do not know the difference between clarity and fatuity.

These shortcomings are counterbalanced, in part, by the potential contributions of integrative reviews to scholarship. Reality is a web, not a collection of parallel lines. Those who fail to see the interconnections run the risk of one-dimensional vision. Thus, broad reviews hold a greater promise of bringing us closer to complex truths than the many important but one-sided studies upon which they are based.

My second justification for skipping across traditional disciplines is practical. Its essence is captured in Plato's cave fable, in which the inmates mistake shadows for the realities of the sunny world above. In some way or another, we are all tethered in a cave of political illiteracy. To begin seeing the light, we must question some of our most fundamental assumptions. We must then dig up facts in thousands of informative, but limited, articles and books. We must also, as we go along, transform the myriad of new images into one coherent whole. But life is short; even those who already question basic political premises are not often in a position to sift through and assemble the pieces of the political jigsaw puzzle. Somehow, they must grope for a realistic world view on the basis of partial and fragmentary evidence. The record of both ancient and modern democracies is unequivocal: all too often their citizens vote and act against their convictions and interests. Such gaps can only be closed by means of shortcuts: the information that emerges from the vast specialized literature must be integrated and convincingly presented in a single book.

My own record, I am afraid, is no exception. Twenty years ago I felt that the United States stood for democracy and justice. Had the opportunity presented itself, and much as I hated guns and regimentation, I would have gone to Vietnam. I had little patience with the people who would have us betray the cause of freedom by building fewer missiles and bombs. I have had since then the rare opportunity of researching the subject on a full-time basis for over six years, free from the obligations of teaching or making a living. Although these years of study and contemplation detracted nothing from my commitment to liberty, they forced me to drastically revise my views of Cold War America.

These years have also convinced me that the voyage into a better future must begin with a careful study of the past. The Soviet Union is no more, but others could readily take its place as Chief Enemy of the Republic. The Cold War is at a low ebb now, but the forces which created and sustained it are still commanding the dikes. If we wish to avoid another half a century of racing with Russia, Japan, or some other nation, if we wish to avoid another half a century of crimes against nature and our fellow passengers to the grave, if humanity is to realize the age-old dream of continual progress, these forces must be contained. The containment manual can only be culled from the pages of history, and, especially, from the pages of Cold War America.

A few words are in order about the general organization of this book. From 1945 through 1991, American policy makers explained the arms race in something like the following terms. We have been forced, they said, to choose between two unpleasant alternatives: a sure totalitarian takeover of the free world or life in the shadows of the arms race and nuclear war. Chapters 1-3 show that both totalitarianism and the arms race are indeed highly objectionable. Following a brief introduction to the weapons of this period (Chapter 4), the book goes on to examine the claim that the United States and its democratic allies *had* to choose between the arms race and totalitarianism (Chapters 5-8). The book does so by reviewing (5) the ideas that have allegedly guided our military policies, (6) the Soviet-American military balance, (7) the history of the Cold War, and (8) American policies in the Third World. Taken together, these four chapters show that the dilemma between the arms race and totalitarianism has been strictly imaginary. In the real world, the West could have lived in peace *and* freedom. The book then goes on to examine the causes of collective misbehavior in military affairs, environmental issues, and other areas (Chapter 9). The book concludes by sketching a simple new road into a safer, freer, more prosperous and just, future (Chapter 10).

Readers who know little about the Cold War and American politics, as well as readers who wish to closely follow the central argument of this book, may choose to read it from cover to cover. Others may prefer to view this book as a collection of essays on a wide variety of topics. For instance, historians of the Soviet-American military balance may be interested in my unconventional treatment of this issue. Likewise, environmentalists and social reformers with no interest in military affairs might still wish to look

up Chapters 2, 3, 9, and 10. Finally, the unusually broad scope of
this book allows it, on occasion, to place familiar subjects in a new
light. Specialists might therefore go quickly through well-worn
material and slow down when they come across unfamiliar reflections.

At one stage or another, this book benefited from the comments
of Jerry Bails, Peter H. Burr, Nathalie Marshall-Nadel, James B.
Michels, Christina W. O'Bryan, Alvin M. Saperstein, William A.
Schwartz, George Ziegler, and members of my immediate family.
I can only hope that this book justifies, in some small measure, the
many sacrifices that Donna, Eric, Ethan, and Helen were asked to
make on its behalf. All four have my love and heartfelt thanks.

Chapter 1

TOTALITARIANISM

It's incredible to me that after fifty years of Soviet power, paradise should be kept under lock and key.

Nikita Khrushchev[1a]

And now the forces marshalled around the concept of the group have declared a war of extermination on that preciousness, the mind of man. By disparagement, by starvation, by repressions, forced direction, and the stunning hammer-blows of conditioning, the free, roving mind is being pursued, roped, blunted, drugged. It is a sad suicidal course our species seems to have taken.

And this I believe: that the free, exploring mind of the individual human is the most valuable thing in the world. And this I would fight for: the freedom of the mind to take any direction it wishes, undirected. And this I must fight against: any idea, religion, or government which limits or destroys the individual. This is what I am and what I am about. I can understand why a system built on a pattern must try to destroy the free mind, for that is one thing which can by inspection destroy such a system. Surely I can understand this, and I hate it and I will fight against it to preserve the one thing that separates us from the uncreative beasts. If the glory can be killed, we are lost.

John Steinbeck[2]

Throughout the Cold War, the omnipresent doomsday clock stood as a reminder of the abiding peril of nuclear war. Other doomsday clocks could be visualized too. If we take the environmental situation as a whole, we can imagine a doomsday clock which has been relentlessly moving toward midnight since World War II.[3] This is not the place to establish the reality and magnitude of this peril; we only need note in passing that it is in this context that one hears speculations about whether humanity shall go out with a whimper or a bang.

One can imagine yet a third doomsday clock and a third way of going out. The clock I have in mind is a totalitarian clock. The peril is not to our physical, but spiritual, existence; not of something new, but of something as old as the human species. "The atom bomb . . . is equaled by . . . the threat of totalitarian rule . . . By one, we lose life; by the other, a life that is worth living."[4]

This chapter demonstrates the existence of this third clock. It raises a few theoretical issues concerning freedom and slavery. It portrays the dark reality of life under the totalitarian yoke and, by presenting this reality almost side by side with the reality of nuclear war and the arms race (Chapters 2, 3), it attempts to show that we must never forget either one or the other.

What is Freedom?

I shall begin by proposing a practical definition of freedom. If given the chance to think this matter through, most people might concede that freedom is made up of at least six components.

Political freedom encompasses such rights as voting, running for political office, sitting on juries, or belonging to opposition political parties.

Civil liberties encompass freedom of speech, religion, and movement; freedom to leave and enter one's country and place of residence as one sees fit, to listen to any kind of music, read any book, etc. Civil liberties require the rule of law (an orderly political system which guarantees and protects these liberties) as well as adequate checks against abuses of power by governments and other organizations.

Economic freedom encompasses the right to act in the marketplace as a free agent, choose any line of employment, and start a business of one's own, with minimal interference from government, other organizations, and private parties.

When people feel alienated, oppressed, or exploited because they are not governed by members of their own nation, ethnic group, religion, or other collective, they lack *collective self-determination*. Most Tibetans residing in Tibet feel less free now than they did before China conquered their ancient homeland. In Kuwait, some women feel oppressed and exploited because their lives are largely governed by men. In 1979, to take another example, the political affairs of Estonia were largely controlled by Russians; those of Romania by Romanians and Russians; and those of Russia by Russians. Consequently, at that time, most people in these three places perceived Russians as freer than Romanians and Romanians as freer than Estonians.

Social justice encompasses: 1. Extension of the franchise of political, civil, economic, and intellectual liberties to every member of society. For instance, the U.S. today is freer than it was in the past in part because it no longer sanctions slavery and indentured servitude and because it grants women the right to vote and run for political office. 2. People can suffer social injustice not only at the hands of their government, but also at the hands of their fellow citizens, and this too can detract from their personal freedom. Most of us would agree that people who suffer job discrimination or who are looked down upon because of their national origin, skin color, sex, sexual orientation, age, religion, or bad eyesight, are not as free as they could be, and therefore that one's social acceptance influences one's freedom. 3. Access to such basic necessities as food, clothing, shelter, health care, safe environment, and educational opportunities. The needless sufferings of Charles Dickens' children (and reality was worse than Dickens' sugar-coated stories), constitute flagrant violations of freedom. Parents who must prostitute their child to save their family from freezing or starving are not as free as their fellow passengers to the grave who squander a million dollars on their child's wedding. Likewise, all other things being equal, children whose physical, intellectual, and moral development has been stunted through starvation, lead pollution, or life in a crime-ridden ghetto, cannot be said to be as free as well-fed children growing up in a safe, nurturing environment.

Intellectual freedom is the least obvious component of freedom. We have no difficulty grasping that a man behind bars is not free, and only little difficulty perceiving that adverse social circumstances curb freedom, but we find it difficult to see intellectual cages. Nonetheless, these invisible cages are just as real as their physical and social counterparts.

We can sense the importance of intellectual freedom by diverting our attention from our own familiar surroundings to other cultures. Consider, as one extreme example, Native Australians before they came in contact with European culture. Though they lived in greater harmony with nature and though their society's chances of survival were higher than ours, anthropological research suggests that even the most questioning minds among them, compared to the minds of a few of their English conquerors or a few ancient Greek intellectuals, were limited by their culture. The same can be said of other cultures, and, to a certain degree, of all of us. To the extent that our behavior, feelings, store of knowledge, and worldview have been distorted by past indoctrination; to the extent that we take anything for granted merely because we imbibed it from our elders, superiors, or tradition; we are still, like our ancestors, dancing around the fire.

But although absolute intellectual freedom is not given to anyone, some individuals manage to come nearer to this ideal than others. Here we are chiefly concerned with the fact that some societies and nations place more hurdles on their members' road to intellectual freedom than others. Some societies are more inclined than others to teach their members not only how to think, but what to think; to cover up and restrict their access to "undesirable" information and ideas; or to shape their desires, thoughts, and behavior by propaganda and lies.[5]

The question "What is freedom?" has been debated for thousands of years. A few examples will suffice to show the range of opinions and some of the irreconcilable positions that have been taken by some participants in this perennial debate. Some communists attach overriding significance to social justice and consider the other five components trivial or obfuscatory. Fascists consider collective self-determination as the only important component, while proponents of cosmopolitanism think that human beings would be freer if they did away with nation states and came to think of themselves as citizens of the world. Some libertarians hold that only political, civil, and economic rights are important, and some behavioral psychologists confidently assure us that freedom itself is an illusion.

But we cannot go into all these ideologies here. We can only observe that, with the possible exception of cosmopolitanism, these ideologies tend to ignore the deep-seated aspirations of most people. We all like to believe that reality is simpler than it is; that it readily lends itself to neat, compartmentalized solutions. But reality is infinitely more complex than these singleminded ideologies allow. Once they let go of ideological cliches, most individuals perceive freedom in terms similar to the ones described above. Naturally, different people assign different weights to the six components. In practice, however, most people do accept the importance of all.

Assuming that these six components come close to telling us what freedom means in practice to most people, there remains the problem of freedom ranking—determining that a given society is as free as, freer than, or less free than another.

A good starting point is provided by the realization that utopias exist only in their creators' minds: in the real world, no nation or society is totally free or unfree. For example, there may have been little intellectual freedom in some tribal societies of the past, but their adult *male* members may have enjoyed extensive political rights (e.g., free elections of tribal chiefs), civil liberties (e.g., no prisons, speaking out without fear), economic freedom (e.g., choosing to be hunters or medicine men), social justice (e.g., equal opportunity for leadership positions, rough equality in material possessions), and collective self-determination (e.g., not being dominated by members of another ethnic group). Likewise, Americans are overall freer than Jordanians, but, as of this writing, not as free to smoke hashish.

By its very nature, then, freedom-ranking of some countries is exceedingly difficult, requiring detailed studies and involving somewhat arbitrary and subjective value judgments. In 1980, for instance, it was hard to say which was freer, Sweden or the United States; the Soviet Union or China; Guatemala or Cuba. In such cases, consensus is unlikely and even a single observer might be hard put to come up with definite conclusions. But these fine distinctions should not blind us to the fact that some nations are, overall, freer than others.

Here we are only concerned with the freedom ranking of widely divergent political systems such as Canada and Mexico; Sweden and China. In such cases, you might conclude that a given country was freer than another by studying the six components of freedom in each. Unless you are blinded by ideology, you will quickly discover that Sweden in 1980 outclassed China in all six components (including these two countries' treatment of minority groups—which falls under both collective self-determination and social justice; for instance, compare the treatment of Lapps in Sweden to that of Tibetans in China). Hence, you would probably conclude that Sweden was freer than China.

In most cases, however, a few telling signs can obviate laborious comparative research, e.g., elections where one party gets 99 percent of the votes; thousands of prisoners of conscience; persecution of small farmers, intellectuals, or ethnic minorities; mass production of busts of a living political figure; prohibition on speaking a particular language; or mass emigration.

Life in a Dictatorship

One classical example of a dictatorship is provided by Rome under the emperor Gaius Caligula.[6] Caligula assumed power in 37 A.D. (at age 25) and was assassinated in 41 A.D. Caligula took his own sister from her husband and treated her openly, and incestuously, as his wife. Later, he attended a friend's wedding and appropriated the bride to himself, disregarding both her and his friend's wishes. He killed and tortured most of his friends and relatives. He forced parents to attend the executions of their sons. He killed many of his victims slowly, with numerous slight wounds. "Strike so that a man feels he is dying," was his constant order.

"I wish the Roman people had but a single neck," he said once when his subjects annoyed him; and there is little doubt that he would have chopped this neck sooner or later, if only he could.

When short of money, he would force people to make him their heir; then, complaining that they ridiculed him by continuing to live, he would have them executed in mock trials. To save money, beasts kept for gladiator shows were sometimes fed human beings instead of cattle.

The point in recounting these misdeeds is not the monster Caligula, but the ubiquity of Caligulism on history's bloodstained pages. The only known solution to such abuses is the replacement of arbitrary power with a system of checks and balances. According to legend, such a system was first introduced more than 25 centuries ago by the Athenian Solon, a man who was in a position to assume dictatorial rule but chose, instead, to legislate democracy, greater social justice, mild redistribution of wealth, and the rule of law.

The Nature of Totalitarianism

Caligula's approach to the exercise of power was based on a rational but erroneous premise. The keys to a tyrant's survival, he unscientifically believed, were hate and fear. "Let them hate me, so they but fear me," he used to quote from a favorite poem. It did not occur to him that if he concealed his crimes and fiendishness; controlled all important facets of the nation's political, economic, social, and cultural life; placed informers among his subjects so that they would be afraid to conspire against his life; justified his brutality with lofty words, ideals, ideology, or scientific pretensions; shaped his subjects thoughts and feelings; and made them love this carefully contrived but absurd image of himself instead of hating him; that he could commit his monstrosities for decades, enjoy his victims' affections, be fondly remembered after his death, and receive kind, heartfelt eulogies from a great number of distinguished historians.

If, in addition, he himself believed what he told his subjects, if he believed that the crimes he committed supported some higher purpose (Nazism: the glory of the race; Stalinism: social justice; Skinnerism: saving American culture from overpopulation, nuclear war, and environmental destruction), then his actions and utterances would have been more consistent and carried greater conviction, thereby further improving his prospects of survival in power.

The application of these insights, or totalitarian principles, marks the difference between dictatorial and totalitarian systems. In both systems, individuals are not free and in both they are under the threat of being treated as the Romans were treated by Caligula. But, though in real life the lines of demarcation between both systems are blurry, these principles are thoroughly applied only in a totalitarian system. Rome during Caligula's reign is a classical example of pure dictatorship; China during the Cultural Revolution may be the closest our species has come to pure totalitarianism.

Iraq under Saddam Hussein provides an intermediate case between dictatorship and totalitarianism. According to one writer, "fear is the cement" that held the country together.[7a] Pervasive internal security forces, a multitude of informers, one party state, a single ideology, random executions, a single-minded ruthlessness, and unending purges further solidified the regime's foundations. A large painted figure of Hussein towered over the "entrance of every Iraqi village," often emitting "a lurid fluorescent glow."[7b] For over ten years, the regime has been embroiled in self-imposed, devastating military conflicts with Iran, some of Iraq's ethnic minorities and, more recently, an alliance of Western and Middle Eastern nations. In some cases, children of suspected dissidents were arrested and tortured; their mutilated corpses then sold back to their grieving families. Children's eyes were reportedly gauged in order to force confessions out of their adult relatives. Hussein's family and a few associates held a great deal of the country's political and economic power. In a typical episode, Hussein's uncle usurped someone's land. When the victim threatened to take the matter to court, Hussein's uncle told him: "Why waste your time? If we are in power, you will . . . only hurt yourself. If we are overthrown, you won't get one centimeter of my flesh, because there are so many people waiting to cut me up."[8]

Totalitarianism is not new. Sparta, the Aztec Empire, and the Holy Inquisition lasted centuries precisely because they adhered to many totalitarian principles. The Third Reich applied these principles with near-perfection and might have still been with us were it not for its shortsighted foreign policies.

Totalitarianism comes in two basic types, gruesome and docile. Past totalitarian states fall into the former category—harsh, heartless regimes in which the unhappy vast majority is held in check through a mixture of mind control and intimidation. Stalin's Russia, Hitler's Germany, and Mao's China practiced gruesome totalitarianism. In fictional form, Orwell's *1984* magnifies these twentieth century nightmares.

Our vision of docile totalitarianism is derived from fanciful future projections, not from actual realities. In America, two of the best known works of this genre are Aldous Huxley's *Brave New World* and B. F. Skinner's *Walden Two*. Huxley's *Brave New World*, for instance, depicts the final stage in the gradual, ongoing descent of the West into the abyss of docile totalitarianism. In sharp contrast to Orwell's *1984*, in Huxley's *Brave New World* overt coercion is rarely encountered. Instead, the rulers retain total control through a deft combination of genetics, mind control, and escape valves. Their subjects are content in their slavery. For them, life's meaning can only be found in pleasurable sensations. Their thoughts, actions, and feelings have been ably shaped and engineered by the best that the science of that future day can offer. While the puppeteer quietly pulls every string, the puppets lead lives of blissful ignorance.

The Soviet Union: 1917-1984

From 1945 to 1984, the only putative external threat to Western democracies came from the so-called communist countries, especially from the Soviet Union and China. Because conventional wisdom throughout most of this period insisted that the Soviet Union was Chief Enemy of the Republic, I shall largely confine my remarks to this particular country and period. Post-1984 Soviet developments will be taken up in a later section. Let us begin with a few generalizations.

Throughout most of its history, Russia had been a dictatorship. As in Rome under the Caesars, the level of criminality depended on the particular individual, or group of individuals, in power. At times, their actions would have made Caligula himself green with envy. At other times, their actions were relatively mild. But because Russia did not possess a system of checks, balances, and free elections, the specter of untold horrors always lurked in the background.

Under the Bolsheviks, some of the totalitarian insights mentioned earlier were superimposed on this dictatorial framework. During Stalin's long reign, especially, the system came fairly close to letter-perfect gruesome totalitarianism. Thus, power was traditionally secured not only through terror and intimidation, but also through propaganda and lies and through near-total control of the economy, media, and educational system. Crimes which secured the power and privileges of a fairly comfortable ruling class were justified in terms of a high-sounding ideology. Any genuinely critical discussion of this ideology was considered a heresy. Any mention of the obvious fact that many national policies had little to do with this ideology's stated objectives of equality, freedom, and peace, was suppressed.

The rulers were shaped and handsomely rewarded by the system they governed and there is no reason to believe that they were endowed with critical minds. Most likely, then, they did not see that Marxism was, despite its many insights and despite its justified anger at heartless exploitation, a mistaken nineteenth century political and economic theory. They saw it, rather, as solid scientific truth, much as we view the theory that the earth revolves around the sun. This firm belief lent their actions conviction and consistency they might otherwise not have possessed. Bertrand Russell saw this disturbing aspect of Soviet communism already in 1920:

> Bolshevism is not merely a political doctrine; it is also a religion, with elaborate dogmas and inspired scriptures. When Lenin wishes to prove some proposition, he does so, if possible, by quoting texts from Marx and Engels. A full-fledged Communist . . . is a man who entertains a number of elaborate and dogmatic beliefs . . . which may be true, but are not . . . capable of being known to be true with any certainty. This habit of militant certainty about objectively doubtful matters is one from which, since the Renaissance, the world has been gradually emerging, into that temper of constructive and fruitful skepticism which constitutes the scientific outlook.[9]

This habit of militant certainty, combined with effective command of every major aspect of the nation's life, contributed to this system's stability. No fundamental changes were likely unless the leaders themselves chose to relax their grip on their subjects or unless they were made to do so through foreign intervention.

Let us try to bring to life this abstract characterization of pre-1985 Soviet Union by means of a few unrelated episodes:

I. Between 1917 and 1984, the Soviet system lacked elementary freedoms. But it went to great lengths to create a facade of democracy—such things as a seemingly independent judiciary system, free elections, and autonomous republics. Many Soviet citizens sensed the truth, but felt they couldn't make the system live up to its professed ideals. Resigning themselves to the realities of absolutism and to the pretensions of democracy, they quietly went about their private lives.

Yet after decades of oppression, some people were still brave enough to stand up and say: "I've had enough. Kill me if you want, but I will no longer put up with your lies." Viktor Tomachinsky's case provides one heartrending example. One day in 1981, this 35-year-old auto mechanic and poet was seen handing invitations to a court hearing in which he planned to sue the Secret Police and the Department of the Interior. They had promised him, he charged, an emigration visa; they later reneged, causing him serious monetary losses. The following day he pressed this charge in a Moscow court, and one can well imagine the judges' amazement at his daring challenge. The judges dismissed the case on the grounds that they did not have jurisdiction over the matter, without explaining what private citizens could do to protect themselves from governmental abuses of power.

As he might have suspected, Tomachinsky's symbolic gesture cost him his life. The Secret Police (the co-defendant in the daytime proceedings) came for him that night. Two years after this nocturnal visit, his wife was told that he died of pneumonia.[10] Maybe he did, but murder at the hands of his government appears a far likelier explanation for his untimely death. It is also a matter of speculation whether he was summarily shot or whether his government thought it expedient, as did Orwell's Big Brother, to break his independent spirit first by torture.

II.   Someplace in Washington, there is something called the Arms Control and Disarmament Agency. Although it was allegedly created to promote peace, informed observers knew from the outset that it was going to do nothing of the kind. As we shall see later, things could and should be different in Western capitals. But the point I wish to make here is that, throughout the Cold War years, many Americans realized that this agency could not properly carry out its mission and that the search for peace could not be handed over to this or any other government bureaucracy. Hence the peace movement, civil disobedience, and the bouts of massive demonstrations one saw from time to time in the Western World.

The Soviet Union had an official peace bureaucracy too, which, even more than ours, received its orders from the top. And there too, despite the propaganda and absolute secrecy about military affairs, a few conscientious individuals felt that the Soviet Union ought to have an independent peace movement. In coming to that conclusion, they were probably influenced by the glowing reports in the Soviet official media concerning autonomous peace organizations in the West.

Unlike its Western counterparts, this group did not plan acts of civil disobedience, e.g., sit-ins at missile sites or transportation routes. It only intended to promote trust between the USSR and the USA.[11] Its members insisted that they were not dissidents and that their goals were identical to officially avowed goals of the Soviet government. All the same, in a functional totalitarian system any independent political group, regardless of its goals, undermines the status quo. A week after the group's formation, its members were threatened with persecution, loss of jobs, and home arrests if they failed to comply with orders to cease and desist. As an additional warning, two of the group's members were imprisoned for fifteen days.

For all these idealists knew at the time, their professional lives could be ruined by their actions. The Secret Police kept complete dossiers on every man, woman, and child, and it is practically certain that these individuals were blacklisted. For example, membership in this group might end a scientist's prospects of meaningful employment. Still worse, some of these individuals faced the danger of finding themselves entrapped in a prison, mental asylum, or forced labor camp.

Despite the threats, these idealists persisted. Now, I have heard many unkind words about Western peace activists, but I have rarely heard anyone suggest that they are insane. Not so, however, in the early 1980s' Soviet Union. There, to sacrifice your career, your future, and possibly your life for peace, some practical people might have said, you must have been crazy. And this is what the Soviet government said too. Two months after the group's formation, just before its chairman, Sergei Batovrin, was scheduled to meet a few American peace activists, he was arrested on the trumped-up charge of evading military service. Later, Batovrin was forcibly confined to a mental asylum for a month and compelled to take depressant drugs. He was released after vigorous Western protests, but the "treatment" for his courageous and peaceful nonconformism was continued on an out-patient basis.[12]

III. Some time in the late 1930s, a Communist Party conference was under way in Moscow. At the end, the usual tribute to Comrade Stalin was made, followed by the customary standing ovation. At that point, an unusual complication developed. The presiding secretary was new at the job, replacing a man who had just been Gulagized. The secretary dared not stop clapping and thereby appear insufficiently worshipful of the Great Comrade, nor could his subordinates dare be the first to stop. The big shots on the podium, and the rank and file in the hall, kept clapping their hands vigorously with make-believe enthusiasm. Only after *eleven minutes* did one man on the podium stop, and only then, in an instant, did everyone else stop too.[13]

This act of courage, fatigue, or common sense led to the customary nocturnal visit. We may surmise that a confession was wrung out of him on an unrelated charge by prolonged physical and psychological torture, that he was sent to a concentration camp in the frozen North, and that there he was treated worse than most slaves had been treated in the U.S.—beaten, humiliated, worked to exhaustion, and slowly starved to death. (The lot of this particular man might have been less or more fortunate than the one I imagined here, but this would have been a typical treatment.)

Mikhail Gorbachev, the Soviet Union's last president, may have survived a similar incident as a young student and Communist Party activist. According to one report,

> An acid test of the young student's basic human decency was posed by the infamous Doctors' Plot of 1953, when Stalin ordered several Jewish doctors in the Kremlin arrested on bogus charges of poisoning the leadership. . . . There was a Jewish student in Gorbachev's study group, Vladimir Lieberman, a brilliant orator and highly decorated war veteran. An ugly confrontation took place in a lecture room before Gorbachev's whole class. One student tried to implicate Lieberman in the Doctors' Plot, and spewed forth garbage meant to cast doubt on him. Lieberman himself rose to make an eloquent defense: "Should I, as the only Jew among you, take on the entire responsibility for all Jews?" Everyone fell silent. Gorbachev, eyes blazing, jumped to his feet, and for once he allowed his anger to surface. "You're a spineless beast!" he shouted at Lieberman's accuser. These were times of terror and suspicion everywhere. Just one denunciation was enough not only to be expelled but to earn a one-way ticket to a labor camp.[14]

IV. Although Tomachinsky, Batovrin, and the clapping-weary official were courting trouble, their tragedies still show the level of sheepishness to which the average Soviet citizen had to sink in order to thrive or even survive. Moreover, it is worth keeping in mind that most of Stalin's victims were no more defiant than their fellows. Many were picked because someone coveted their spouses, jobs, or apartments and pressed secret charges against them on fabricated grounds. A joke about Stalin's mustache, a casual praise for America's highways, a hazardous escape of a decorated soldier from a Nazi prison camp, or the misfortune of being a namesake (to say nothing of being a relation) of an Enemy of the Fatherland,[15a] invited death, torture, or the chilling horrors of Gulag. At times, arrests were made simply because someone needed to fill a predetermined quota (just as slave traders were not interested in establishing guilt, but in filling their ships).

The following quotation, taken from a 1988 issue of a Soviet journal, suggests that miscarriage of justice was commonplace in the Soviet Union, even in cases with no political overtones:

For fourteen years in a row, the same man was murdering young women. . . . Every year the number of victims grew. During that time, fourteen innocent people were convicted in eleven separate court cases. By the time the real guilty party was caught, one of the convicted had already served ten years in prison; another, after eight years of confinement, had gone completely blind and was released as "not posing any danger;" a third, given the death sentence, had lost his life; and a fourth had tried to take his own life but was pulled alive from the noose. . . . It turned out that those who tried to defend themselves during the inquiry were beaten. They slammed the head of one against a safe; they struck another in the face with his own shoe. A third they beat with a copy of the Criminal Code . . . They turned one adolescent witness upside down and shook him "to shake the nonsense out of him."[16]

V. Some apologists for the pre-1985 Soviet system justified its ruthlessness on the grounds that it was the only way to feed, clothe, and shelter everyone. Just give Marxism-Leninism time, they said, and you would see what it would do. Once material prosperity had been achieved, the apologists assured us, the rulers would relax their grip. Some people believe that affluence purchased at such a price—death for a fraction of the population, horrible slavery for another fraction, regimented life for the rest—is not worth it.[17] But let us, at this point, try to evaluate the regime by its own standards of excellence: economic achievements, improved material living conditions, and social justice.

It must be conceded that significant improvements have been made. According to one 1982 CIA study,[18] from 1950 to 1980, material living standards tripled, while the overall rate of economic growth was comparable to growth rates in Western democracies. In the same period, significant progress had been made towards a more equal distribution of income, wealth, and privilege. By the early 1980s, the average citizen ate twice as much meat as did his counterpart twenty years earlier, more than the average Norwegian, Israeli, or Italian.[19] By 1984, the average Soviet ate more and better than his predecessors, worked less (41 hours a week), was assured gainful employment, earned more money, and consumed more goods. Yet, despite this record, it can still be said that, in comparison to the achievements of mixed economies like Sweden's and Canada's, Soviet communism largely reneged on this promise of material prosperity (and on Khrushchev's more extravagant brag that Soviets would soon become more prosperous than Americans).[20] In particular, by 1984, after a lifetime of regimentation and misery, Soviet citizens still fared worse economically than the people of any advanced industrial democracy on earth.

American workers were 2.5 times more productive, and American citizens three times more affluent, than their Soviet counterparts.[21] Most residents of Soviet cities lived in tight (the average urban dweller had one hundred or so sq. ft. of living space), shabbily constructed apartments, but even this was considered a luxury. According to the official press,[22a] some 20 percent of city residents in the Russian Republic lived in communal apartments. That is, two out of every ten families shared one apartment, with the parents and children of each family occupying a single room and all members of both families sharing small kitchen and bathroom facilities. A Russian acquaintance of mine now residing in the U.S. described the hardships such a situation created for him. After a messy divorce, he says, husband, wife, and mother-in-law had to go on living together because none could find another residence.[23]

Luxury consumer goods such as cars were beyond the reach of most people. Even more essential goods were inferior in quality or unobtainable. In the early 1980s, only 65 percent owned refrigerators,[24a] by which Soviets meant a cooling unit only one-third the volume of its American equivalent and lacking a freezer compartment.[20] For every hundred people, the U.S. had approximately 76 telephones, Finland 62, South Korea 19, and the Soviet Union 11.[24b]

Many consumer goods were in short supply. The shabby service had to be experienced to be believed. For example, a typical Soviet woman spent on average two hours waiting in shopping lines every day of her adult life (besides the time everyone had to spend waiting in line at the bank, bus station, airport, government ministries, and elsewhere).[20] In 1983, some Soviet provinces suffered from a chronic eyeglass shortage. In one province, thousands were on a waiting list for months.[22b] Humor captures the absurdity of the system better than dry descriptions: "What will happen to the

Sahara if it is taken over by the Soviet Union?" went one Russian joke. "It will run out of sand."

By 1990, the Western media were openly informing their readers that "the Soviet Union is an utterly backward nation, lagging far behind the West in virtually every facet of life while squandering its rich natural resources and poisoning its environment."[25] Per capita income in the Soviet Union was one-tenth that of Northern Europe. One out of five families has been on a waiting list for an apartment for more than ten years. Many regions were on the verge of ecological breakdown. Most basic consumer goods were still in short supply.

VI. The Soviet agricultural program entailed collectivization and the deliberate massacre, Gulagization, and starvation of millions of peasants. Although the mass terror disappeared by the mid-1950s, although Soviet people did not depend on food imports for their survival[19] (before the early 1990s' partial breakdown of the Soviet economic system), Soviet agriculture remained grossly inefficient. The inefficiencies stand out enough when Soviet agriculture is compared to agriculture in countries like Argentina (which were often not free but which gave their people, even during dictatorial phases, greater economic freedom). When the early 1980s' Soviet and Western systems are compared, the differences are striking. About 25 percent of the Soviet workforce was on the farm (and only 3 percent of the American,[24c]) yet Soviet yields were smaller. One likely reason for this comparative backwardness was clear long before the communists came to power. A nineteenth century writer observed: "Give a man the secure possession of a bleak rock, and he will turn it into a garden; give him a nine years lease of a garden, and he will convert it into a desert."[26]

Apologists for Soviet regimentation used to scoff at this view, explaining the scandal of Soviet agriculture by denying this scandal's existence[27a] or by arguing that there was something peculiar about the Soviet Union; for instance, its soil and climate were just not good enough. Such explanations were silenced by another statistic. Grudgingly, the regime let some people farm small private plots on a part-time basis, mostly by hand. In 1973, these private plots occupied less than 1.1 percent of the nation's agricultural lands, but produced 27 percent of the total value of farm output,[20] with private plots yielding about eight times as much as comparable collective fields.[28]

It follows that the pre-1985 Soviet Union might have solved its agricultural problems by restoring individual ownership of land or by introducing other political and agrarian reforms[29] (a program under way in 1992). For decades, though, the totalitarians at the top were comfortable, well-fed, and conservative. After all, they might have felt, you give those *muzhiks* a centimeter, they may want a kilometer.

Ivan Khudenko did not propose private ownership of land. His approach was more along the lines of an Israeli kibbutz (ironically, an institution which is itself Marxist-inspired): a small group of people farming cooperatively by sharing labor, machinery, and profits. In 1972, he was given some men, unused marginal farm-land, and machinery to test his ideas. The experiment succeeded and labor productivity on Khudenko's farm was *twenty* times higher than on neighboring farms. Shortly after, an order was received from high-up to close down Khudenko's cooperative and not pay his co-workers anything for a whole year's work.

Khudenko sued the government for back pay for himself and his workers. Through some slip of the authorities, or through the exemplary courage of the judges, he won. He then took the court order to the bank to collect the money, where the Secret Police finally caught up with him. He was charged with an attempt to take state funds under false pretenses, and this time the judges were good team players. The death penalty was naturally considered. Eventually the judges decided, in view of his family situation and other mitigating personal circumstances, that a six-year jail sentence would be sufficient punishment for his crime. Two years later Ivan Khudenko died in jail.[30]

By the late 1980s, even though the centralized bureaucracy was under siege from reformers at the Kremlin and on the farm, its tentacles were still paralyzing the nation. Although its labyrinthine intricacies were being explored by the Soviet press itself, and although productivity was no longer a life-threatening crime, the stagnation persisted. For instance, an enterprising peasant rented an island from a government-run farm. By 1987, he turned it into a profitable cattle farm. Predictably, the farm was closed down.[15b] By late 1990, the impasse between the bureaucracy and reformers contributed to peacetime food rationing in the Soviet Union.

VII. I remember reading, when I was about eight years old, an entertaining Soviet short story. The plot, which takes place some time after the October Revolution, describes an episode in the lives of a working couple. Both are former peasants now residing in a city. By the time we meet them, the husband is literate. An anti-illiteracy campaign is afoot, and the wife is strongly encouraged by the Party (through her husband) to learn to read and write. She staunchly refuses until she discovers a letter in her husband's coat, apparently from a woman. She then becomes obsessed with the idea that her husband is cheating on her. Too embarrassed to show this letter to anyone, she resolves to learn to read so that she can decipher this mysterious letter herself. Her husband gives her daily lessons, and in a few months she reads the letter. To her disappointment (or relief, I can't remember which), she finds out that it was merely an official letter from a female Party education commissar—a letter which accompanied the reading primer.

Years later it dawned on me that this story was not mere literature, but propaganda written by an exceptionally gifted "engineer of the human soul." Clearly, in this story and in thousands like it, the Party pledged a better future in which, among other things, workers would be literate and well-educated. Did the party keep this pledge by 1984, 67 years after the Revolution?

Some quantitative progress was made. Under the czars only 25 percent of the people were literate; by 1984, most people were. By 1987, more than 70 percent of the Soviet population over ten years of age completed secondary education and 12 percent completed college.[31a] The overall quality, however, was substandard. Conformity, blind patriotism, and hero worship were fostered from an early age. Critical thinking and creativity were stifled. A 1950 textbook for a Soviet teachers' college defined "initiative" as the "search for the best way to fulfill an order."[32] And so, with few exceptions (such as music and mathematics where creativity was not perceived as a threat to the regime, dissident literature which deliberately aimed at undermining the regime, and sporadic achievements in other areas) the Soviet cultural output was unimpressive. This low quality was especially conspicuous in the sciences, in part because the scientific method involves a critical search for the truth, a search which is inherently incompatible with dogmatism and authoritarianism. A clear conflict existed between the national interest in first-rate culture and science and the rulers' interests in stifling them. And here too, the rulers had the last word.

VIII. Their system, the Soviets used to claim, promoted freedom, truth, equality, justice, peace, and prosperity. It abided by the rules of good and scientific living laid down by the all-wise Lenin and the almost-as-wise Marx, and therefore it was, by definition, the best system on earth. So, while they admitted that they still had a long way to go, they publicly subscribed to the observationally absurd notion that they were the front runners. Hence, falsities and pretenses permeated the entire system.

Some 2,300 years ago, the Athenian Agathon said that "one thing is denied even to God: To make what has been done undone again."[33] Although familiar with dictatorships and Spartan totalitarianism, poor Agathon would be hard put to imagine the practice of molding the past. Yet, Soviet history books often omitted key events and figures which contradicted the conventional dogma prevailing at the time they went to press. Occasionally, such histories went as far as creating new facts to fit the old theories (instead of—as might be expected in a disinterested academic discipline— creating new theories to fit the old facts).

Some time after the execution of Lavrenti Beria (Chief of the Secret Police), subscribers to the *Great Soviet Encyclopedia* received an essay on "the Bering Sea," along with instructions to cut out the entry "Beria, L." and replace it with the new, perfectly fitting, article.[34]

A powerful tool in the Soviets' brand of creative history was omission—inconvenient events simply never happened. By 1984, most Soviets were still unaware of the massive American aid their country received during World War II. Similarly, Stalin's fellow revolutionaries were not only murdered, they were also purged from, or diabolized in, the nation's collective memory.

IX. The confrontation between Galileo and the Roman Catholic Church has been much talked about. The Church, you will recall, claimed that the sun goes around the earth, citing some passages from the Scriptures in favor of its position. Galileo claimed the reverse, citing observations and common sense in favor of his position. As a result, Galileo was tried, threatened with torture, publicly humiliated, placed under house arrest, and prohibited from publishing his books. In the opinion of some historians, this incident contributed to the centuries-long decline of Italian science. Lesser known but more extreme incidents occurred countless times in Soviet history. One state ideology supposedly provided the rulers with justification for their power. Therefore, novels, poetry, music, physics—every branch of the arts, humanities, and sciences —had to conform to this ideology first, and only then to petty bourgeois ideals like truth and beauty.

Genetics was among the victims. Some passages in the Marxist-Leninist "scriptures" implied that acquired characteristics could be inherited. They implied, for instance, that the body building efforts of parents could improve the physique of their future children. Geneticists claimed that they could not, citing observations and common sense in favor of their position. This unintentional heresy led to the denunciation, persecution, torture, or death of many geneticists. The "science" of Marxism, not the science of genetics, was applied to Soviet agriculture (genetics played a key role in improving agricultural productivity in this century), with the predictable, highly disastrous, consequences. Some geneticists were rehabilitated later and steps were taken to put genetics on its feet again. Yet even by 1992, Russian genetics—like Italian science—has not fully recovered.

Empirical sociologists were particularly apt to challenge the state ideology. For instance, they might find that blue-collar workers were alienated from their jobs, or that Soviet society was divided into distinct classes—theoretically impossible findings according to the Marxist-Leninist gospel. Stalin, who was a fairly consistent fellow, banned empirical sociology. In 1968, the Institute for Applied Social Research was set up in Moscow. Some sociologists then proceeded to assemble some facts about Soviet society (including a few theoretically impossible facts). This prompted the rulers to set up an "investigating committee," to force the Institute's director into early retirement, and to fire about one-third of the staff. The changed policy of the Institute, according to its new director, was this: "Sociology is a Party science. . . . The Marxist sociologist . . . cannot pose as an 'impartial research-er.'"[20a] In other words, at that time, in that Institute, objectivity and the scientific method were to be servants to the state religion.

A similar logic applied to creative artists. Here is an older (1958) excerpt, taken from the newspaper of the writers' union:

> What sort of reason can anybody have in our socialist conditions to pine for "freedom of creativity?" . . . The reason can only be sought in philistine individualism, a mortal sickness distinguish-able from the plague perhaps only in that outbreaks of it still occur. Anybody who feels himself restricted by his part in the common cause should look deep in his own heart: he will prob-ably find a wretched individualist lurking there.[31b]

X. Perhaps more sinister than the attack on truth was the indi-rect attack on empirical rules of evidence, on reason, and on lan-guage. This attack was based on the ingenious insight that human beings too confused to observe, reason, and communicate clearly tend to be subservient subjects. Such individuals find it hard not only to realize that history is being rewritten in front of their eyes, but that past events are immutable. They believe that yesterday's friends are today's foes, and disbelieve evidence showing that their real enemies are the people who so ruthlessly manipulate them.

If Marx had any goal, it was the elimination of injustice and inequality. But Stalin and his Party faithfuls (the pigs in Orwell's *Animal Farm*) had absolute power, and there was nothing, and no one, to prevent them from being a bit more equal than others. How to resolve then the conflict between the creation of a new privileged class with Marx's ideal of a classless society? Nothing is simpler. You need only decree that "equalization in the sphere of require-ments . . . is a piece of reactionary petty bourgeois absurdity."[20b]

Marxism was forcibly imposed on Czechoslovakia in 1948. Twenty years later, the Czech communist government set about establishing communism with a human face. After the typical war of nerves and intimidation, the Soviets brutally crushed the Prague Spring. A typical Czech newspaper article, written fifteen years after the invasion (and only six years before the collapse of Eastern

European communism), described the invasion as "internationalist assistance that the fraternal countries gave to the people of the Czechoslovak Socialist Republic in August 1968." It was consistent with "the fundamental interests of the working people of the Czechoslovak Socialist Republic . . . and of the international working class as well." The attempt to establish communism with a human face resulted in part from "serious errors of a subjective sort, such as the inconsistent observance of Leninist norms of intra-party life, unjustified self-confidence, unrealistic assessment of the potential for further development, and attempts to accelerate that development in an artificial manner. . . . Underestimating the importance of . . . ideological and political upbringing work, replacing it with administrative interference, and ignoring the working people's critical remarks, demands, needs, and experience were also serious mistakes." The Czech Communist party in 1968 was "politically heterogeneous, divided, indecisive, and simply weak and incapable of repelling the frontal attack of right-wing internal and reactionary external forces."[22c]

Totalitarian Foreign Policies

Soviet Foreign Policies: 1917-1984

The historical record strongly suggests that Soviet communists had, for the most part, continued the expansionist foreign policies of their tsarist predecessors, and that they were willing to resort to ruthless methods to further their objectives. At the same time, and despite occasional lapses, by and large their foreign policies showed a considerable degree of restraint and rationality. In particular, the desire to avoid the cataclysmic consequences of nuclear war played a key role in shaping Soviet international behavior.

The ruthless and expansionist elements are evident from a great number of historical episodes, including treacherous Soviet conduct during the Spanish Civil War,[35] the reported sacrifice in 1945 of one million soldiers in order to reach Berlin before the Western armies,[36a] breaking a written obligation to evacuate northern Iran and only doing so under strong American threat to use force,[37] Stalin's approval of the invasion which precipitated the Korean

War,[1b] occasional threats to use nuclear weapons (regardless of true Soviet capabilities and intentions at the time such threats were made, prospective victims such as the United Kingdom could not take them calmly), the reckless gamble to assure Cuban independence and redress America's meaningful nuclear superiority by placing nuclear missiles in Cuba,[1c] the brutal crushing of the Prague Spring, the hardships these so-called communists imposed on independent trade unions in Poland, and the Afghanistan War. A typical occurrence—the Russo-Finnish Winter War—gives the flavor of pre-1985 Soviet foreign policies as a whole.

In their 1939 non-aggression pact, the Nazis and Soviets secretly agreed that Eastern Poland, Finland, and the three then-independent Baltic States (Estonia, Latvia, and Lithuania) should come under the Soviet Union's "sphere of influence." The Soviets proceeded to invade and occupy Eastern Poland and, by threatening the Baltic states with a similar fate, were able to annex all three without the direct use of force.

Stalin faced a more difficult situation in Finland. This small country was closer to the Russian heartland, so a fascist rise to power in Finland, or a German takeover, would have posed a genuine security risk for the Soviet Union. Long before the October Revolution, Finland (like the three Baltic states) was part of the Russian Empire. Perhaps the Soviets felt that they had some legitimate claims over Finland and that this was an opportune time to bring her back into the fold. The people of Finland were freer than the people of the other four nations which the Nazis conceded to the Soviets' sphere of influence. The Finns were more likely therefore to fight for their national independence and greater individual freedoms and to exert a higher price for their subjugation. Thus, war could weaken the Soviet Union and tarnish its reputation. Moreover, the Soviets had no territorial or other claims against Finland. In fact, a non-aggression pact between the two nations was to remain in force until 1945.

In late 1939, the Soviet Union tried to coerce Finland into making territorial concessions. Finland accepted some key Soviet demands but rejected others. Trusting their overwhelming advantage, the Soviets failed to foresee the critical role this confrontation with their diminutive neighbor was to play in their history (especially by leading Hitler to believe that it would only take "one powerful blow" to topple the clay-footed Soviet giant[38]). According to Khrushchev, if the Finns "didn't yield to our ultimatum, we would take military action. . . . All we had to do was raise our voice a little bit and the Finns would obey. If that didn't work, we could fire one shot and the Finns would put up their hands in surrender. . . . None of us thought there would be a war."[1d]

When the Finns didn't obey, the Soviets alleged an attack by Finland (they did not have to search far in history to learn this trick; four months earlier Poland had "invaded" Germany). Finland suggested arbitration. The Soviets indignantly refused. Three days later they attacked Finland on a massive scale. Finland decided to fight back.

Obviously, this wasn't an even match. The Soviets outnumbered the Finns at the outset four to one in troops, eight to one in airplanes, and 36 to 1 in tanks. The Soviets also had a much larger population and resources. During the Winter War, the Finns received considerable material support from Sweden, moral support from the entire world (with the exception of most Nazis and communists), and little else. Yet they withstood the Soviet Goliath successfully throughout that cold winter. By March of 1940, the Finns had to agree to a dictated peace. The Soviets, for their part, had more pressing concerns. The Winter War had already cost them one million soldiers,[1d] and they must have assumed that through peace they would be able to accomplish what so far they failed to attain through war—turning free Finland into the Finnish Democratic Republic.

As if Finland had not suffered enough—almost 1.8 percent of its people dead or wounded, 11 percent refugees, some 11 percent of its territory lost—the Soviet Union started blackmailing her again shortly after the signing of the March 1940 peace treaty. This time Russia tried to dictate Finland's foreign and domestic policies, and it demanded reparations for the war Finland "started." Finland was negotiating a defensive alliance with Sweden and Norway, but all three were browbeaten by the Soviets and prevented from concluding it. This psychological warfare and the fear of approaching doom probably contributed to Finland's subsequent decision to join the Nazi invasion of the Soviet Union, a decision which alienated Finland's erstwhile democratic supporters, cost numerous lives, and justifiably weakened her postwar position.[39]

By war's end, Finland managed to retain her political and economic institutions. It continued to be a free and prosperous country, albeit with the obvious problem of its big neighbor still breathing down its neck. The threat of Soviet aggression always lurked in the background, though it receded with time. The Finnish press, for example, could not be openly critical of the USSR, Finland could not conduct a truly independent foreign policy, and virtually all her military preparedness plans were aimed at deterring, and if need be, bitterly fighting, any overt Soviet aggression. Perhaps we can sum up this delicate David and Goliath duet by saying that, from 1945 to 1989 Finland was not as free as Switzerland, but that it was incomparably freer than Cuba, South Korea, or El Salvador.

By late 1989, the Soviet Union formally recognized Finnish neutrality and declared that it had no moral or political right to interfere in the affairs of Finland or Eastern European nations.[40a]

Before leaving the subject of pre-1985 Soviet foreign policies, we need to review three commonly held misconceptions.

The first tends to merge Soviet desires with madness. The Soviets, so this popular misconception goes, were willing to take any risk, including the risk of nuclear war, to achieve their objectives.

To be sure, given their expansionist record and imperial history, a turbulent past replete with invasions and occupations of their homeland, the added security afforded by buffer states between their homeland and potential enemies, the propaganda value of external threats in fostering internal cohesion, and the rise of Russia's political and military status in the international pecking order thanks to its centuries-long policies of foreign conquest, Pre-Gorbachev Soviet foreign policies could hardly be characterized as humanitarian or as showing much concern for other peoples' aspirations for national independence. By the same token, with few possible exceptions, these policies were not reckless. Like others, the Soviets would have liked, if they could, to rule the world. But as long as they couldn't do so without undue risks to themselves, they were evidently willing to reconcile themselves to the status quo and to adopt policies that were likely to secure what they had and to maximize the chances that, history willing, in the long run they would have more.

In my opinion, this view—that Soviet foreign policies until 1985 were expansionist in intention but restrained in execution—offers the most plausible interpretation of the historical record:

> After Stalin's death . . . the Soviet Union became committed . . . to the prevention of nuclear war. Moreover, the Soviets believe that any major military clash with the United States will tempt the enemy to use nuclear weapons. They also feel that it would be almost impossible to contain a limited nuclear war. Therefore, in Soviet thinking, it is important to avoid a direct military confrontation with the United States at almost any price. . . . Hence, the thrust of Soviet foreign policy can be best expressed as neither war nor peace. It is a formula that still stresses the security of the homeland and its empire as the uppermost priority of foreign and military policy. The leaders are still committed to the expansion of influence and power, and to a global definition of what they consider legitimate interests. At the same time, they are determined to prevent a nuclear war for any reason whatsoever, and to avoid dangerous confrontations with the United States."[41]

A second misconception confused Soviet intentions and Soviet capabilities. Like other nations, Russia wished to increase its power and, if possible, achieve world hegemony. In the 1950s, this might not have seemed an utterly absurd hope. But by 1984 the internal contradictions and inefficiencies (a sample of which has been described in this chapter) that afflicted the system put such dreams squarely in the realm of the impossible. The overall East/West correlation of forces (Chapter 6) and, since the early 1960s, the diminishing international influence and stature of the Soviet state, lend strong support to this view. During this period, the Soviets suffered serious reversals in China, Indonesia, Algeria, Ghana, and Egypt. Their ideological hold over many of the world's intellectuals and workers had considerably diminished (who could conceive in 1984 of countless individuals of the caliber of George Bernard Shaw, H. G. Wells, or H. G. Muller endorsing Soviet-style socialism?) Their once near-total control of communist parties in Western Europe and elsewhere shrank or evaporated. Their misguided decision to aid a collapsing but friendly regime in Afghanistan led to a years-long quagmire, which, by 1989, culminated in withdrawal reminiscent of the French and American defeats in Vietnam. Unlike Britain, America, or any other empire, they did not derive economic gains from their vassals; in fact, their involvement in Eastern Europe, Cuba, and Vietnam constituted an economic burden. On the positive side, their domestic policies were beginning to undergo reforms which could make their nation stronger, they achieved, perhaps, practical nuclear parity with the U.S., and they gained temporary influence in Angola and Ethiopia. In 1981, a former U.S. ambassador sarcastically summed up the historical record and the fallacy of mistaking intentions with capabilities: "Expansionism indeed!"[27b]

The last misconception concerns parallels between Nazi and Soviet occupation policies. Some comparisons are instructive. Both systems were pseudo-scientific and totalitarian, both believed that the end justifies the means, both preferred collectives to individuals, and both were capable of unspeakable callousness. To a certain degree, both were afflicted with nationalistic fervor. But it takes a great deal of closed-mindedness to ignore the real and significant differences between Soviet and Nazi occupation policies.

Undoubtedly, most Czechs would have been better off if left alone, and most Poles happier, but there is positively no question that they, and Eastern Europeans in general, were far better off under the Soviets than they were under the Nazis, or, in some instances, under their own fascist governments. Also, even though the realities for most ethnic minorities were often bleaker than the official disavowal of racism might suggest, they were incomparably better than they were under Nazi occupation. By 1984, the Soviet practice of obtaining slave labor from occupied countries had long ceased. Eastern Europeans enjoyed a greater degree of autonomy and self-rule. The situation was even more striking in the economic sphere:

> The Soviet imperial system . . . does not . . . imply economic exploitation . . . In the immediate postwar years the East European economies *were* effectively subordinated to that of the

USSR, but . . . the situation has now changed and Soviet subsidies to Eastern Europe may have amounted to $87 billion for the period 1960-80. . . . Uncommonly among historical empires, the USSR as the dominating power generally lags behind its East European dependencies in standard of living, economic development and educational levels. Yet the Soviet Union heavily subsidizes Eastern Europe.[42a]

Similarly, the USSR's financial commitments in the early 1980s' to Cuba, Vietnam, Mongolia, Kampuchea, and Laos were substantial and represented "a considerable drain" on an economy which was "already badly strained in several key areas."[42b] Other analysts believe that these subsidies only posed a marginal difficulty for the Soviet Union.[43] But regardless of the details, there is a consensus on the key point: from 1974 until Soviet satellites were set free, the relations between the Soviet Union and its satellites were devoid of economic exploitation.

Needless to say, this last point is not only strikingly divergent from Nazi policies, but from the policies of most Western democracies. Before German unification, East Germany provided the clearest illustration of these Soviet policies. According to one source, East Germany's per capita gross national product was comparable to that of Britain, while its industrial accident rate was about one-third that of the Western average. Most workers had approximately five weeks of paid holidays. In general, though material living standards of East Germans were far lower than those of West Germans, they were considerably higher than those of Soviet citizens. For example, practically every East German household owned a refrigerator, but only two out of three Soviet households owned one.[28]

China and Tibet, 1950-1991

Some people believe that ruthlessness and expansionism are temporary features of totalitarianism. Past Soviet foreign policies, they say, sprang from legitimate security needs, especially the Soviets' determination to prevent, once and for all, future invasions of their homeland. Although this view cannot be readily dismissed (because it deals with motives, not with observable actions), I believe that expansionism and ruthlessness are not incidental features of totalitarianism. Theoretical considerations which lead me to this belief will be reviewed later. Here I should like to lend this belief empirical support by briefly considering two other case histories of totalitarian foreign policies. I shall take up contemporary China first, then move on to ancient Sparta.

In 1950, a year after the communists had assumed power in China, they invaded Tibet, their smaller and weaker neighbor. Since then, Tibet has ceased to exist as an independent nation. This was a flagrant violation of Tibet's rights for self-determination. However, with an international order governed by anarchy and brute force and with a backward theocracy ruling Tibet, it may be unfair to blame China for trying to build an empire of her own, improve her national security, or modernize and improve the lot of the Tibetan people. So I shall confine my remarks to Chinese occupation policies after organized and armed resistance to the invasion ceased.

Once they took charge, the communists ironfistedly imposed a Maoist brand of totalitarian hell on the deeply religious Tibetans. A few dry statistics speak for themselves.

"In Tibet, 100,000 political prisoners toil in Chinese labor camps . . . more than 50 anti-Chinese uprisings have flared in 25 years. A half-million Chinese occupation troops—one soldier for every 12 Tibetans—keep order. . . . [By November 1983], at least 35 leading dissidents were executed in public, 3500 more were arrested."[44] In 1959, nine years after the Chinese takeover, a nationwide uprising was followed by an escape to India of some 100,000 refugees, including Tibet's political and spiritual leader, the Dalai Lama. The Chinese occupation led to "an estimated one million Tibetans dead from imprisonment and starvation. Tibet's 6254 monasteries . . . [are] gutted and in ruins; the Tibetan people themselves vehemently anti-Chinese." "A flood of Chinese immigrants has moved into Tibet, taken the best land for destructive, collectivized agriculture, decimated the already scarce forests, and wantonly slaughtered Tibet's once abundant wildlife."[45] As usual, the mass killings can be gleaned from population statistics, which "reveal a disproportionate dearth of males in Tibet."[46] The Dalai Lama summed up the situation: "The Chinese claimed that they came to Tibet to 'liberate' us from the past and modernize the country. In fact they have brought the greatest suffering to our nation in its 2100 years of history."[44]

Sparta and the City States of Ancient Greece

Although the Spartan state contained some democratic and oligarchic elements, it can be best characterized as totalitarian. It depended, for example, on a much-dreaded secret police. Except on official business, Spartans were forbidden to travel abroad and foreigners were prevented from traveling in Sparta.

Some historians believe that Sparta's foreign policies were not fundamentally expansionist. According to this view, her imperialistic ambitions, if they existed at all, were satisfied by subjecting, or bringing under her influence, her immediate neighbors. Other historians believe that when Sparta was the foremost military power in Greece (following her victory in the Peloponnesian War), she did harbor imperialistic designs against other Greek city states. According to this view, she failed to carry them through because of her parochial, incompetent, arrogant, and cynical foreign policies.

The scanty record is clearer on the question of heartlessness: Spartan foreign policies were extremely ruthless, even by Grecian standards. In foreign states in whose internal politics the Spartans had a say, Sparta "took care that they should be governed by oligarchies in the exclusive interest of Sparta."[47] These oligarchies, which were hated by the majority of the people in the states where they had been set up, were often supported by Spartan garrisons. Two incontestable examples are the bloodthirsty oligarchies the Spartans established and propped up in Athens in 404 B.C. and in Thebes in 382 B.C.

The Soviet Union, 1985-1991: End of an Era

For almost seven years, the USSR has experienced radical political, cultural, social, and economic transformations. By December 25, 1991, this revolutionary period culminated in the formal resignation of Mikhail Gorbachev (this quiet revolution's chief architect), the dissolution of the Soviet Union itself, and its partial metamorphosis into the Commonwealth of Independent States.

Early in this twilight period, moves were made to foster a genuinely pluralistic society. Meaningful steps towards economic democracy were taken. Committed reformers attained power in free elections. Pluralism, checks, and balances were no longer dirty words in the Soviet political vocabulary. Soviet newspapers were gradually becoming not only readable, but actually entertaining and informative. Bukharin, Kamenev, and Zinovev had been legally rehabilitated. Intellectually honest attempts to study Khrushchev's influence on Soviet history were published in the official press. *Novi Mir* serialized Pasternak's *Doctor Zhivago*. By 1989, excavations of mass graves were afoot. *Gulag Archipelago* was recommended reading in high school. A new history text put "the total number of deaths in the repression at about 40 million."[40b] The most popular Soviet magazine published an article by an American peace activist which was highly critical of *both* the United States and the Soviet Union. "The Soviets," concluded a 1989 *Komsomolskaya Pravda* article, "must share some of the blame for the Cold War." Soviet troops left Afghanistan, even though the Kremlin must have realized that this fierce neighbor of theirs might consequently retreat to inquisitional feudalism and vehement anti-Russianism.

In the foreign policy domain, a new theory and practice were upheld which were, according to one Western analyst, "profoundly different" from those of the Cold War.[31c] From 1985 through 1991 the Kremlin preached, and gave every evidence of practicing, what it called *new political thinking*. This policy constituted a sharp break from the Soviet past. The theory itself is not new. Humanitarians have been fighting for something like it since the dawn of history; ecologists for decades. No major world power, however, has ever before practiced this creed for as long as seven days (let alone seven years).

According to this new thinking, we are all residents of a global village. There is one world or none. There is much more which unites the world's people than that which sets them apart. No nation is an island; all nations are increasingly dependent upon each other.[31d]

The nations of the world today resemble a pack of mountaineers

tied together by climbing rope. They can either climb on together to the mountain peak or fall together into an abyss. This
new political outlook calls for the recognition of one simple
axiom: security is indivisible. It is either equal security for all,
or none at all.[48]

To survive the nuclear arms race, environmental decline, and
economic chaos, global interests must be placed above the interests
of nations and classes. Since all the world's nations are interdependent, and since successful solutions to the world's ills require
cooperation, the old international pecking order, might is right, and
parochial interests must be given up.[31e] This is not to say that
serious conflicts among nations and classes are about to vanish,
only that the overriding reality of interdependence mandates subor-
dinating them to global concerns and peaceful resolutions.

This *new political thinking* called for massive reductions in
military spending, and for using the savings to improve human
needs. On the nuclear question, it advocated abolition as a long
term goal. Recognizing realities, it espoused mutual interim reductions, leaving each nuclear weapons state with just enough weapons
to deter nuclear blackmail or attack. This new political thinking
proposed international cooperation to combat terrorism and a peaceful resolution of regional conflicts. Unlike some propaganda of
earlier years, the Russians gave every appearance of willingness to
let this new way of thinking guide their actions. From 1985 to
1991, they accepted, for instance, disarmament proposals which
were, by conventional wisdom (but not by the new thinking) grossly skewed against them. They recognized Finnish neutrality.
They permitted the re-unification of Germany, a decision which
could turn the German military machine into the single most powerful conventional power in the Eurasian continent (even after proposed sizable reductions in Germany's 600,000 strong armed
forces). Countless other examples could be cited, all showing that,
at least for a few years, the new thinking *was* the beacon of Russian
international policy.

The significance of these developments has been hotly disputed.
Some observers believed that if reformers in Russia and in the
newly formed Commonwealth of Independent States as a whole are

not forced to retreat or retire, if the West comes around to giving these reformers the help they so richly deserve, if the Republic of Russia, at least, survives as a single political unit, these developments could prove to be one important legacy of this century to the next.

Others took a more skeptical view. They rightly insisted that by the beginning of 1992 Russia was still authoritarian. They pointed to the unpredictability of Russian domestic policies and to the move by late 1990 towards greater regimentation. They argued that economic turmoil in the newly formed Commonwealth of Independent States will force the leaders to restore tyranny. Russian reformers, in their view, were not driven by democratic impulses, but by patriotism and international competition. If they succeed, Russia would simply enter the 21st century as a smaller, but far more cohesive and assertive, rival. Others, these critics went on to say, tried to democratize Russia and failed. Why then should current reformers succeed? For a time, Russian autocrats would wait in the wings. Somewhere along the line, they would re-emerge as the dominant political force in Russian politics, as they did following Khrushchev's famous thaw, and as they almost did in 1991. Authoritarianism is too well-entrenched in Russian culture. Millions still worship Stalin. What, these skeptics went on to say, could you expect from survivors of Stalinist purges and self-proclaimed Leninists? How can anyone believe followers of that sickly intolerant Lenin, whose real goal, in Trotski's words, was not the dictatorship of, but over, the proletariat? How can anyone deal with former disciples of a man whose thoroughgoing authoritarianism caused so much anguish in his day, whose shortsightedness and arrogance set in motion the Stalinist steamroller, and whose bust still haunts the Russian landscape like the plague?

In view of recent Russian actions, skepticism about the Russians' sincerity rings hollow. Given the presence of hardliners in the Kremlin, what else, one wonders, could Russian reformers do to convince their Western enemies?

But the controversy about the future of democracy in Russia and other members of the Commonwealth of Independent States is grounded in reality. So far, openness has been purchased at a very heavy price. When Gorbachev came to power in March of 1985, he inherited a stable—albeit stagnant—regime. When he resigned, the Commonwealth of Independent States was in deep crisis. The economy and living standards were in decline, anarchy and apathy were threatening the very foundations of the political and economic order, crime was on the rise, and the average citizen was openly disillusioned and restive.[49,50]

At this writing, therefore, I would place greater odds on the future of a one-mile tightrope walker than on the future of Russian democracy. No one can say where Russia, the Ukraine, and their sister republics will be 25 years from now. There is an outside chance that Russia might become reasonably free, and perhaps even, in view of its socialist heritage, its clear recognition of the importance of economic justice, its adoption of a genuinely enlightened foreign policy outlook, the outpouring of creativity which might follow in the wake of centuries-long suppression, and its cultural diversity, that it might develop into a freer, more livable and peaceful place than many Western democracies are today. Alternatively, it could revert to Stalinism or it could end up someplace between these two extremes. The emergence of bellicose nationalism could be imagined too. In view of the tailspinning economy, the deepening ethnic strifes, the challenge which ongoing reforms pose to powerful groups in Russian society, the speed and unprecedented nature of these reforms, the sacrifices they require from the Russian people, the pathetic failure of many powerful Russian reformers to understand the realities of Western politics, and the West's disinclination to help these reformers in what could be in any event a hopelessly difficult task, no one can be sure what the future, in this case, will bring.

Fortunately, this uncertainty has little bearing on the central argument of this book, whose chief concern is Western, not Russian, freedom and politics. Though my indictment of Western military policies would be more convincing under the premise of lasting Russian democratization, its chief conclusions stand even if the reformers fail. For this reason, I shall concede this point to mainstream historians of the Cold War, and assume, throughout most of this book, that from 1985 through 1991 Russia posed as great a threat to Western security and independence as it did throughout the preceding 40 years. In particular, to make the flow of my narrative a bit less meandrous, I shall largely ignore the excitement, chaos, anxiety, and hope that characterize the later period and assume that both periods were fundamentally alike.

The Myth of Authoritarian Efficiency

To those of us who love freedom, authoritarianism's moral inferiority to democracy is self-evident. We find it much harder to explain authoritarianism's greater inefficiency and heartlessness. Why, you may have asked yourself, is there less social justice under dictatorial and totalitarian rule than under freedom? Why are the sciences and humanities so typically backward in any totalitarian society that ever existed? Why is the standard of living and the economy in general so far behind those of free nations? Why are dictatorial and totalitarian foreign policies more outwardly ruthless?

Some people assert that authoritarian societies are, in fact, more efficient and just than democracies. But this is a myth because freedom is not only more humane, but also by far more efficient. This incontestable observation has been amply documented above, and will be further documented later in this book. At this point, I shall accept this observation as true and try to explain it.

Fortunately, we need not go far in our search, for the explanation is *freedom* itself: *properly working* democracies are more just and, at the same time, more efficient, because they are freer.

Why, for example, is there greater distributive justice in a properly working democracy than in a typical dictatorial state?[51] First, thanks to their freer communications media, educational system, and other information resources, citizens of a democracy are more aware than their authoritarian counterparts of the extent to which poverty and economic inequality exist among them. Second, even if both knew what was going on, the former are freer to do something about inequality through protests or elections of more responsive candidates. In a democracy, then, there is a built-in self-correcting mechanism against injustice, a mechanism which is absent in a totalitarian state. Obviously, even in the most advanced contemporary democracies this mechanism is often subverted. But as long as a measure of free access to information and open elections exists, this mechanism can only be subverted in part. Conversely, an authoritarian ruler may introduce greater equality and social justice, but this does not stem from inherent qualities of the system itself. It stems, rather, from a rare combination of qualities (including foresight, generosity, and the political skill to override the inevitable opposition to just reforms) in a single ruler.

Whence the mediocre quality of totalitarian science? There is an inherent contradiction between the type of human being the system wishes to create and the type of human being needed for the creation of good science. To attain political stability, a totalitarian system inculcates dogmas, conformity, meekness, and subordination; to achieve excellence, a scientist must be open-minded, innovative, and mettlesome. To be sure, some individuals can uncritically accept social and political dogmas while retaining flexibility in their own field of specialization, so there is some first-rate science in such totalitarian countries as Stalinist Russia. But these isolated islands of excellence in an otherwise barren intellectual seascape can be best viewed as a tribute to the human spirit—which can sometimes prevail under the most adverse circumstances—and not as a tribute to a rigid social system.[36b]

Whence the persistent follies of totalitarian societies? In part, wisdom depends on a system's willingness to acknowledge, and learn from, mistakes, not on inflexible adherence to divine authority. Most policy makers find it hard to acknowledge mistakes and abandon failing policies (see Chapter 9). In totalitarian societies, policy makers can suppress evidence that they made a mistake and shoot anyone who somehow finds out the truth and who proceeds to recommend the needed changes, so unwise policies are likely to persist unchallenged far longer than necessary. In contrast, in functional democracies the truth comes out more readily and it leads to criticism and debate. If elected leaders commit many errors or if they rigidly adhere to failing policies, they and their policies may well be voted out of office. We see here again democracy's built-in corrective mechanism which assures wiser, more efficient, and more just policies.[52]

Why do dictatorial occupations tend to be more blatantly ruthless than democratic ones? Or why, to take a related question, do some democracies show greater responsibility towards nature?

How can one account for the garish ecological conditions in some ex-Soviet and East European regions?   If transparent atrocities against foreigners or the environment are committed, the public is more likely to learn about them in democratic than in totalitarian states and is in a better position to bring these atrocities to an end. So, regardless of their personal wishes, politicians in properly working democracies are going to think harder than their totalitarian counterparts before taking actions which may violate public sentiments about fair play, public health, nature, or the national interest.

We could go on answering such questions, but enough has been said to drive home the point that claims of comparative authoritarian efficiency and justice are a myth. This conclusion is not meant to encourage complacency. As we shall see later, the West must remain on its guard and it must still emerge from the plutodemocratic quagmire. Nor is this conclusion meant to imply that individual Westerners were somehow better than Russians, Chinese, Iraqis, or Indonesians, for they were decidedly not. This conclusion is only meant to support the belief that our political traditions are superior to theirs, and that the remedy to our ills cannot be found in universal slavery, as some people suggest, but in greater freedom.

For many years I took the myth of authoritarian efficiency seriously. I was always revolted by any form of slavery, but was troubled by the insistence of some otherwise intelligent people that totalitarianism is more efficient; that it can win wars and therefore that freedom in the end will be lost; that it can tackle humankind's most pressing problems better and therefore that freedom ought to give way to slavery. Disconfirming evidence kept flying in my face, but the myth itself still troubled me because of an unresolved theoretical difficulty: in totalitarian systems things are often worked out in advance, through a master plan, and by a single central planning authority. In contrast, in existing democracies there is less direction from the center, things are often arranged at the last possible moment, individuals go their separate ways, and there is no single planning authority. A totalitarian system, in short, appears as a beehive or as soldiers marching to a single drum; democracy appears as a colony of penguins or as a multitude of shoppers in a middle eastern market.

Beehives and parades look more efficient than penguin colonies and middle eastern markets. By the same token, it seems more sensible to determine in advance the number and types of cars a nation needs and then produce them according to a single master plan, instead of letting seemingly blind market forces determine the outcome. It appears that way, I think, because we cannot help drawing an analogy between individual decisions and social policies. For an individual, centralized planning often makes sense. Why then shouldn't the same logic apply to societies too?

New social policies differ in principle from individual decisions. Because social policies involve complex systems, they lead to many unintended consequences. Because they involve actors who are capable of foolish and selfish actions, their formulation and implementation are often flawed. Human societies, in other words, are fundamentally different from bee colonies. Bees act largely by instincts; human societies select policies which often must be revised through a process of trial and error. As a rule, bees act in ways which promote the colony's well being; people sometime act in ways which benefit them and harm society. Hence, practical efficiencies of human societies are strongly influenced by these societies' abilities to learn from their mistakes, curb socially harmful individual actions, and promote beneficial ones. As we have just seen, such abilities are more readily found in democracies than in authoritarian systems.[53]

Summary

Individual freedom is comprised of political freedom, civil liberties, economic freedom, collective self-determination, social justice, and intellectual freedom. Individuals in freer political entities enjoy greater freedom than individuals in less free entities. Caligula's Rome provides one example of the arbitrariness and injustice of life in a dictatorship. Totalitarian societies often retain the repulsive features of dictatorships, but add to them a far greater degree of control over the political, economic, educational, and informational system, and thus, over the hearts, minds, and bodies of the citizenry. They range between two extremes—gruesome and docile. From 1917 to 1984, Soviet totalitarianism was often characterized by terror, intimidation, repression, ruthlessness, economic inefficiency, technological backwardness, big and small lies, enforced orthodoxy, dogmatism, and indoctrination. Soviet foreign policies often manifested expansionist and ruthless elements, as evidenced, for instance, in the 1939/40 Russo-Finnish Winter War. Throughout the Cold War, these untoward elements were tempered by Soviet rationality, eagerness to avert nuclear war, domestic weaknesses, foreign policy setbacks, a modicum of moral accountability, and the economic costs of empire—unlike Western powers, the Soviet Union was unable or unwilling to derive economic gains from its dependencies. Chinese and Spartan foreign policies further suggest a close link between totalitarianism and ruthlessness abroad.

From 1985 through 1991, Russia and, to some extent, other former Soviet Republics, have been undergoing a stepwise revolution. Bolshevism had been partially replaced with "new political thinking"—an ideology which underscored the importance of international cooperation in averting environmental decline, nuclear war, human suffering, and economic chaos; since the world's nations are dependent upon each other for prosperity and even survival, their common humanity should take precedence over parochial and national interests. Throughout this period, Russian actions were consistent with this new way of thinking—so much so that no analyst had been able to predict from one year to the next the extent of democratization, openness, dissolution of empire, and disavowal of the use of force within and outside Soviet borders. By the close of 1991, the fortunes of Russian society, of the new Commonwealth of Independent States as a whole, of openness, and of democracy remained uncertain.

The belief that authoritarian governments are more efficient than democracies is observably mistaken. Properly working democracies not only tend to enjoy superiority in the moral sphere, but also in the economic, military, scientific, and cultural spheres. Only checks and balances, unrestricted dissemination and exchange of information, a free marketplace of ideas, and popular elections can control selfish abuses of power and safeguard the crucial process of learning from past mistakes. Given the ethical repugnance and practical inferiority of dictatorial and totalitarian systems, the desire to curb, avert, or roll them back can be justified on both moral and utilitarian grounds.

Chapter 2

CONSEQUENCES OF
NUCLEAR WAR

Oh, cease! must hate and death return?
Cease! must men kill and die?
Cease! drain not to its dregs the urn
 Of bitter prophecy.
The world is weary of the past.
Oh, might it die or rest at last!

Percy Shelley[1]

Types of Nuclear Bombs

Throughout the ages, two curious reversals of opinion took place concerning the transformation of one chemical element into another. Ancient and medieval alchemists believed they could strike it rich by finding a stone or a substance capable of transforming cheap metals into gold. But because they had failed and because their successors adopted the new atomic theory (which "proved" that such transformations were unrealizable), the alchemists' belief in the philosopher's stone came into disrepute.

But the physical impossibility of one age often becomes the everyday occurrence of another, and twentieth century atomic scientists have learned to transform some distinct chemical elements into others. Thus, the alchemists' dream came true, but with two unexpected twists. First, the end product of modern nuclear transformations is not only gold, but an astonishing variety of substances. Second, these transformations do not derive their primary social or economic significance from their end products, but from the enormous amounts of energy they produce.

There are two basic types of nuclear weapons. In an A-bomb (atomic or fission bomb), atoms of heavy elements (uranium-235 or plutonium-239) break up (fission) into lighter elements and release energy. In an H-bomb (hydrogen, fusion, or thermonuclear bomb), two isotopes of the lightest element (hydrogen) are fused into a heavier element (usually helium, the next lightest) and produce an enormous explosion.

There is a curious hierarchical relationship among the explosive components of nuclear bombs. Because fission is set in motion by conventional explosives, every A-bomb contains both fissionable materials and conventional explosives. In turn, the best available evidence to date suggests that fusion of hydrogen isotopes can be set off only at enormous temperatures (hence the name "thermonuclear bomb"). Though it might be possible in the future to produce the required temperatures through laser beams or other processes, at present they can be produced only through the explosion of a fission bomb. An H-bomb explosion, then, is a three-layered process that takes place almost at once—a conventional explosion which sets off a fission explosion, which then sets off a fusion explosion.

Several variations of these two bombs exist. In the neutron bomb the initial radiation component (see below) of the explosion is enhanced and the blast and heat components are reduced. In a more important variant, the H-bomb's core is surrounded by a shell of uranium-238. This adds, at little additional cost, considerable explosive power. The result in this case is a four-layered series of explosions: conventional, fission of uranium-235 (or of plutonium-239), fusion of two hydrogen isotopes, and fission of uranium-238.[2a,3a]

For any given weight of explosives, the yield of nuclear bombs is roughly 3.5 million times greater than the yield of conventional explosives. In the 1980s, the average American nuclear warhead weighed about 100 kg and had an equivalent yield of some 350,000,000 kg (or 350,000 metric tons) of TNT.[2b] Such enormous amounts of energy can be more conveniently expressed in thousands of metric tons of TNT (kilotons, abbreviated as kt), or in millions of tons (megatons, or Mt). For example, the average American warhead's yield was 350 kt, or 0.35 Mt.

Nuclear and conventional explosions also differ in their physical effects. Conventional bombs destroy by producing a blast. At their center, they can only reach a maximum temperature of some 5000°C and they emit no ionizing radiation.[4] Incendiary bombs destroy and kill by starting fires and by burning people alive, not through blast and ionizing radiation. While nuclear bombs produce far more destructive blasts per unit of weight than conventional bombs, they also produce devastatingly high temperatures (similar to those at the center of the sun) and radiation levels.

Effects of a Single Nuclear Explosion

The physical characteristics and effects of a single nuclear explosion are determined by many variables, including the type of bomb used, its yield, the height at which detonation occurs, weather conditions, and the type of target. Any brief description is therefore abstract and simplified. Moreover, because humankind's experience with nuclear explosions over cities has been limited, only a rough sketch of the effects of a single nuclear explosion can be drawn here.

Ultraviolet Pulse

For a person standing outdoors some distance from ground zero, the first indication that a nuclear explosion has occurred is a blinding flash of intense ultraviolet radiation.[3b] The duration of this flash depends, among other things, on the explosion's yield; in a 1 Mt detonation, this flash lasts about one-tenth of a second.[4] This flash can dazzle observers miles away (especially if they happen to look in the direction of ground zero) and temporarily blind them.[5a]

Electromagnetic Pulse (EMP)

Although this pulse is similar in character to the waves which transmit radio and television signals, it is millions of times stronger and it is of a very short duration—less than one-thousandth of a second. Wherever this pulse occurs, it can be absorbed by power lines, antennae, long wires, and other collectors, and carried to the electrical and electronic devices to which these collectors are attached. EMP can therefore lead to temporary interference in communication and power systems, and it can disable electric power supplies, telephones, telegraphs, radars, radios, computers, and other electronic devices. In the event of an all-out war, EMP could incapacitate or severely cripple a nation's military and civilian power and communication systems, thereby complicating retaliation and recovery in the affected area.

EMP's direct effects on people are negligible: only the few people who happen to hold a pipe, long wire, or similar collector at the moment of explosion could die of severe shock.[4]

The EMP of surface or low-altitude explosions (the types of explosions that could be used to destroy missile silos and level cities) affects a comparatively small area. But a few strategically placed explosions some twenty miles above the earth could blanket an entire continent and, because EMP travels with the speed of light, they could do so in an instant. Both the USA and the USSR have had many spare bombs, so it is almost certain that each would have tried to achieve this blanket effect in the event of an all-out war.

In addition to EMP, a nuclear explosion can alter atmospheric conditions and disrupt transmission of radio and radar signals.[4]

Heat

Some 35 percent of the bomb's energy is given off as heat (thermal radiation). At the moment of explosion, the bomb itself becomes as hot as the sun. Within a fraction of a second, a fireball—a luminous spherical mass of air and bomb's residues—is formed. The diameter of a 1 Mt bomb's fireball at its most luminous stage is about 1.5 miles. The diameter of a bomb one-fortieth that yield (12.5 kt, the yield of the Hiroshima bomb) is a quarter of a mile. A fireball can be seen from a great distance. A 1 Mt high-altitude explosion can be seen from as far away as 700 miles.[4] Its fireball rises fast, like a hot air balloon, grows in size, and cools off. In just one minute after the explosion, it assumes the familiar shape of a mushroom cloud,[3c] some 4.5 miles above the point at which the explosion has taken place.

The fireball's effects depend on distance, the bomb's yield, and weather conditions. Everything within the fireball, or close by, evaporates or melts. On a clear day, a direct exposure to the brief heat pulse given off by the fireball of a 1 Mt explosion can cause severe (third degree) burns as far as 5 miles away from ground zero. For a 12.5 kt explosion, the corresponding distance is some 1.3 miles.

The heat pulse given off by the fireball starts fires over a large area. Fires may also start as an indirect result of the blast. These fires increase the number of casualties. Under certain conditions—a clear, dry summer day, for example—these small fires might coalesce into larger fires, rage hours after the explosion, and burn or asphyxiate everything in their path, including human beings still alive in their homes or in underground shelters.

Blast

Some 50 percent of the bomb's energy is taken up by the blast. The blast wave travels more slowly than thermal or ionizing radiations, so a person standing in the open one mile from the site of a 12.5 kt explosion will have seen the fireball, been burned, and been exposed to initial ionizing radiation when, some two seconds after the explosion, the blast wave reaches him and he hears the explosion.

The blast lasts a few seconds. As is the case with all nuclear bombs' effects, its severity and physical characteristics depend on the bomb's yield. Its chief direct effect is overpressure, which is experienced by human beings in its path as a sudden, shattering blow immediately followed by hurricane-like winds.[6a]

As every scuba diver knows, people can withstand overpressure fairly well. The direct effects on the human body of the overpressure created by nuclear explosions are comparatively mild, including, on occasion, damaged lungs and ruptured eardrums.[4] Winds, on the other hand, can kill or injure human beings by sweeping them off their feet, tossing them about, or hurling them into solid objects. The wind of a 1 Mt air burst would kill most people in the open at a distance of 3.3 miles or less from ground zero.[7]

The combined impact of overpressure and strong winds of a 1 Mt bomb would demolish most buildings within a range of 2.5 miles from ground zero and break most windows within a range of 13 miles.[7] The collapsed buildings, uprooted trees, overturned cars, and flying objects would take a heavy toll in human lives. Some of the flying and overturned objects in this upheaval (such as ovens or wood stoves) may start fires.

Most human beings at a distance of one mile or less from ground zero of an explosion as small as the Hiroshima bomb will die from the effects of the blast alone: crushed in collapsed buildings, knocked out by flying objects, hurled by the winds, or incinerated.[6a]

Ionizing Radiation

Some 15 percent of the bomb's energy is taken up by ionizing radiation. From the psychological point of view, and from the point of view of humankind's long-term future, radiation is perhaps the most frightening direct effect of nuclear explosions. We can sense blast, heat, and fire, but we can't detect ionizing radiation (except at very high intensities when it produces a tingling sensation[4]) without the aid of special instruments; we can be irradiated to death without knowing it. Unlike fire and blast, ionizing radiation not only damages our health, but, through its potential impact on fetuses and on reproductive cells, it may damage the health of our descendants. Though the heat and the blast wreak incredible havoc, their direct effects are gone within seconds, or, in the case of the fires they cause, within hours or days. In contrast, poisonous radioactivity may linger for years.

X-rays are the most familiar type of ionizing radiation. Owing to their ability to penetrate the human body, they are widely used as a diagnostic tool. But even when used in minuscule doses (as in dental examinations), X-rays can cause slight problems by damaging, or ionizing, the chemical constituents of our bodies.

Two overlapping schemes are used to classify the ionizing radiations produced by nuclear bombs. The first, which will not be taken up here, is based on their ability to penetrate matter. The second scheme is based on their order of appearance.

Initial radiation is released within the first minute of an explosion. It accounts for about 5 percent of the bomb's energy. The initial radiation of a 12.5 kt explosion will knock unconscious people standing in the open at a distance of less than half a mile from ground zero. These people will die from radiation sickness within two days (even if they somehow managed to escape the heat and blast). People standing in the open three-quarters of a mile away will die within one month.[6b]

Given these three powerful effects—blast, heat, initial radiation—the chances of survival are slim for anyone within a one mile radius of a small nuclear explosion. With larger explosions, or with multiple detonations in one area, the lethal range is greater. Those who manage to survive all three must still deal with *radioactive fallout* (also called *residual radiation*). Fallout takes some 10 percent of the bomb's energy. Fallout is emitted by fission products such as radioactive iodine, weapon residues such as plutonium and radioactive hydrogen, and substances in the vicinity of the explosion which became radioactive as a result of exposure to the bomb's initial radiation.

Radioactive fallout is usually classified into two components, early and delayed. Early fallout reaches the ground within 24 hours of the explosion. Delayed fallout reaches the ground after 24 hours. Early fallout is also called local fallout because it tends to remain in the vicinity of the explosion site. Delayed fallout is also called global fallout because it can take months or years to come down to earth, during which time it can be carried to all corners of the globe.

Although both global and local fallout are generated by every nuclear explosion, their relative proportions depend on several conditions. For example, because rain washes down some radioactive particles, there would be more local fallout and less global fallout when an explosion is followed by a hard rain.

Another condition which needs to be mentioned is the height of the explosion. In a surface burst—an explosion occurring at or near the ground—earth and other materials are vaporized by the fireball and carried upwards with it. As the fireball expands and cools, some of these substances coalesce with some fission products into highly radioactive particles ranging in size from fine dust (resembling talcum powder) to marbles.[4] The marble-sized particles come down shortly after the explosion. The dust may come down within hours, after it has been carried by the winds as far as a few hundred miles. In contrast, if an explosion occurs at a high enough altitude so that the fireball does not touch the ground—an air burst—the radioactive particles in the rising mushroom cloud are much smaller and lighter, they tend to remain airborne for much longer periods, and they may be carried thousands of miles from ground zero before they settle.

Hundreds of unstable radioactive isotopes are released in a nuclear explosion. Their half-lives (the time it takes for half their radioactivity to decay) range from fractions of a second to thousands of years, but the overall radioactivity given off by this fiendish mixture decays rapidly. Roughly, during the first six months after the explosion, for every sevenfold increase in time, the radiation dose received is decreased by a factor of 10. Thus, after 7 hours, it is 1/10 of the dose given off by the same radioactive mixture of fallout particles at one hour; after 49 hours (approximately 2 days), 1/100; after 343 hours (14 days), 1/1,000, and after 2,401 hours (100 days), 1/10,000.

Local fallout poses more serious problems than global fallout because it is concentrated in a much smaller area and because it settles quickly, before much of its radioactivity has decayed. However, global fallout has its fair share of adverse effects too. Some radioactive substances released by a bomb, e.g., strontium-90 or plutonium, remain radioactive for many years, taking their toll on the global environment. For a single bomb, the global effect is negligible. But the effect was significant during the 1950s and early 1960s, when hundreds of nuclear bombs were exploded in the atmosphere. It may be deadly if thousands are exploded in an all-out war.

Because surface bursts cause considerable local fallout and because the radioactive particles in this fallout can be carried by winds many miles from ground zero before they come down to earth, surface bursts can cause many deaths among people who have not been directly exposed to the blast, heat, and fires. For example, if a 1 Mt bomb explodes at or near the surface in Detroit, and if the winds on that particular day blow steadily towards Cleveland, the local fallout in Cleveland, some 90 miles from ground zero, will be strong enough to kill any Clevelander who spends much time outdoors during the two weeks following the explosion. Staying indoors during that period, but not in a fallout shelter, might still cause severe radiation sickness.[5b] Assuming northwesterly winds on the day of explosion, it might take six years for radiation in Cleveland to decay to safe levels.

The medical effects of ionizing radiation depend on the dose. A strong dose (over 5,000 rads) of radiation, such as the initial radiation given off near ground zero, can knock people unconscious on the spot and kill them within a day or two. In contrast, the health of people receiving a weak dose (less than 100 rads) will be little affected in the near term (although years later they will be a bit more likely to suffer cancer, vision impairment, and other long-term effects of radiation).

Intermediate doses (100-500 rads) cause radiation sickness. The severity of this sickness and the chances of surviving it depend, among other things, on the total radiation dose accumulated (the higher the dose, the more severe the symptoms and the lower the probability of survival), and on the age of the victim (the very young and very old are especially vulnerable).

Within this intermediate range of exposure, a victim may develop a variety of symptoms, including loss of appetite, nausea, vomiting, intestinal cramps, diarrhea, apathy, fever, and headache. When the accumulated dose is on the low side of this intermediate range (100-200 rads), only a few mild symptoms are felt. They disappear within days and recovery is apparently complete. As the accumulated dose rises, more symptoms appear in more severe form. Because there is no effective cure for radiation sickness, a rough prognosis can already be made in the first two days: if you suffer from a severe case of nausea, vomiting, and diarrhea during this time, you are unlikely to survive.

After the first two days, the victim may begin to feel better, though still experiencing fatigue and lack of appetite. This apparent recovery is often deceptive, for the number of blood cells during this two-week period often falls to dangerously low levels. This results in resurgence of some of the old symptoms. New symptoms often appear as well, including internal and external bleeding, increased susceptibility to infections, and temporary hair loss (mostly from the scalp). Depending on many variables, but especially on the radiation dose, the victim may die at this stage or gradually get better.

Recovery of people exposed to radiation in this intermediate range is often incomplete. For years after the exposure, their chances of experiencing infections, cancers, cataracts, and reduced body vigor are higher than they were before the exposure. The incidence of stillbirths, deaths during the first year of life, mental retardation, malformations, and cancer among human beings exposed to intermediate radiation during their embryonic stage of development will be higher. There might also be an increased number of genetic defects among the survivors' descendants.[8]

Hiroshima

At the close of World War II, two fission bombs were dropped over the Japanese cities of Hiroshima and Nagasaki. The explosion in Hiroshima has been studied in greater detail, in part because it occurred three days earlier and caused greater destruction. The following narrative will be largely confined to Hiroshima.

There is a great deal of uncertainty regarding some effects of the Hiroshima bomb. For example, estimates of the number of dead vary by a factor of three and there is a genuine scientific controversy about the bomb's long-term genetic consequences. These doubts can be ascribed to the complexity of the subject, to its emotional impact on all its would-be dispassionate students, and to the wartime presence in Hiroshima of thousands of forced laborers from other parts of Japan and from occupied Korea[9] and the consequent difficulty of estimating the number of people who died as a result of the explosion. Disregard for individual suffering on the part of the totalitarian Japanese government of those days, and the years-long censorship imposed by the American occupation forces on research into anything connected with the explosion and its aftermath, further complicate efforts to ascertain the bomb's effects.[10a] But despite the uncertainties, the picture presented below is accurate enough to tie our earlier abstract descriptions of the bomb's separate effects into a meaningful whole.

On the clear morning of August 6, 1945, the Hiroshima bomb exploded about one-third of a mile above city center. Its approximate yield was 12.5 kt. Some 350,000 people were in Hiroshima at that time.[11a] Perhaps as many as 70,000 were instantly killed from the immediate effects of blast, heat, and initial radiation. Shortly after, many more were killed by fires. In the following months, many survivors died from radiation sickness, burns, indirect blast injuries, or from a combination of all three and of the general adverse conditions prevailing in Hiroshima at the time (including inadequate medical care, shelter, and food supplies). By year's end, five months after the explosion, some 140,000 people, or two-fifths of all city residents, were dead.

Almost all buildings within a radius of 1.3 miles from ground zero were reduced to rubble by the blast. Much of this rubble was then reduced to ashes by the huge firestorm which raged for half a day after the explosion.[11b] More than two-thirds of all buildings in the city were destroyed.

Survivors' recollections of victims and landscapes right after the explosion bring these dry statistics to life:

> There were shadowy forms of people . . . some . . . looked like walking ghosts . . . some strange thing had deprived them of their clothes . . . one thing was common to everyone I saw—complete silence.[12a]

> Hiroshima was no longer a city, but a burnt-over prairie. To the east and to the west everything was flattened. . . . How small Hiroshima was with its houses gone.[12b]

> The . . . people . . . all had skin blackened by burns. . . . They had no hair . . . and at a glance you couldn't tell whether you were looking at them from in front or in back . . . their skin . . . hung down. . . . Many . . . died along the road . . . like walking ghosts.[13a]

> I climbed Hijiyama Hill and looked down. I saw that Hiroshima had disappeared. . . . looking down and finding nothing left of Hiroshima—was so shocking that I simply can't express what I felt.[13b]

Even for those who had apparently recovered, this ordeal was not over by the end of 1945. Some survivors suffered ruptured eardrums and disfiguring scars. All survivors were at greater life-long risks of cancer and vision impairment. Individuals exposed at the prenatal stage of development were likelier to suffer mental retardation and other problems. When these and other late effects are taken into consideration, the total death toll may be about

200,000, or over one-half of all Hiroshima residents on the day the bomb went off[6c] (a lower estimate puts this figure at about one-third of city residents[4]).

Many survivors report reduced vitality and greater vulnerability to external stress, disease, and infection.[13] Although these claims describe borderline conditions which cannot be easily quantified and studied and which may be psychological in origin (and thus unrelated to radiation and other physical effects of the bomb), to the survivors these debilitating conditions seem real enough.

The experience entailed emotional and social costs. Many survivors lost family members and close friends. Some felt guilt because they lived while their loved ones perished. These feelings were often exacerbated by an inability to help sufferers, or by failure to act courageously under trying circumstances. They lived under overhanging clouds for years: Will cancer or cataract strike? Should they go ahead and have children despite the perceived genetic risks?

Forty-six years after the event, a social stigma is still attached to the bomb's survivors. Because of potential health problems, survivors suffer job discrimination. Job discrimination, social stigma, and possible genetic effects lead to reduced marriageability. These adversities created feelings of alienation, bitterness, and inadequacy:

> When . . . we interviewed the Hiroshima survivors, we found that they had no desire to speak of their experiences: those experiences, even after the lapse of twenty-six years, were still too terrible to talk about. Yet terrible as they were, we heard the victims express, time and again, the same thought: "Our agony that August day was nothing compared to the agony we have suffered in the long quarter of a century that has passed since then. If you tell our story, all we ask is that you tell the truth."[9]

Yet grim as these experiences were, they offer only a partial picture of a future nuclear war between two nuclear-weapon states. As an air burst, the Hiroshima bomb generated little local fallout. So, unlike the prospective victims of an all-out nuclear war, the people of Hiroshima were spared the devastating impact of lingering high levels of radioactivity. The explosion in Nagasaki—the only other nuclear bombing during the war—was an air burst too, so no fallout from other surface bursts drifted to Hiroshima. In contrast, in an all-out nuclear war, many areas, regardless of whether they are hit directly, will have to contend with such radioactive imports. And by today's standards, the Hiroshima bomb—with only one-thirtieth the destructive power of humanity's average warhead[14]—is comparable to a mere battlefield weapon.

We must also keep in mind the enormous number of nuclear bombs which might be used in an all-out war. Beyond a certain point, their overall impact—especially on such complex entities as the biosphere, world economy, and human societies—may be qualitatively different from a mere sum of the constituent parts (see below). Also, many bombs are more destructive than one bomb. So a town the size of Hiroshima then, or of Madison, Wisconsin today, would be hit by more than just one bomb. How many then? The following story throws some light on this question.

In 1960, President Eisenhower sent a few people to the appropriate headquarters to inquire about America's war plans. One of his messengers picked a Hiroshima-sized Soviet town. Unlike Hiroshima, nothing about this town made it stand out as an attractive military target. Yet the plans allotted it one bomb with 320 times, and three bombs each with 80 times, the explosive yield of the Hiroshima bomb.[2c]

Hiroshima survivors were also comparatively fortunate in the amount and quality of help they received. True, Japan's rulers did not rush to their aid,[10b] but help did eventually come. After an all-out war, it will be too dangerous to walk about. There will be too few people able to help and too many needing help, so most victims will receive no help at all.

Effects of a Large Nuclear Explosion

A 1979 U.S. government study examined the consequences of a 1 Mt (yield of 80 Hiroshima bombs) surface burst in downtown Detroit.[5] This is not an unusually large bomb; in an all-out Soviet-American war, Detroiters would have been extremely fortunate to get only four.

Such an explosion will create a crater 1,000 feet in diameter and 200 feet deep. This crater will be surrounded by a rim of highly radioactive soil which will have been thrown out of it by the blast. Up to 1.7 miles from ground zero, no significant structure will remain. Everyone within this area—70,000 in 1979—would have died in a flash. There will be less devastation, fewer deaths, and fewer injuries as the distance from ground zero increases. Still, miles away the damage will be considerable. The survivors in Greater Detroit and areas dozens of miles away will be faced with a serious fallout problem which, in some places, will linger for years.[5b]

Of some 4.3 million Greater Detroit residents in 1979, some 250,000 would have died, an additional 500,000 injured shortly after the explosion, and the final casualty toll would have been much higher.[5] Owing to the bomb's size, and owing especially to severe local fallout, the long-term physical and emotional effects on the survivors were likely to be more grave than they were in Hiroshima.

With a 1 Mt air burst no crater will be formed, there will be little local fallout, and some strong buildings and structures will remain standing. However, many more immediate casualties are expected (in 1979, 470,000 dead, 630,000 injured). With one of the largest bombs in the Soviet arsenal (25 Mt), a single air burst could destroy almost all houses in Detroit, kill or injure approximately three-fourths of all the people, and destroy most heavy industrial buildings and machinery.

Gigantic bombs have never been exploded over a city, so it is hard to predict their actual impact. One can get some idea, however, from a 1954 atmospheric test explosion conducted on an uninhabited, remote, Pacific island. The bomb exploded 7 feet above ground. The plan called for a 7 Mt yield, but, unexpectedly, the actual yield exceeded 15 Mt.[15] The explosion took place just before dawn and was seen by a man in a Japanese fishing vessel some 75 miles away, who, like all his shipmates, was unaware of what was going on. To him the white-yellow fireball looked like the rising sun, and he rushed downstairs to tell his mates that the "sun was rising in the west." A few hours later, fallout, in the form of white ash, started falling on the fishermen's vessel, hair, and clothes. All suffered radiation sickness. Some recovered, most partly recovered, and one or two died later as a result.[15a]

The fallout traveled to an inhabited island 120 miles away. Its 82 inhabitants were unaware of the danger and took no protective measures when the lethal clouds arrived (there wasn't much they could do, except to bath frequently and stay near the shoreline where the waves would have washed the radioactivity off). They were evacuated and treated two days after the explosion, but by then every islander had been sufficiently exposed to become ill. Starting nine years later, many islanders developed thyroid cancers, other thyroid abnormalities, and other cancers. Although official sources overlook this point, we may hazard a guess that the lives of these 82 human beings were tragically affected by these events.

It turns out, however, that these islanders were lucky to have survived at all. Had they been in one of their fishing spots at the northern tip of the island during those two days, they would have received lethal doses of radiation and died within two weeks.[15a]

Following this larger-than-expected Bikini Atoll test, nine American operators were trapped in an underground bunker. Though this bunker was located twenty miles from ground zero, protected with three-inch thick concrete walls and roof, and buried under ten feet of sand, it kept rolling back and forth when the ground shock arrived, as if it were resting on a "bowl of jelly."[15] This was followed by a radioactive hailstorm. Fortunately, these operators were evacuated early and quickly enough to escape exposure to high levels of radioactivity.

The total contaminated area was more than 350 miles long and 60 miles wide. An area of 7,000 square miles—almost the size of New Jersey—was contaminated to such an extent that, had a similar explosion taken place on land, lethal doses would have been received by all people staying in the open within this area. All people remaining indoors, but not in fallout shelters, would have fallen seriously ill.[4] In 1979, twenty-five years after the explosion, some islands in this atoll were still too radioactive to be visited.[3d]

The final word on the effects of large nuclear weapons belongs to an observer of this notorious test explosion:

I do not propose to chant a tale of horrors. I can only tell what it was like for me in 1954 in a concrete bunker twenty miles from ground zero. Draw your own twenty-mile radius. I can only tell you what happened to the Japanese fisherman seventy-five miles away and the . . . natives 125 miles away. Draw your own 125-mile radius."[15b]

Effects of a Limited Nuclear War

Limited nuclear wars have been a subject of speculation throughout the Cold War.[15] In such wars the theater of operations, or the targets, are limited. One example involves a nuclear war which leads to destruction of the entire European continent west of the Soviet border but which leaves Soviet and American territories intact; another example entails a war in which military installations are destroyed and cities are spared.

The effects of limited wars need not be described here. Limited wars always carry the grave risk of escalation, so a description of a full-scale war should suffice to convince sane people that a limited nuclear war has not been a viable strategic option. Besides, a limited war occupies an intermediate position between a single explosion and a full-scale war; its consequences can be assessed by extrapolating upwards the effects of a single explosion, given above, or by extrapolating downwards the effects of a full-scale war, given below.

Consequences of Nuclear War

Novel and complex events like nuclear wars are notoriously unpredictable, suggesting that contemporary scientific research can only portray a highly uncertain picture of a post-nuclear world. This incertitude is strikingly confirmed by the historical record. Thus, scientists in this century have repeatedly underestimated the health hazards of ionizing radiation. They became aware of serious electromagnetic pulse (EMP) effects around 1960, of nuclear risks to the ozone layer in the early 1970s, and of the potential for nuclear winter in the early 1980s (see below). Thus, the picture portrayed here is either too grave, or, more likely, not grave enough.

A depiction of war between two or more nuclear-weapon states can be conveniently divided into two parts. First, knowing what one bomb can do, we can make reasonable assumptions about the number of bombs that will be used in war and about their yields and likely targets. The rest is an exercise in extrapolation. If, for example, one average explosion over one typical city kills 100,000 people and contaminates 50 square miles, then 100 explosions over 100 cities would kill 10 million and contaminate some 5000 square miles.

The second part is more conjectural. It deals with economic, environmental, and other broad, interdependent consequences of an all-out nuclear war.

Direct Consequences

The direct effects of nuclear war can be presented as a series of projections of increasing severity.[3,5,6,11,16]

I. If only two well-armed countries (e.g., Cold War America and Russia) are involved in the gloomy encounter, and if each detonates less than 10 percent of its total nuclear arsenal over the other's largest cities, the mildest imaginable outcome is 35 million dead and 10 million seriously injured in each country, with one-half the total industrial capacity of each side destroyed.

Within 40 years of the war's end, local and global fallout may cause 1 million thyroid cancers, 300,000 other cancers, 1.5 million thyroid abnormalities, 100,000 miscarriages, and, perhaps, 300,000 genetic defects.

We have noted earlier the higher incidence of severe disfigurement, vision impairment, increased susceptibility to disease, chronic malaise, and other lifelong emotional and social problems among Hiroshima survivors. Even in the most optimistic projection of an all-out war, some 150 large cities are hit, leaving thousands of times as many immediate survivors and personal tragedies as in Hiroshima.

Even the most optimistic war projection must assume the use of surface bursts. Although surface bursts cause less immediate urban destruction than air bursts, they can best serve the presumably important strategic objectives of destroying well-protected military installations (like land-based missiles in the American Midwest) and of contaminating an opponent's homeland. In the event of a Russian/American war, the use of surface bursts would, in turn, result in contamination of an area of some 25,000 square miles (the size of West Virginia) in either country. Much of this contamination will cover lands where cities once stood. The survivors could be faced, therefore, with the unpleasant choice of living among the ruins of contaminated cities, building new cities, or waiting years, decades, or centuries for the old cities to become safe again.

II. A likelier projection still confines the war to two major nuclear-weapon states, but assumes more bombs and more targets. This projection entails the death of about 100 million people in either country, the virtual destruction of the industrial and military capacity of both, long-term radioactive contamination of 50,000 square miles, and, during the first 40 years, 5 million thyroid cancers, 13 million other cancers, 7 million thyroid abnormalities, 10 million spontaneous abortions and, possibly, several million genetic defects. In this projection, practically all surviving Russians and Americans would have suffered like Hiroshima survivors.

III. A less likely outcome can be obtained by doubling the figures in projection II. In this case, because about 90 percent of all Americans and 80 percent of all Soviets (the Soviet Union was more rural) die within one month of the fatal encounter, far fewer survivors and personal tragedies are expected.

IV. This projection assumes that half of all nuclear bombs in existence during the 1980s would have been used to destroy cities in the USA, Commonwealth of Independent States, Europe, Canada, North and South Korea, Australia, South Africa, Cuba, China, India, Pakistan, and Southeast Asia. In this extended projection, at least 1 billion people die within one month of war's end. Within 100 years, some 9 million people contract cancer, 24 million people are rendered sterile, and, possibly, 11 million children are born with genetic defects. The number of personal tragedies, and the number of square miles that are contaminated for years, are proportionately greater than in the preceding projections.

On each of the projections above we need to superimpose the possible destruction of civilian nuclear power plants and installations. Such destruction will accomplish several strategic objectives. Since conventional and nuclear electricity-producing plants are vital to industrial economies, their targeting will reduce an adversary's chances of economic recovery. Owing to thē close linkage between the civilian and military nuclear industries, bombing of civilian facilities would weaken an adversary's chances of regaining war-related nuclear capabilities. Such bombing would further reduce a nation's chances of recovery by contaminating and rendering uninhabitable huge tracts of land for decades. It follows that many nuclear power plants and installations are likely to be vaporized by surface bursts during an all-out war.

We can begin to take in the horrors of such wholesale destruction by recalling that a peacetime accident in a *single* nuclear power plant could be catastrophic.[17a] An accident in a single reprocessing facility, a breeder reactor, or a near-ground radioactive disposal site could have even more ominous implications. Thus, one accident involving a radioactive waste disposal site in the Ural Mountains reportedly caused the death of thousands[18] and required evacuation of an area of some 600 square miles.[19,20] The names of 32 towns and villages in this region have disappeared from Russian maps.[19] The region is deserted and sealed off—to inhabitants, most visitors, and a river.[21]

Radioactive materials produced in nuclear power plants decay more slowly than the by-products of nuclear bombs,[3] so the devastation of nuclear power plants would considerably increase the area which would remain unsafe for human habitation after the war. For breeder reactors, reprocessing facilities, and near-ground radioactive waste-disposal sites, the picture is even grimmer: certain portions of the Commonwealth of Independent States, the eastern half of the continental U.S., the states of Washington and California, and considerable portions of Western Europe, could be contaminated for decades. Even centuries later, it might be advisable to check radioactivity levels before buying land in these regions.

The wartime vaporization of most nuclear power facilities will increase (by about one-third) average global fallout and its long-term effects. Moreover, because radioactive materials from this source are longer-lived than materials produced by nuclear bombs, their relative contribution to the global fallout will increase over time. For instance, ten years after the war, total radioactivity in global fallout would be three times higher with such vaporization than without it.

Some people find it hard to believe that something as unpleasant as this could indeed take place, but war and politics obey their own logic. A junior Soviet officer who defected to the West tells us that, due to shortage of uranium and plutonium in the Soviet Union, "not all Soviet rockets have warheads . . . so that . . . use is being made of radioactive material which is . . . waste produced by nuclear power stations."[22] By the 1980s, at the latest, both sides had enough accurate warheads, so they may have adopted the more efficient course of spreading radioactive dust by targeting nuclear power installations. Needless to say, if rumors regarding the intentional destruction of Iraqi nuclear power facilities during the Persian Gulf War turn out to be true, they support the view that nuclear power plants will be targeted in an all-out war. It also goes without saying that in the future, nuclear states may be far less cautious than the USA and the USSR have been.

In sum, if this comes to pass, large areas of the northern hemisphere will be contaminated for years and global fallout will pose greater risks for longer periods of time. As a result of both, there will be greater loss of lives, property, and land than previously believed. Unquestionably then, and regardless of whatever else one might think about them, nuclear power plants and installations constitute a grave risk to a nation's security.

On each of the projections above we also need to superimpose the specter of "salting." Radioactive substances differ from each other in longevity and in the kind of radiation they emit. Cobalt-60, a radio-isotope of ordinary cobalt, continues to emit high levels of deadly penetrating radiation. After five years, more than half its radioactivity is still present. Cobalt-"salted" bombs will cause more deaths and suffering than ordinary bombs, and they will contaminate larger areas for longer periods of time.

The open literature does not indicate whether the bombs of any nuclear-weapons state contained cobalt or similar materials. It should not be supposed, however, that a nation would refrain from "salting" simply because some of the cobalt-60 produced by its own bombs would harm its land and people. Consider, as just one example, atmospheric tests of nuclear weapons. According to a United Nations' estimate, they may be responsible, among other things, for 150,000 premature deaths.[6d] In this case, despite the known risks to everyone (including residents and politicians of the testing countries themselves), testing continued for years and was stopped only because the Western public, not Western politicians, had enough (see Chapter 7). Historical occurrences such as this suggest that rationality and good will are not always present in international relations. Therefore, "salted" bombs might have been used in an all-out nuclear war.

Indirect Consequences

I. *Genetic Risks.* We have noted earlier that nuclear war may cause harmful mutations and other genetic defects, thereby causing millions of individual tragedies for centuries after the war. In this section I would like to draw attention to the implications of these defects to the human gene pool as a whole.

Two modern developments (which have nothing to do with nuclear war) need to be mentioned in this context. First, owing to medical advances, genetically unfit individuals are more likely to survive and reproduce now than in former ages. Second, the modern environment contains many mutation-causing substances. Both developments may gradually raise the incidence of deleterious genes in the human gene pool and thereby bring about a gradual decline in its quality. Some geneticists go as far as to prophesy a genetic twilight, in which the quality of the human gene pool erodes to the point where everyone is "an invalid, with his own special familial twists."[23]

Now, if it turns out that nuclear war increases the number of genetic defects, war might reduce the quality of the human gene pool to some unknown extent. Moreover, if the specter of genetic twilight is real (many geneticists believe that it is not), nuclear war might hasten its coming.

II. *Environmental Consequences.* In view of the complexity and interdependence of ecological systems, efforts to forecast the effects of nuclear war on particular ecosystems and on the biosphere as a whole are plagued by uncertainties and controversies.

For instance, some by-product of nuclear war—of which we are now totally ignorant—might destroy or seriously damage the biosphere's capacity to support human life. Bearing these doubts and unforeseen consequences in mind, we must turn now to the mixture of facts, inferences, and guesswork which make up this subject.

There will be fewer people and less industrial and commercial activity long after the war, hence some serious environmental threats will be ameliorated. By killing billions and destroying industrial infrastructures, nuclear war might, for instance, halt or slow down the suspected trend of global warming. On balance, however, the war's overall environmental impact will almost certainly be on the negative side.

Radioactive fallout will contaminate soils and waters. We shall probably learn to adjust to these new conditions, perhaps by shunning certain regions or by carrying radioactivity meters everywhere we go the way our ancestors carried spears. Still, this will lower the quality of human life.

Nuclear explosions might create immense quantities of dust and smoke. The dust and smoke might blanket, darken, and cool the entire planet. Although the extent of the damage is unclear,[24] it would be far more severe during the growing season—late spring and summer in the northern latitudes. One Cassandran and controversial prediction sounds a bit like the eerie twilight described in H. G. Wells' *The Time Machine*. This "nuclear winter" projection forecasts freezing summertime temperatures,[25] temporary climatic changes (e.g., violent storms, dramatic reductions in rainfall), lower efficiencies of plant photosynthesis, disruption of ecosystems and farms, loss of many species, and the death of millions of people from starvation and cold. However, even these pessimists expect a return to normal climatic conditions within a few years.[26a,27]

To appreciate the next environmental effect of nuclear war, we must say a few words about the ozone layer. Ozone is a naturally occurring substance made up of oxygen atoms. Unlike an ordinary oxygen molecule (which is comprised of two atoms and is fairly stable) an ozone molecule is comprised of three atoms and it breaks down more readily.

Most atmospheric ozone is found some 12 to 30 miles above the earth's surface (in the stratosphere). Stratospheric concentrations of ozone are minuscule, occupying less than one-fifth of one-millionth the volume of all other gases in the stratosphere. If all this ozone could be gathered somehow at sea level to form a single undiluted shield around the earth, this shield would be as wide as the typical cover of a hardcover book (one-eighth of an inch).[28] However, minuscule as its concentrations are, the ozone layer occupies a respectable place in nature's scheme of things.

Some chemicals which are produced routinely by modern industrial society may react with stratospheric ozone, break it down, and lower its levels. Such depletion may have two adverse consequences. First, stratospheric ozone selectively absorbs sunlight in certain portions of the ultraviolet and infrared spectrums, so its depletion will cause more of this radiation to reach the earth and change global temperature and rainfall patterns. Second, by absorbing more than 99 percent of the sun's ultraviolet radiation, stratospheric ozone shields life on earth from its harmful effects (some scientists feel that terrestrial life could not evolve before this protective shield took its place). Ozone depletion might allow more ultraviolet radiation to reach the earth's surface, thereby disrupting natural ecosystems, lowering agricultural productivity, suppressing the human immune system, and raising the incidence of skin cancer and cataracts.[28] Since 1985, extensive temporary reductions of the ozone layer have been observed in polar regions, but their causes (man-made or natural) and implications remain uncertain.[29] From 1981 to 1991, the ozone shield over the Northern Hemisphere has been depleted by 5 percent, thereby allowing a 10 percent increase in ultraviolet radiation on the ground.

The connection between nuclear war and the ozone layer is simple: the heat created by nuclear explosions produces huge quantities of nitrogen oxides in the surrounding air.[25] In addition, the launch of solid-fuel missiles may release huge quantities of chlorine and nitrogen compounds.[30] These, in turn, are precisely among the chemicals that could cause significant depletion of the ozone layer and lead to the two adverse consequences described above.

In the first days and weeks after the war, smoke and dust will prevent the increased ultraviolet radiation from reaching the earth's surface. But ozone levels will reach their nadir in 6 to 24 months, long after most of the smoke and dust have settled back to earth.[25,26b] Ozone levels will probably be restored to above 90 percent of former levels within five years after the war.[26b] Hence, "nuclear winter" and ozone depletions are not expected to appreciably offset each other.

Under the altered conditions created by a nuclear war, as many as 50 percent of the earth's species might become extinct,[26c] some pest populations might temporarily increase,[26d] and most natural communities might undergo radical transformations.

III. *Economic Consequences.* To see the complexity of modern industrial economies, ask yourself how self-sufficient you are, in comparison, say, to a native North American of some 500 years ago. Most likely you depend on a highly complex web for sheer physical survival, let alone travel, leisure, education, and similar luxuries. Your food, water, heating fuel, and other necessities often come from outside sources, and their continuous arrival depends on an intricate, finely tuned network. In the event of total war, this network would be blown to smithereens in minutes.

The pool of workers and skilled professionals will be reduced by death and illness to a fraction of its pre-war levels. Oil refineries, power plants, factories, food production facilities, and other industrial and commercial facilities will be destroyed. Fallout will render immediate reconstruction impossible, for the survivors in the combatant countries will have to spend the first weeks or months indoors, underground, or in shelters.

Without enough fuel to run tractors, fertilizers and pesticides to grow crops, and people to work the fields; without adequate means of shipping raw materials to farms and factories and of shipping food and industrial products to consumers; and without money or some other accepted standard of exchange; national economies may be in shambles.

Some areas may be highly contaminated. Many regions may be frozen solid during the first growing season after the war. The survivors may be physically ill or sick at heart. They may not possess the necessary strength and courage, like Job, to start all over again. Why, they may wonder, should they work like slaves to rebuild a modern society that might end again in death?

The present complex system of international trade will almost certainly vanish. International aid, including grain and food exports, might cease. Millions of people in countries which depend on food imports or specialized exports will suffer a great deal.

It is impossible to predict the long-term consequences of all this. Perhaps a modern economic system similar to our own could be re-created in 20 to 50 years, bringing much of the anguish and chaos to an end. Perhaps recovery would never take place, the world sinking instead to something like the decentralized economies of the Dark Ages.

IV. *International Consequences.* The combatant countries might never recover their international standings. They could terrorize the world for a while with whatever remained of their nuclear arsenals, but with social and economic collapse these arsenals might fall into disrepair. In the long run, moreover, a nation's international position depends on factors such as human resources, economic performance, moral fiber, and education, all of which could be irreversibly weakened after an all-out war. So one hundred years after the war, people in what was Russia may speak Chinese or Urdu. If descendants of the people who used to live there a century earlier are around, their social status may resemble that of Japanese bomb survivors. The same forecast might apply to North Americans, Japanese, or Germans, and their neighbors.

It is also possible that nation-states everywhere will collapse or, alternatively, that they will survive and that eventually major partners to the nuclear exchange will regain their international standing.

V. *Human Health.* When we look at our health from a historical perspective, one fact clearly stands out from all the rest: Westerners today are healthier than ever before. In 1900, tuberculosis alone accounted for some 11 percent of all American deaths. Now tuberculosis has practically disappeared from the American scene.[31] Other infectious, communicable, and debilitating diseases, including gastroenteritis, diphtheria, poliomyelitis, typhoid, smallpox, plague, malaria, pellagra, and scurvy, have been reduced or eliminated.

Statistics fail to convey the impact of these advances on our world outlook, society, history, or quality of life. But statistics do give us some idea of how much better our health is here and now than it was at any time in the past or than it is in many less developed countries now. In the United States, a baby born in 1987 was expected to live on average 75 years, some 28 years longer than an American baby born in 1900[32] or an African baby born in 1975.[17b] On average, Westerners today are freer from a host of debilitating diseases and their chances of realizing their biological potential are higher.

These remarkable differences between us and our ancestors, and between us and many of our less fortunate contemporaries in poor nations, are not for the most part attributable to better cures. They spring from advances in our understanding of the causes of diseases and, consequently, in our ability to combat them effectively by preventing their occurrence. Prevention strategies include such things as sanitation, widespread immunization, nutritional supplements, chlorination of drinking water, and drying or spraying swamps as part of the fight against malaria. In contrast, in past centuries people were more susceptible to disease because of poor nutrition, poor education, and inadequate shelter. No complex infrastructure for controlling epidemics existed. Owing to poor sanitation, typhoid, cholera, plague, and many other epidemics spread unabated. In the absence of antibiotics, deaths from diseases like pneumonia and syphilis were commonplace.

It follows that modern advances in health are ascribable to new knowledge and to the development of a complex infrastructure of prevention and health-care delivery. After a nuclear war the knowledge may remain. But much of the infrastructure will be destroyed, precisely at the point when it is most sorely needed by the irradiated, starved, and emotionally and physically stressed survivors. At least for a few years, survivors of warring nations might revert to the good old days of their forebears, or to the good contemporary days of their less fortunate brothers and sisters in the Third World. Epidemics of all sorts might break out. Many people who depend for survival on medical help (like diabetics and regular users of dialysis machines) will be dead in a short time.

We do not know whether it would take years, decades, or centuries to rebuild the health system, nor even whether anything like it will ever be put together again. We do, however, know that for the first few years after the war the health of most survivors will be adversely affected.

VI. *Human Populations*. The direct effects of war on human populations have already been discussed. Here I shall only superimpose the war's indirect effects on projection IV above, a projection which entailed one billion deaths in targeted countries as a result of near-term effects of nuclear bombs: blast, heat, initial radiation, and local fallout (the effects of the other three projections would be correspondingly lighter). The death toll will continue to climb for years after the war, as a consequence of widespread famine in targeted nations, famine in numerous non-targeted Third World countries whose people partly depend for survival on food or food-related imports from targeted nations, general deterioration of the health care and disease prevention system, lingering radioactivity, paucity of shelters, temporary but severe climatic changes, and the likelihood that some grief-stricken survivors will prefer death to a prolonged struggle for sheer physical survival. Several years after the war, the world's population may go down by another billion people.

The longer-term impact of total war on human populations depends in part on whether social conditions resembling our own are re-established. If not, human populations could keep declining for decades. But even if such conditions are re-created, further reductions seem likely during the first few decades because young children, infants, and fetuses are more vulnerable to the stresses of a post-nuclear world (radiation, starvation, death of parents, etc.), and so proportionately more individuals in these age brackets will die. In addition, many people may refrain for years after from having children, so the death rate is likely to be higher than the birth rate. (I have confined the discussion here to dry statistics not because they are the most interesting, but because books like this one cannot possibly convey the countless individual tragedies these numbers imply.)

It must be admitted that all this will be a nasty Malthusian solution to overpopulation and rapid population growth. Consequently, for at least half a century after the war, overpopulation and rapid population growth will no longer make appreciable contributions to such ills as environmental deterioration, species extinction, nationalism, and over-organization.

VII. *Social Consequences*. Like other cataclysmic events, nuclear war might bring about radical social alterations. It is impossible to foretell what directions these changes will take. Behavioral norms might change and human life might be held in greater or lesser esteem. Pride in our humanity, in our rationality, in our superiority over the beasts, might decline. Scientists and politicians might be lynched. Books might be burned. Laws decreeing all free inquiries punishable by death might be enacted. Machines might be outlawed or confined to museums. On the other hand, war might come to an end and enlightened humanitarianism might surge at last.

Organized social systems might be broken down and replaced by anarchies, tribal groups, or small decentralized communities. Some of these communities might be open, like ancient Athens, and some closed, like Sparta. Perhaps the most ironic possibility is the emergence of totalitarianism from the ashes of the once-free world. This might happen, for instance, if the military or police are given broad powers to handle the crisis, and if they retain and expand those powers. At any rate, freedom in this new world might have few defenders. Would anyone think democracy worth defending if it contributed to such carnage? Alternatively, authoritarian political systems might become freer.

VIII. *Extinction*? Extinction of humankind is often mentioned in this context. However, based on what we know now of the effects of nuclear war, extinction is highly improbable: under any likely set of assumptions, it seems that some of our kind will be able to pull through the hardships and survive. But because extinction cannot be completely ruled out, and because it is the worst imaginable outcome of nuclear war (actually I find it hard to imagine at all—no people walking this earth—forever), it should be rendered even more improbable by reducing the risk of nuclear war.

Reality of Nuclear Peril

At one tense moment of the Cold War, one analyst assured his readers that "because of the costs of nuclear war and the increasing possibility of satisfying almost any reasonable interest by nonviolent means, nuclear wars will not be fought."[33]   It would presumably follow from this position that the Cold War has been just a game— costly and ridiculous to be sure, but not deadly. Hence one did not need to worry about the arms race, demonstrate or engage in acts of civil disobedience against it, or lose a job or an election for opposing it.

Other analysts disagreed. No one, they said, "can estimate with any confidence the likelihood of a nuclear war. Given the historical record and the possible finality of nuclear disaster, it is simply reckless arrogance to assume that there is 'no' danger and to act accordingly."[34a]

This more pessimistic view strikes me as more nearly correct. I believe that, even now, we can be overtaken by nuclear war and that we ought to do everything we can to eliminate this specter. I find it hard to believe that anyone is willing to commit himself to the proposition that anything whatever will not happen simply because it defies reason. The record is crystal clear: in history, anything goes. I shall bypass therefore a detailed refutation of this kind but unrealistic optimism. Instead, I shall describe a few actual circumstances that could still lead to war. Taken together, these episodes establish the reality of the nuclear threat.

Nuclear war could be started deliberately.   For instance, Chinese officials may decide to do away with both Russia and the United States by firing submarine missiles at Russian cities from American territorial waters.   Terrorists may one day be able to carry out a similarly deceptive exercise with a couple of suitcase bombs.   Nuclear proliferation raises the chances that nuclear weapons will eventually fall into irresponsible hands. What might happen when a Saddam Hussein acquires a bomb? Would he not be tempted to use it in the event of imminent removal from power? Even worse, one can well imagine a collapse of the international economic system and the rise of rabid militarism in one or another major industrial power.

But it is not only dictators, terrorists, and fanatics who might deliberately launch a nuclear war. No human being is wholly predictable, and everyone—including heads of nuclear-weapon states—can acquire a couple of unwholesome obsessions. More- over, humankind's fate depends on much more than the sanity of a few politicians. For example, at any given moment throughout the 1980s, there were some 20 American missile submarines cruising quietly 200 feet under the surface of the world's oceans, each carrying enough bombs to obliterate, at the very least, 16 to 24 metropolitan areas.[34b] So, while at sea, each submarine was a small superpower. Had the captain and a few other officers in one submarine become deranged and decided to fire, we should have all been getting ready to say our last prayers.[35,36] These officers, and their thousands of American and foreign counterparts at sea, on land, and in the air, were screened carefully. So it is unlikely that anything like this would have happened. Still, someday, some-place, somebody might have had strange ideas and might have been in a position to carry them through.

Nuclear-weapon states can also be drawn into war through miscalculation and against their will. By all accounts, we came fairly close to total war during the 1962 Cuban Missile Crisis. "The smell of burning flesh was in the air," Khrushchev remarked after the crisis was over. President Kennedy probably shared Khrushchev's anxiety. The odds that the Soviets would go all the way, he felt, were "between one out of three and even."[37]

In 1962, the USA had a considerable nuclear edge over the USSR. War might have caused complete devastation of the Soviet Union and only a partial devastation of the United States. President Kennedy and his advisors were not perhaps fully aware of this disparity, but the Soviets were.[38] By the 1980s, the Soviets could conceivably obliterate the United States after a massive attack against their nuclear installations (Chapter 6). So they were less likely to "blink," "flinch," or "crawl" (the actual words of some top Kennedy advisors and of at least one highly respected American historian). As one retired politician put it, "if we go eyeball-to-eyeball again, God help us."[39] As already mentioned, of even greater concern is the distinct possibility that future nuclear adversaries might have a more care-free attitude about nuclear weapons than either the Americans or Russians.

Robert Kennedy, who was intimately involved with American decision-making during the Cuban Missile Crisis, observed that "if we had had to make a decision in twenty-four hours . . . the course that we ultimately would have taken would have been quite different and filled with far greater risks."[40a] To this we need only add that, in the next round, war cabinets might be forced to make a decision in less than 24 minutes.

Robert Kennedy's ghostwriter also noted the importance of free and open debate for reaching the right decision. "Opinion, even fact itself, can best be judged by conflict, by debate."[40b] There are excellent reasons for believing that this simple truth is rarely understood by run of the mill heads of states. To show this, we need go no farther than President Kennedy himself. According to one Western analyst, "the optimistic assumptions that underlay the [abortive Bay of Pigs] invasion were not seriously challenged by any of the President's advisers, partly because . . . all the members of the advisory group surrounding the President valued their membership to such a degree that they felt it better to suppress doubts and conform to the dominant optimism rather than raise objections."[41]

"One member of the Joint Chiefs of Staff," Robert Kennedy wrote after the crisis, "argued that we could use nuclear weapons . . . I thought . . . of the many times that I had heard the military take positions which, if wrong, had the advantage that no one would be around at the end to know."[40c] And I think now: What if a person with this kind of mentality is at the helm of a nuclear ship of state the next time around?

During the crisis, the militaries of both nations were on hair-trigger alert: any kind of false alarm or unexpected event could have precipitated an accidental war. Yet, those thirteen days had their fair share of such incidents.[42]

One incident involved the shooting down of an American U-2 reconnaissance plane over Cuba during the crisis, prompting the U.S. to consider a bomber attack on Cuban missile sites. The order to shoot the plane down was either given by a Soviet commander on the spot, or, most likely, by Castro himself,[34c] in violation of strict instructions from Moscow not to shoot at American aircraft.[43a]

At another tense moment of the crisis, a CIA-trained and directed team which had been dispatched earlier from the U.S. blew up a Cuban industrial facility and reportedly killed 400 workers.

According to the Cuban government, this terrorist act was guided by "photographs taken by spying" American planes.[44]

Another incident involved an American reconnaissance plane flying over Soviet territory. This produced, in the same day, a remarkable letter from Khrushchev to J. F. Kennedy, of which the following excerpt is telling enough: "What is this, a provocation? . . . Is it not a fact that an intruding American plane could be easily taken for a nuclear bomber, which might push us to a fateful step; and all the more so since . . . you are maintaining a continuous nuclear bomber patrol?"[40d,45]

During the crisis, the U.S. Navy forced five or six Soviet submarines to the surface in or near the quarantine zone, in at least one case through the use of a depth-charge attack. "According to an American admiral, one Soviet sub was crippled, could not submerge, and was forced to steam home on the surface. What if a Soviet sub had been sunk? Or what if a captain of a Soviet submarine, to protect the lives of his crew, had returned fire in self-defense, sinking a major American vessel and causing injuries and deaths?"[34d]

During the crisis, the Soviets captured a highly placed spy. Before being captured, this man chose to give the signal for an imminent Soviet attack; "he evidently decided to play Samson and bring the temple down on everyone else as well." Fortunately, this signal was suppressed by the courageous mid-level intelligence officers who received it. Had it not been, the "risk and danger to both sides could have been extreme, and catastrophe cannot be excluded."[34e]

Some powerful people appear capable of being moved by ordinary human emotions like compassion, loving-kindness, and a concern for humanity's future. Khrushchev, despite some serious misdeeds, belonged to this group. This is clear from the quotation above, his overall record (he was a forerunner of Gorbachev), his political autobiography, and the following, rather typical, retrospection about the Cuban Missile Crisis:

> When I asked the military advisers if they could assure me that holding fast would not result in the death of five hundred million

human beings, they looked at me as though I was out of my mind or, what was worse, a traitor . . . So I said to myself: To hell with these maniacs. If I can get the United States to assure me that it will not attempt to overthrow the Cuban government, I will remove the missiles.[43b]

We can only wonder about the outcome of a nuclear crisis in which *both* protagonists are practitioners of mainstream confrontational politics (e.g., George Bush and Saddam Hussein).

Moreover, it so happens that Kennedy's Cuban gambit is merely the best known—but by no means the only—incident in which nuclear weapons were used as instruments of coercion (see Chapter 8). Nuclear diplomacy has been employed by the world's powers on more than nineteen occasions, often in pursuit of comparatively trivial objectives. If anything like the Cold War returns, the chances of something like the Cuban Missile Crisis overtaking humanity again are far greater than most history books would have us believe.[34]

Like so many other complex evolutionary processes, nuclear arms races may be sowing the seeds of their own destruction. For example, in a future race, there is a remote chance that one day one side might develop the technical means of knocking out the other's nuclear forces in a surprise attack. This might prompt the other to adopt a "launch-on-warning" strategy of firing its missiles when a disarming first strike is presumed to have taken place. The decision to fire might be made on the basis of data received from machines (radars, satellites, computers, etc.) and interpreted by people. Both machines and people are capable of accidentally plunging the world into a nuclear nightmare.

Finally, World War III could start through sheer accident. A specialist on the subject recently concluded that "the risk associated with . . . [nuclear weapons] accidents is potentially very great."[46a] Rather than racking my brain for hypothetical examples, I shall describe a few actual near-accidents. In drawing your conclusions from these episodes, please remember that this is a partial list—a few memorable episodes taken from hundreds; we still lack information about accidents in countries such as the USSR, China, France, or Israel.[46] Recall also that the only two major nuclear accidents on record took place in the Soviet Union, not in the United States.[19,20] To many people, this has been one of the most disconsoling thoughts on this subject—that humankind's future depended on the ability of far-from-perfect political systems to avoid accidents and to learn from their mistakes. Remember also that our next nuclear opponent may be far less cautious and rational than the Soviets.

In one incident, an American bomber carrying a high-yield H-bomb crashed over North Carolina. All but one of the bomb's five safety devices were triggered by the fall. Had the fifth gone off too, the bomb might have exploded. Such an unexpected explosion could conceivably be taken for a surprise Soviet attack requiring nuclear "retaliation."[47a]

In a 1961 incident, American bombers were on their way to obliterate the Soviet Union but were recalled two hours later when it turned out that a moon echo had been mistakenly interpreted as a Soviet attack.[47b]

In 1980, an American missile was reportedly almost launched because its maintenance crew neglected to disconnect a vital wire. One of the two officers in charge claimed that by pulling a plug at the last minute he and his fellow officer "saved the world"[48] (the Air Force denies this story).

In 1959, According to Khrushchev, a Soviet missile had overshot its test target and headed toward Alaska. Fortunately, it carried no warheads and ended up at the bottom of the sea.[49]

Reagan's harsh rhetoric may have made the first half of the eighties the most explosive in the postwar decades. From 1981 to 1983, in particular, the Soviets believed that the United States was planning to attack them. Because the U.S. was unaware of these Soviet forebodings, it might have taken inadvertent actions which would have dangerously aggravated the situation. In this and similar cases of false perceptions, according to a former American official, "no timely or adequate efforts were made to dispel the tensions before events were allowed to run their course. We were all lucky."[50]

Taken together, all these circumstances prove beyond doubt that nuclear war could happen.[51] This in turn raises the question: If contemporary nuclear arsenals are not dismantled, or if the Soviet

Union's place as our chief antagonist is taken up by Russia or some other nation, what is the probability that nuclear war will happen?

Because they depend on intuition, reasonable estimates can differ by a large margin. If we arbitrarily assume that in every given year there is only a 1 in 1000 chance of nuclear war, then the probability that war will erupt in the next 15 years is about 1 percent, in the next 30 years, 3 percent, and in the next 100 years, 10 percent. If the chance is 1 in 100, the respective long-term probabilities are 14 percent, 26 percent, and 73 percent. If the chance is 2 in 100, they are 26 percent, 45 percent, and 87 percent. My own intuition is that, even now, the chances in any given year of an all-out nuclear war are something like 1 in 100, and that the probability of nuclear war in the next 15 years is greater than 14 percent. But regardless of one's intuitive estimates, it is clear that, given the enormous stakes, such chances should not be taken lightly. Better still, they should not be taken at all.

After a long journey we come up with three melancholy conclusions. Even the mildest imaginable outcome of nuclear war will be an unparalleled calamity to countless individuals, to civilization, and to the human species. Nuclear war could have broken out in the past; luckily, it did not. And, despite the recent dissolution of the Soviet Union, if nuclear proliferation is not brought to an end, or if the nuclear arsenals of current nuclear-weapon states are not drastically reduced or eliminated, nuclear war could very well happen. Bertrand Russell's famous lines still capture humanity's predicament:

> I cannot believe that this is to be the end. . . . There lies before us, if we choose, continual progress in happiness, knowledge, and wisdom. Shall we, instead, choose death, because we cannot forget our quarrels? I appeal as a human being to human beings: remember your humanity, and forget the rest.[52]

Summary

Nuclear bombs wreak far greater damage than conventional explosives. They owe their greater destructive power to immediate blast, heat, and radiation, and to the lingering effects of radioactive fallout. The combined effects of the Hiroshima bomb killed over half of city residents, turned the lives of many survivors into a lifelong nightmare, and leveled the entire city. Owing to its greater yield, the effects of a typical contemporary bomb are expected to be greater. Although the aftermath of an all-out nuclear war among major nuclear powers cannot be described with certainty, it would surely be the greatest catastrophe in recorded history. In any combatant country, it may kill half the people, afflict many survivors with a variety of radiation-induced diseases, destroy industrial and military capabilities, and contaminate vast tracts of land. Such a war might also lower the quality of the human genetic pool, damage the biosphere, cause a breakdown of national and international economic systems, destroy the health care and prevention system, and move surviving societies in unpredictable directions. Although extinction of the human species is unlikely, it cannot altogether be ruled out. History, psychology, and common sense strongly suggest that nuclear war is more probable than most of us would like to believe. This, and the cataclysmic quality of nuclear war, imply that humanity can scarcely afford another half a century in the shadow of a nuclear holocaust.

Chapter 3

COSTS OF THE ARMS RACE

Imagine that you are creating a fabric of human destiny with the object of making men happy in the end, giving them peace and rest at last. Imagine that you are doing this but that it is essential and inevitable to torture to death only one tiny creature—that child beating its breast with its fist, for instance—in order to found that edifice on its unavenged tears. Would you consent to be the architect on those conditions?

Fyodor Dostoyevsky[1]

Life endured under the shadow of nuclear war, and the horrible price humankind will pay if war actually breaks out, are the most obvious costs of nuclear competitions. They are not, however, the only costs. To put our subject in a proper perspective, we need to examine other costs.

For the sake of brevity, this chapter will focus on the costs and risks which the Cold War has exacted from the American people. The reader should bear in mind, however, the many sacrifices endured by other nations. It also goes without saying that the cost of future military competitions may dwarf the price humanity has already paid for the Cold War.

Military Costs

By the mid-1980s, America's postwar military position had steeply declined.

At the end of War World II, the United States was the world's foremost military power. Among other things, it was the only Allied country which fought a large-scale war on two separate fronts, provided vital support to its allies, and developed atomic bombs. As we shall see (chapter 6), since the late 1960s the USA has enjoyed an edge over the USSR in fighting conventional wars, but this edge had little meaning in the nuclear age. Nuclear weapons are the Great Equalizers: any country possessing enough of these fairly cheap bombs, as well as adequate means of delivering them (e.g., missiles), is militarily second to none. Long ago, the Soviet Union had enough; China in the 1990s constitutes a borderline case; countries such as Japan and Germany might acquire a sufficient quantity in the future. So the U.S. had been reduced from a peak of unquestionable superiority to the much less secure position of first among equals.

A second aspect of America's steep military decline is not comparative (our military position vis-a-vis potential adversaries), but absolute. At the close of World War II, the U.S. was impregnable. During the war, it had erected some fortresses on the West Coast in fear of a Japanese invasion and suffered its share of setbacks. Nonetheless, it was the only major combatant whose land and civilian population were virtually untouched. During the 1950s, even though the Soviets possessed perhaps the capability to destroy a few American cities with nuclear bombs, the U.S. would have survived. In the years that followed, however, the Soviets could devastate the U.S. and there was nothing we could do to stop them except make it clear that we could, and would, retaliate in kind. To be sure, this deterrent posture may have decreased our chances of oblivion, but it did not eliminate our essential vulnerability.

Nuclear weapons proliferation posed an even greater security threat. Newcomers to the "nuclear club" (Israel, South Africa, India, and Pakistan[2]), prospective members (e.g., Brazil, Argentina), and nations capable of rapidly acquiring nuclear weapons (e.g., Japan, Germany) may act less responsibly than America, Russia, Britain, France, and China. If visited by economic hard times, fascist takeovers, or environmental catastrophes, these newcomers may be more tempted to use nuclear weapons. And, while nuclear weapon states have a country to lose and are unlikely to engage in nuclear blackmail, elusive criminals, terrorists, or madmen may come by a handful of bombs and be more tempted to use them. The proliferation of nuclear weapons within the military organizations of all nuclear weapon states poses additional threats. In the U.S., for example, at one time nuclear weapons could be fired only from bombers stationed in a few places and handled by a relatively small number of men who belonged to a single service. In the 1980s, these weapons could be launched from all kinds of bombers and missiles located practically anywhere (in one service alone—the U.S. Navy—from some 250 ships and submarines[3]); they were operated by many more people (some 100,000 in the U.S. alone[4]); and these people belonged to more independent units of our Armed Forces. Clearly, the chances of accidental or unauthorized firing under such conditions were greater in the 1980s than they were before.

Thus, thanks to the nuclear arms race, the United States' military position in the mid-1980s had declined from clear superiority to equality, and from virtual invincibility to troubling vulnerability.

By lavishing stupendous resources on the arms race, we weakened the economic and educational base upon which our long-term military might depended. The West spent sizable resources, including manpower, on non-productive weapons and on huge standing armies. Had some of these resources been diverted to civilian research and development, industrial equipment, or education, Western economies would have been stronger. The military implications of such spending were more serious for the Soviet Union, whose economy was less than one-quarter as large as the West's. But excessive military spending might still have adverse consequences for Western security, for often in international relations yesterday's friends are today's foes. Thus, twenty years from now, if the U.S. is still around, its chief adversary could well be a country other than Russia. If that other country spent much less on defense than the U.S., and more on its educational and economic base, then its long-term military position and its ability to wage conventional wars might improve more rapidly than either the United States' or Russia's.

Conventional Wars

All other things being equal, it is plausible to suppose that the more arms a nation has, the likelier it is to engage in conventional wars and military adventures. Armed conflicts can therefore be viewed as one indirect cost of the arms race.

The Vietnam War serves as one powerful reminder of the stupendous costs of major non-nuclear conflicts. This war caused millions of deaths, injuries, and individual tragedies, cost billions of dollars, weakened the USA's international standing, and cast a dark shadow over America's foreign policies. It was also the most notorious case of environmental warfare in history—agricultural crops and natural ecosystems were deliberately destroyed, much of the countryside was disfigured with numerous craters, and some species of wild plants and animals were probably made extinct.[5a]

> The war in Vietnam left in its wake extensive impoverished grass-land instead of forests, widespread erosion and dust storms, major declines in freshwater and coastal fisheries, and severe losses of wildlife, especially from the forest canopy—wounds from which the land may not recover for a hundred years. . . . War-damaged environments fostered the spread of bamboo thickets . . . rodent populations, and "bomb crater malaria."[6]

Although it is too early to assess the consequences of the Persian Gulf War, the few guarded details which have so far escaped the censor's pen are troubling. Heavy casualties, human anguish, and resurgent jingoism have often been associated with military conflicts, but modern technology is introducing additional twists. A conventional war of only a few weeks' duration imprinted itself on the collective memory of the survivors. It killed, maimed, or injured 1-3 percent of the long-suffering Iraqis and Kuwaitis. It craterized the landscape. It set in motion short-lived rebellions, eventually forcing well over 10 percent of Iraq's people to flee their homes and seek refuge abroad. If rumors about the bombardment of operating nuclear facilities prove true, this war may have caused long-term radioactive contamination of some tracts of land. This war left in its wake an enormous oil spill which imperils the ecology of the Persian Gulf. In the last days of the war, Iraq's rulers carried out their pre-war threat of setting on fire some 550 Kuwaiti oil wells. Consequently, (1) severe health and ecological problems are expected over hundreds of thousands of square miles in Kuwait and outlying regions, (2) for a few years, the smoke may block sunlight and cause a slight cooling of the northern hemisphere, and (3) over the long term, the vast quantities of carbon dioxide may make a small contribution to global warming.

Economic and Human Costs

In 1986, the world's military spending exceeded $900 billion.[7] From 1983 to 1988, America's share of the world's total hovered around one-third.[5b,7] By 1987, according to official U.S. statistics, the military establishment cost the average American household some $3,500 a year.[8a] Others insist that the actual price tag was much higher and that, in fact, the bulk of our tax dollars went into Cold War-related activities. According to one source,[9] if we include among these activities interest payments incurred by earlier military spending, veterans' benefits, gifts of foreign arms to our allies, and construction of nuclear weapons, in 1986 the arms race cost the average American household well over $5,000 a year. In the Soviet Union, the burden has been far heavier. First, throughout most of the Cold War, the costs of the arms race had been laughingly under-reported by the Soviet government. Second, owing to the greater poverty and technological backwardness of the Soviet Union, Soviet citizens paid a higher price for the arms race than American citizens.

The figures are just as staggering when you consider the manpower requirements of the military. In the 1980s, the Department of Defense kept over two million Americans in uniform, it employed an additional one million civilians, and it indirectly provided jobs for more than three million workers in war-related industries.[8b,10] (These figures do not include retirees, e.g., the 1.5 million military retirees on the public payroll[8b]). In 1980, some 50 percent of the world's scientists were engaged in war-related research and development. Between them, the military-industrial complexes of just the USA and USSR commanded the services of 750,000 scientists.[11]

Besides the money and manpower it absorbed, the military establishment consumed non-renewable natural resources. For example, in the mid-1980s, the military accounted for 1.5 percent of total energy consumption in the U.S.

The economic burdens of the arms race could be perhaps brought to life with a few tangible examples. In the 1980s, it cost as much money to construct a single nuclear submarine as to educate 160 million school-age children in less developed countries.[12] The U.S. military consumed half a million dollars per minute,[7] and every minute 30 children in the world either starved to death or died from diseases that could have been easily prevented through vaccination.

In fact, peace could alter the human condition, *if* only the one trillion dollars ($1,000,000,000,000) or so the world still spends each year on wars and war preparations could be diverted to more productive channels. Each year, some 15 million children under the age of five starve to death or fall ill and die because they are underfed or improperly fed; of these 15 million Tiny Tims, 9 million could be saved for a mere $65 million.[13a] Every year, half a million of the world's children become partially or totally blind because their diet lacks vitamin A; it would cost a mere few million to rid humanity of this scourge.[13b] A mere speck of the world's military spending could save Brazilian rain forests and African elephants. These funds could be diverted to clean our air and waters, keep the world's growing deserts in check, conserve energy, and protect the biosphere. They could be used to avert the looming crisis of international debts and national deficits. They could be used for space exploration, development of non-polluting energy sources, and medical research. In America, they could be used to raise the U.S.'s international standing in infant mortality from number 24 to number 1, thereby saving every year the lives of some 20,000 American infants. They could help Americans reach the Dutch level of unwanted teenage pregnancies, thereby reducing the number of these yearly individual tragedies from 900,000 to 300,000. They could be used to improve fire safety (currently, the incidence of fire-related deaths in the U.S. is one of the highest in the world). They could be used to rescue most of the 100,000 Americans who die every year from avoidable workplace-related diseases.[13c] They could be used to combat the scandal of hunger in the world's richest country. By 1985, at least 20 million Americans (including over 10 million children) were hungry, mostly because of cuts in government aid since 1980 (cuts which coincided with the most massive peacetime arms buildup in American history).[13d] They could be used to bring down America's homicide rate (10 times higher than England's). They could be used to stimulate our economy and save our farms from soil erosion and corporate takeovers. They could be used to put healthy food on our tables. They could be used to renovate our cities, our decaying bridges and highways, and our declining industry. In short, if the money humanity squanders now on warfare and killing machines could only be judiciously diverted to meet human needs, living conditions on this planet could be radically improved.

Some observers suggest other adverse economic costs of the arms race, such as inflation. But because these costs are controversial and uncertain, I shall ignore them here. However, there is no question that brain power, manpower, and other resources which are presently soaked up by the arms race could be used for more productive purposes, thereby vastly enhancing the quality of human life on this planet.[14]

Environmental Costs

Apart from wars, the most serious environmental impact of the military arises from its nuclear programs:

I.   The radioactive waste these programs produce must be stored safely for thousands of years, a problem that has so far proven intractable. Although by 1991 there has been only one major nuclear accident in a military waste disposal site in the Urals and one near-accident in the state of Washington,[15] over the next few millennia there will be many opportunities for additional accidents, especially if the quantities of waste and the number of countries producing them continue to rise. By 1988 the U.S. Department of Energy confirmed decades-long charges that nuclear weapon plants and laboratories threaten the environment and public health. In a published report, the Department stated that radioactive and toxic chemicals produced in these sites have often contaminated public water supplies and that they may cause cancers, miscarriages, and other diseases in residents of nearby cities.[16] In the U.S. alone, it may cost as much as $150 billion to *partially* quarantine this kettle of rancid fish.[5c]

II. As we have seen (Chapter 1), accidental explosions of large nuclear bombs cannot be ruled out.

III. Until worldwide atmospheric tests of nuclear bombs came to a virtual stop, they degraded environmental quality.

IV. Although the environmental consequences of the more recent underground tests are believed to be comparatively light, serious long-term consequences cannot be ruled out.

V. Nuclear submarines routinely release radioactive substances into the oceans.

VI. Accidents involving satellites powered by nuclear reactors may cause radioactive contamination. So far the global impact of such accidents has been negligible. But if space is militarized, and if large nuclear reactors are deployed in satellites, this problem could become more serious.

The environmental impact of the military is by no means confined to nuclear pollution. According to one source, military-related activities accounted for some 20 percent of environmental degradation on this planet.[17a] Thus, production of bombers deplete non-renewable resources; disposal of poisonous chemicals pollutes the biosphere; and the launch of solid-fuel missiles may deplete the Earth's ozone layer.[18] Similarly, in the U.S. alone, by 1989 well over 14,000 military sites suffered from toxic contamination.[17b]

We may note in passing that the environmental costs of the arms race would have been much higher had the public in the West given the military establishment the freedom to do as it liked to the biosphere and to public health. For example, large-scale atmospheric tests of nuclear bombs would still be an everyday occurrence, an MX missile racetrack would now cover portions of Nevada and Utah, and a military "antenna farm" would cover 41 percent of Wisconsin.[19]

Moral and Psychological Costs

Though it is impossible to quantify, or prove the existence of, the costs described in this section and the next, they may well be severe.

Many people realized the fundamental irrationality of a race that did violence to all contestants and that could, in principle, be replaced by less suicidal forms of competition. They suspected that this race had nothing to do with its avowed goals of preserving freedom, security, independence, and social justice. In the long run, these irrational and irrelevant aspects of our species' collective behavior could erode such individual standards of morality as truthfulness, tolerance, and fair play, thereby tearing apart essential strands in the delicate fabric that holds our civilization together.

Moreover, we shall remain free only as long as we remain willing to defend our open society against its enemies here and abroad. But if open societies are responsible in part for the madness of the arms race, if they are incapable of showing greater responsibility on this crucial issue than closed societies, are open societies worth defending at all? And if the worst comes, and if human beings can erect a new civilization from the radioactive ruins of the old, would they not relinquish freedom?

Militarism, Imperialism, and Plutodemocracy

The vast standing army the U.S. has kept in place since World War II constitutes a sharp break from the country's historical traditions. This break contributed to an unprecedented, and ominous, militarization of American society.

The military bureaucracy is made up of individuals whose training and habits diverge, in some ways, from democratic practices and ideals. For instance, a distinguished general felt that, should the U.S. find itself in anything like the Vietnam War again, the President should try "to silence future critics of war by executive order."[20]

The military establishment is a collection of vast and powerful organizations such as the U.S. Navy, the civilian branch of the

Department of Defense, and the war-related sectors of the Boeing Corporation. In the absence of adequate safeguards, such organizations are driven to pursue their own narrow interests, not the public's. Some of the needed safeguards are missing and others which are in place are being eroded. Gradually, or abruptly under extreme circumstances, this erosion might lead to a military dictatorship.

As employer of millions of people and spender of billions of dollars, the military establishment enjoys considerable political power. This power leaves its mark even in such unlikely places as academia. In 1982, for example, the Department of Defense funded 13 percent of all university research,[21a] thereby diminishing academic freedom.[22]

A former Deputy Assistant Secretary of Defense and his co-author tell us that "we are surrounded by distressing evidence that civilian control of today's booming military establishment is a good deal less than a generally prevailing reality."[21b] This is attested by the military's effective propaganda machine, by the huge cost over-runs which plague the system, and by countless incidents. A major general, for instance, conducted an unauthorized bombing campaign during the Vietnam War. Another general conducted an unauthorized espionage operation in the offices of the Assistant to the President for National Security.[21b] Similarly, in the mid-1980s, military figures played key roles in the Iran-Contra Scandal.

The military establishment skillfully uses the broadcast and print media to enhance its objectives and political power. Coupled with the number and complexity of election issues, this can lead people to vote against their own, and their country's, interests. J. W. Fulbright, former Chairman of the U.S. Senate Committee on Foreign Relations, felt that the problem was already grave in 1970:

> I had . . . no idea of the extent to which the Pentagon had been staffed and armed to promote itself . . . to shape public opinion and build an impression that militarism is good for you. A most unsettling aspect of these various campaigns was the scant attention the disclosure of their existence attracted. . . . This complaisant acceptance of things military is one of the most ominous developments in modern America.[23a]

To be sure, the U.S. is not a garrison state, nor is it at a grave risk of becoming one by the year 2020. We have too many safeguards in place, and our generals are as committed to the system (as they understand it) as most of us are. The chief danger might not be a coup, but an insidious, gradual transformation of our values and institutions.

The arms race, then, constituted an experiment. It could have culminated in a dictatorship or a full-fledged plutocracy. Alternatively, even if it continues for another century, Western democracies might survive it unscathed. There are good reasons to believe, however, that the arms race has already weakened Western democracies and that, even now, it may eventually undermine them:

> The incursions the military have made in our *civilian* system . . . muffled civilian voices within the Executive branch, weakened the constitutional role and responsibility of the Congress, and laid an economic and psychological burden on the public that could be disastrous. . . . Militarism as a philosophy poses a distinct threat to our democracy. . . . [A military take-over] may not seem likely now, but it is by no means so inconceivable that we need not warn against it and act to prevent it.[23b]

Since 1945, most of the Third World's people have not been free. They were severely exploited by a cabal of homegrown tyrants and foreign businesspeople. They lived in abject poverty, with no decent education, medical care, or food. Their lives were comparatively short. Similarly, in the USSR's European satellites, millions were denied fundamental civil liberties, prosperity, and a livable environment. As we have seen, the money spent on the arms race could be used to improve living conditions in the Third World and former Soviet satellites. But the fortunes of these billions of people were tied to the Cold War in more subtle, though no less important, ways. Throughout the Cold War, the Soviet Union attributed the subjugation of its European satellites to the arms race and to its fear of Western invasion. Likewise, the United States used the Cold War to justify its consistent interventions in Third World countries in favor of repressive regimes like Somoza's or Diem's, and against their communist or democratic opponents. For instance, before the CIA toppled a democratic government in

Guatemala, the American people were told that Guatemala was a "beachhead for Soviet Communism" in the Americas. The price the world's people paid for such interventions is incalculable. As we shall see later, U.S. policies in Guatemala alone were responsible for the deaths of at least 5 percent of the population, to say nothing of condemning most surviving Guatemalans to a life of quiet desperation. To be sure, imperialism existed before the Cold War started and may continue long after its demise. Without the Cold War, it had, perhaps, a better chance of fading away.

In principle, democracies subscribe to such ideals "as one citizen, one vote," "equality before the law," "government of the people, by the people, for the people." But unlike Israeli kibbutzim or some early Christian communities, they rarely practice economic egalitarianism. The greater economic power of the very rich can in turn be translated into a disproportionate political power. Since ancient times, therefore, democracies were prone to drift or revert into *plutodemocracies*—democracies in which the rich few enjoy greater political power than the poorer many.

For the last twenty years or so, the United States has been gradually moving in the plutodemocratic direction. It is inconceivable, for instance, that in a functional democracy the great majority would knowingly increase the buying power of billionaires at its own expense. Yet American voters have been electing and re-electing politicians who did just that.

It may be that this drift towards plutodemocracy is traceable in part to the arms race. The arms race creates pockets of wealth and corruption which might not otherwise exist. A preoccupation with external enemies may diminish our vigilance against plutocratic encroachments. A few of the billions used now for war preparation could be used to educate the people and diminish the influence of excessive wealth, demagoguery, and indoctrination in our body politic.

The Arms Race or Totalitarianism?

On the Western side, the specter of a gruesome totalitarian takeover provided the Cold War's most compelling rationale.

Moreover, the policies it fueled appear to have been astoundingly successful. We have survived the arms race. We have contained and then rolled back totalitarianism. We experienced hardships and persevered, and now, at long last, totalitarian ideologies have suffered decisive setbacks. We have won the Cold War and set the world free. The USA is finally strong enough to establish a new world order.

But, as we shall see, this self-congratulatory interpretation of history is mistaken. It is also dangerous; if it prevails, it could darken the human prospect for another half a century. Despite its reasonableness and appealing simplicity, despite the indisputable horrors of totalitarianism, the dilemma we purportedly faced between totalitarianism and the arms race had little to do with the real world. In the imaginary, self-serving world of our war intellectuals, the West had to choose between the horrors of slavery and the arms race. In the real world, it had to do nothing of the kind. Throughout the Cold War, the West could have taken a road which would have given humanity greater freedom, peace, and prosperity. At this writing, this road is still open and still not taken.

Summary

The United States paid a heavy price for the arms race, in addition to life in the shadow of a nuclear cataclysm. The arms race weakened America's military position by (1) forcing the U.S. to rely on nuclear deterrence instead of relying on its overwhelming military might, (2) making it vulnerable to complete destruction from afar in a matter of minutes, (3) increasing its vulnerability to nuclear blackmail from terrorists and a growing club of nuclear-weapon states, (4) steadily raising the chances of nuclear accidents, and (5) weakening its economic and political system. The arms race contributed to the eruption of numerous conventional wars, thereby helping to bring about deaths, suffering, subjugation, and destruction. By the late 1980s, the Soviet-American arms race still consumed some $600 billion and it still kept millions of people in uniforms and in war-related industrial and research projects. Had all this money and manpower been judiciously diverted, the quality of life of most individuals on this planet, and the human prospect, would have been dramatically improved. The arms race consumed non-renewable natural resources. It contributed to environmental degradation, especially through radioactive pollution. In the long run, the arms race may have undermined individual standards of morality, the resolve to defend freedom and democracy, and the civilian character of our society. The arms race has been used to justify Soviet and American imperialistic tendencies, thereby indirectly killing untold millions of human beings and keeping billions in political, psychological, and economic chains. It may be that the arms race contributed to America's move during the past two decades towards a government of the rich, by the rich, for the rich.

Chapter 4

WEAPONS OF THE COLD WAR

Procrustes in modern dress, the nuclear scientist will prepare the bed on which mankind must lie; and if mankind doesn't fit—well, that will be just too bad for mankind.

Aldous Huxley[1]

A Note on Military Jargon

Throughout this book I use as few acronyms and specialized military terms as I can. These terms are not needed to grasp the general picture. Unlike their counterparts in the natural sciences and mathematics, these terms do not economize or clarify discussions of which they are a part, but needlessly encumber them, thereby making it harder for citizens to critically evaluate military policies. And, once we begin to use the war intellectuals' terms, we tend to think about military affairs in their terms too. For example, it mattered little to the Russians whether a bomb which could destroy Moscow made its home in a Nebraskan or a German missile site. Endowing these bombs with two different names, however, made it easier for our war intellectuals to act as if locations and other trivial characteristics of these bombs made all the difference in the world. This, in turn, was used to support the fallacious argument that the cause of peace was served by negotiating small reductions in one kind of bomb and large increases in another (see Chapter 6).

Western governments and military organizations employ terms like "Minutemen," "Polaris," "initiative," and "shield" (which evoke in most of us positive associations) to promote weapons and policies of mass destruction. This miscalling started early; for example, giving the name "Peacemaker" to a 1940s' aircraft whose deadly cargo could destroy at least one large metropolitan area. This miscalling still continues; for example, giving the name "Peacekeeper" to a ballistic missile which could wipe a few cities off the face of the earth. The least this book can do is break away from this inglorious tradition.

Conventional Weapons

In the 1980s, deployment, production, and research of conventional weapons accounted for some 75 percent of the United States' military budget.[2a,3] These weapons are familiar to most of us, and only call for a few generalizations.

In this century, dramatic increases in the technological sophistication and effectiveness of conventional weapons have taken place. As a result, modern conventional wars are, to a considerable extent, wars between machines and their operators, not between soldiers in open combat. It follows that the side with a more advanced scientific base and a stronger economy has a decisive edge. Because most poor nations have neither, they must import most of their weapons, and they often settle internal political conflicts not through an open fight between the well-armed state and its poorer opponents, but through guerrilla warfare.

A new weapon might confer a decisive edge in conventional warfare on the side which deploys it first. However, soon opponents acquire the new weapon or invent effective countermeasures against it, so the edge is of a short duration. Hence, though new weapons have often helped the side possessing them win battles, in the long run they have harmed the human prospect by steadily raising the costs of war.

Weapon development often leads to obsolescence. Cannons replaced catapults, rifles replaced swords, tanks replaced horses, and modern anti-tank weapons may outdate tanks.

Throughout history, some devices which were not ordinarily viewed as weapons found use in warfare. This practice still continues, albeit at a more advanced technological level. The primitive method of fighting wars by setting forests or fields on fire was replaced by methodically poisoning, plowing over, and setting ablaze large tracts of land. The ancient tactic of defending a city under siege by pouring boiling oil on its attackers has given way to the use of incendiary materials that stick to people's skin and burn them alive.

Chemical and Biological Weapons

Chemical and biological weapons may be used to kill and injure people and other living organisms and to damage non-living materials. Chemical weapons are made of inanimate substances. Biological weapons are living organisms. In comparison to nuclear weapons neither weapon is, at the moment, very effective. They have both been used in the past and will be used in the future, but, except for their psychological impact, and (like all other weapons) their inhumanity, there is nothing particularly unusual or devastating about them. In 1990, the USA and USSR agreed to eliminate their stockpiles of chemical weapons, a decision which may further diminish their importance. On the other hand, their successful deployment in some recent Third World conflicts may increase their appeal, especially for hard-pressed non-nuclear countries.

The chief concern, then, is not with what people can do with these weapons now, but with what they might be able to do with them in the future. In this context, biological research appears more ominous. Over many decades, some biologists have been trying to develop new varieties of disease-causing living organisms.[4] Future advances along these lines might tempt nations or terrorists to vaccinate their people against one such organism in secret, then let it loose, or threaten to let it loose, on the world. Today this is only a script for a science fiction thriller, but we have all learned by now the bitter-sweet lesson that today's science fiction may become tomorrow's commonplace realities.

Nuclear Bombs

Let us move on to nuclear weapons, the "backbone of American military power."[5] In the late 1980s, the entire nuclear program accounted for about a quarter of America's military spending.[3] The nuclear bombs themselves, are, comparatively speaking, cheap; their production probably consumed less than 1 percent of America's total defense budget.[2a] Their yields cover a considerable range; single bombs in the American arsenal could cause roughly as much as 100 times, or as little as 1/100th, the damage in Hiroshima.

A bomb's yield determines, in part, its wartime use. Small bombs are destined for such things as battlefield situations, mines, artillery shells, and anti-submarine operations. Medium bombs are destined against small military targets. Large bombs could be used against metropolitan areas or against large well-protected military targets.

Pound for pound, the Hiroshima bomb had a far greater destructive power than non-nuclear explosives. Since 1945, nuclear scientists have made even more impressive strides in this respect. In the 1980s, a modern bomb weighing as much as the Hiroshima bomb (about five metric tons), could have as much as 150 times its explosive yield.[2b] In fact, by 1980 at the latest, humanity came close to the theoretical limit of weight reductions; as far as contemporary theoretical physics is concerned, further research in this direction was fruitless.

Delivery Vehicles

Bombers and Cruise Missiles

From 1945 through 1991, several types of airplanes could be used to deliver nuclear bombs to a target, depending in part on their starting points. In the event of war between the USA and the USSR, a large number would have taken off from the USA and flown to targets in the USSR and elsewhere. These bombers were large, they could fly to the Soviet Union and back without landing, and they could carry bombs or cruise missiles (see below). Smaller airplanes which could carry fewer nuclear bombs and could not fly so far were stationed in Europe, Korea, and on aircraft carriers.

American bombers were once destined to drop bombs above targets, but, allegedly, the Soviets air defense system could have prevented as many as half of our bombers from reaching their targets. Though the remaining half could still obliterate Soviet cities and military targets many times over, war planners—who like to play it safe—developed countermeasures against Soviet air defense. Of these countermeasures, two deserve special mention.

The so-called stealth bomber should be able to penetrate the Russian air defense system better than existing American bombers.

The second countermeasure equipped bombers with cruise missiles. These missiles could be released hundreds of miles from target, thereby reducing a bomber's vulnerability to Soviet air defense. A cruise missile is a small, pilotless airplane which can fly close to the ground. It is equipped with a built-in navigational system which allows it to deliver its single warhead to target with great accuracy. By early 1992, the USA was deploying cruise missiles by the thousand, with the Commonwealth of Independent States trailing some distance behind. Because these missiles could be launched from airplanes, they maximized the bomb's chances of reaching the target and the crew's safe return (it is not clear, however, whether there will be anyplace safe to return to in an all-out nuclear war). In addition to large bombers, these little unmanned airplanes can be readily launched from almost any platform. As seen in the Persian Gulf War, cruise missiles can also carry a large load of conventional bombs.

Ballistic Missiles

Among delivery vehicles, ballistic missiles have for a long time been held in the highest regard by Western and Soviet analysts. These missiles are equipped with bombs, which, together with the mechanisms that set them off, guidance systems, and some other components, are called warheads. A ballistic missile is essentially a rocket which shoots its warheads out to space and from there propels them toward their targets. From then on, the warhead's trajectory is determined by gravity. Because there is no air resistance in space, warheads there fly with amazing speed—some 25 minutes after a Midwestern missile has been launched, its warheads would begin exploding over Asian or European soil.

At first, ballistic missiles had only one warhead each. Later, new missiles were often equipped with several warheads and many of the old ones were similarly retrofitted. Some ballistic missiles carried as many as ten warheads (ten MIRVs in jargon), and each of these warheads could hit a different target. All the bombs delivered from a single missile have, however, a limited range, and must fall within an area not exceeding some 90 miles in length and 30 miles in width.[6] For instance, bombs from a single missile could destroy targets in both Baltimore and Washington, D.C. (30 miles apart), but not in Baltimore and Pittsburgh (210 miles apart).

Ballistic missiles in the American arsenal could be launched from land and sea. In the 1980s, most Western land missiles were stationed in Europe and in the American Midwest. The European-based missiles were smaller, had a shorter range, were not well protected, and, towards the end of the decade, were being negotiated out of existence. The Midwestern missiles (ICBM in jargon) were placed underground, had a longer range, and were protected by massive concrete silos.

Ballistic missiles could also be launched from submarines. Each missile-submarine carried a number of ballistic missiles, and each missile could be equipped with multiple warheads. On the American side, all missile-submarines were powered by nuclear reactors. Because these reactors enabled missile-submarines to stay under water (without surfacing) for more than two months at a time and to make less noise than conventional submarines, nuclear submarines were harder to detect and destroy.

Strategic Requirements of Nuclear Weapons and Delivery Vehicles

Ideally, all warheads and delivery vehicles must meet the following requirements:

Reliability. Delivery vehicles must take off and discharge their warheads properly; warheads must reach and pulverize their targets. Though the U.S. has never fired ballistic missiles over the

North Pole (as it would have in time of war with Russia), most experts believe that American warheads and delivery vehicles were reliable.

Penetrability. They must get past any obstacle on their way to target. Most ballistic missiles are unstoppable, but a certain fraction of bombers and cruise missiles may have been prevented by Soviet air defenses from reaching target.

Accuracy. They must hit Moscow and not Paris; a missile site and not a preschool two miles away. The U.S. has made great strides in this regard: In 1991, about half of all American bombs, regardless of their point of origin and delivery vehicle, were reportedly able to land within one-quarter mile of target.

Survivability. Enough warheads and delivery vehicles must survive the worst imaginable surprise attack to assure the sufficient destruction of the attacker in a retaliatory strike. Only this, it is believed, can deter nuclear blackmail.

Command, Control, and Communication

A nation's Armed Forces must be continuously integrated into one functional unit. This integration has been achieved through a rigid chain of command which went all the way to the Presidents in the USA and the USSR; through various means of gathering intelligence, including advance warning of impending or actual nuclear attack; and through an extensive communication network.

The most important mission of the American and Soviet militaries in times of peace was prevention of accidental or unauthorized launch of nuclear weapons. For this purpose, a complicated (and so far remarkably effective) network of safeguards and codes has been used. The command, control, and communication network was also believed to be vital to the national interest because it helped assure nuclear retaliation. Though substantial efforts have been expended in this direction, it is doubtful whether this network would have survived a surprise attack in either the USA or the USSR.[7]

For obvious reasons, each side had to know what the other was up to. In part, the needed information has been gathered through traditional activities such as spying and analysis of open publications. In part, it has been gathered through sophisticated technologies such as radar and satellites. Early detection is considered particularly important in deterring nuclear war. Thus, if the Soviets knew that Americans were likely to be forewarned of a surprise attack and save their bombers (by putting them in the air on time), the Soviets might have been less inclined to launch an attack in the first place.

Satellites

Like some nuclear warheads, satellites are carried into space by rockets. But, instead of being propelled back to earth, they are propelled into orbit around it. In the early 1980s, some three-quarters of all space missions had military purposes,[8a] and every third day saw the launch of a new military satellite.[8b] Throughout the 1980s, military satellites were not involved in direct warfare; they only constituted a vital element in integrating the entire military machine. Their integrative functions included (1) reconnaissance, which provided, among other things, surveillance of the entire earth and advance warning of a missile attack; (2) communication, in fact, 80 percent of all military communications were carried out via satellites; and (3) navigation, for example, by helping missile submarines pinpoint their exact location, satellites enabled them to improve the targeting accuracy of their warheads.[8c]

Satellites are gradually being equipped with means of destroying fellow satellites and of defending themselves from attack. If military competitions among major world powers overtake humanity again, these developments could turn out to be critically important to warfare and to the fate of the earth. In contrast, although America's spaced-out 1980s' rush to render satellites capable of missile destruction (SDI in jargon) might produce some unexpected technological spin-offs, the contribution it will make to our national security is sure to be far too slight to justify the costs. Sooner or later, this attempt will be given up as a bad job.

This then is what those exciting first years of peaceful space exploration have come to. Many among us are too young to remember the early promise of humanity's reach to the stars. Some people disdained it even then. Others cannot forget the quarrels which set them apart from their fellow passengers to the grave. But those of us who shared the excitement, those of us whose compassion for their fellows transcends national and ideological boundaries, can only view the 1980s' militarization of space as a letdown from that wonderful moment in 1969 when a man first walked on the moon.

Summary

As much as possible, modern military terms are eschewed in this book because they only served to encumber, obfuscate, and degrade the moral and intellectual quality of discourse in Cold War America. Conventional weapons include such old standards as tanks and rifles and such relative newcomers as anti-tank guided missiles and laser beams. Throughout the Cold War, conventional weapons have been used extensively in international warfare and consumed a much larger fraction of the world's military spending than nuclear weapons. Chemical weapons such as mustard gas may be defined as substances which can be gainfully used to harm human beings, other living organisms, or non-living materials. Recent years have seen a marked increase in their use in local conflicts, but they were not expected to play a major role in a worldwide conflagration. Biological weapons are toxic or harmful living organisms, e.g., disease-causing bacteria or submarine-destroying dolphins. Although they have been relatively unimportant throughout the Cold War, future research might greatly increase their significance and appeal. Despite their overwhelming military importance, nuclear bombs consumed a relatively small portion of America's total military budget; a far greater proportion was expended on the development, production, and maintenance of delivery vehicles. Nuclear bombs could be launched from many corners of the globe; from air, sea, and land; from the ocean's and earth's surfaces and subsurfaces; from aircraft carriers and infantry cannons; from submarines and bombers. They could be delivered to target through bombers, ballistic missiles, cruise missiles, and cannons. These delivery vehicles and the warheads they carried were expected to meet minimum standards of reliability, penetrability, accuracy, and survivability. Each nation has used various means to integrate its armed forces into one functional unit and gain information about the activities of its adversaries and allies. Space satellites played important roles in the military machines of the United States and the Soviet Union, roles which included reconnaissance, communication, and navigation.

Chapter 5

STRATEGIC THINKING IN THE UNITED STATES

It often happens that the universal belief of one age of mankind . . . becomes to a subsequent age so palpable an absurdity, that the only difficulty then is to imagine how such a thing can ever have appeared credible.

J. S. Mill[1]

Nevertheless, such ideas should not be dismissed out of hand as so obviously simpleminded as not to be taken seriously. Simplemindedness is not a handicap in the competition of social ideas.

Charles Frankel[2]

Democrats who do not see the difference between a friendly and hostile criticism of democracy are themselves imbued with the totalitarian spirit.

Karl Popper[3]

Two Interpretations of Western Military and Foreign Policies

Deterrence

Throughout the Cold War, most Americans perceived their country's military policies in something like the following terms. We were caught between a rock and a hard place, and had to choose between the more or less equally distasteful alternatives of either continuing the arms race or laying down our arms. From

1945 through 1991, the free world chose to continue the arms race, and for excellent reasons. Ideally, we would have liked to live without the risks of the arms race and totalitarianism, but the nature of the Soviet state made this impossible. So, in the real world, we could only choose a policy that would have minimized both risks to the greatest extent possible. Unilateral disarmament would have almost certainly cost us our freedom. In contrast, it appeared far less certain that the arms race would have ended up in nuclear war, while its other costs were remote or negligible in comparison to an inevitable totalitarian takeover. Given these unequal probabilities and the equal distaste with which most of us regarded totalitarianism and nuclear war, the choice—unfortunate as it was—seemed clear enough: continue the arms race, cross our fingers, and hope for the best.

This interpretation of the historical record holds that American policies have been defensive and that they have been strongly influenced by ethical considerations. It holds that the U.S. and its democratic allies cherished their freedom and national independence, and that their policies were virtually devoid of aggressive and exploitative motives. Though they would have loved nothing better than being left alone by the militaristic and imperialistic Soviet Union, they were realistic enough to know that, in this less than perfect world, freedom must be defended from its external enemies.

Translated into the realm of nuclear weapons, this essentially defensive posture led to deterrence as the cornerstone of the democratic West's military strategy. Both the Soviet Union and the United States possessed the physical means of decimating each other; neither country could prevent its own destruction. Each relied, therefore, not on defense but on deterrence, for the threat of destruction was mutual: each nation could see to it that its destruction was followed by the destruction of the other. In effect, each side cautioned the other: "You can destroy me and there is nothing I can do to stop you from doing so, but I can destroy you too. Therefore, I appeal not only to your humanity in asking you not to destroy me, but also to your self-interest, for, if you destroy me, I can, and will, destroy you."

Brinkmanship

A radically different interpretation claims that policies of nation states have rarely been influenced by moral considerations or the welfare of the majority of their citizens, and that American policies from 1945 through 1991 were no exception. According to this view, America emerged from the war as the most powerful nation on earth. Its monopoly of nuclear weapons, its military and economic might, its commercial and political foothold in most countries, its belief in itself as a stronghold of freedom, decency, and civilization, its unequal commercial, political, and military relations with most of the world's nations, the dependence that this inequality created for one side and the stupendous profits it brought to the other, and America's willingness to resort to economic blackmail and brute force to achieve its commercial and security objectives, have rendered a good part of the planet's land surface into, essentially, an American empire.

> The international goals of the United States have been clear and remarkably consistent since the end of World War II. Since 1945 U.S. policy has never deviated from its support of the status quo in all noncommunist and nonsocialist countries. This policy is designed to maintain control over the allocation of world-wide resources and available labor and to ensure U.S. access to market and investment areas. No alternative forms of government could be allowed to replace existing friendly governments, since successful alternatives could demonstrate that there were different paths to national economic development from those approved by the United States.[4]

According to this view, the Third World's people did not enjoy illiteracy, malnutrition, malaria, injustice, exploitation, poverty, and hopelessness. If left alone, they were likely to rebel against the dictators who ruled them. With our economic and military assistance, however, our dictatorial friends could easily quench such popular uprisings, provided our support for the dictators was not counterbalanced by another powerful country's support for the rebels. And herein, according to this interpretation, lies the crux of America's Cold War policies.

Only the Soviet Union could conceivably interfere with the status quo. The Soviets did not depend upon us politically or economically, they seemed able to acquire the capacity to intervene in conflicts far away from their shores, and they disliked America's Third World policies. They might take exception, for instance, to the U.S.-created and supported bloody dictatorships in the Philippines, Vietnam, Chile, Iran, Nicaragua, or Greece. They might counteract American culpability in the decades-long imprisonment of the South African anti-apartheid activist Nelson Mandela.[5] They might not sit silently by while the U.S. takes an active part in the massacre of a quarter million Indonesians.[6] They might wish to neutralize American support for Saddam Hussein in Iraq, or for the genocidal Khmer Rouge in Kampuchea.[7] Or they might have curtailed our actions during the Persian Gulf War. Moreover, they might have liked to gain a foothold in these regions for ideological, economic, and balance of power considerations. If left alone, they might have therefore been tempted to provide assistance to Third World insurgents, including, at times, direct military aid and intervention. Our military and foreign policies were aimed at preventing the Soviets from doing so.

Translated into the realm of nuclear weapons, this essentially aggressive posture leads to the unavowed, but nevertheless real, policy of brinkmanship—the policy of pushing a potentially deadly conflict to its limits, of risking a mutual descent into the abyss in order to scare off a more cautious opponent—as the cornerstone of the democratic West's military strategy:

> Chiefly, the arms race is justified . . . and sustained by the geopolitical and ideological struggle between the USA and the Soviet Union, and derives its importance from the USA's determination to dominate and control the Third World and sustain its global hegemony. Within this context nuclear weapons are seen by the USA as being a means of threatening the Soviet Union and thus preventing her from challenging US hegemony.[8]

> It is . . . mainly over the freedom of action of the United States to use a few nuclear weapons, selectively and not against cities, that the nuclear competition unfolds.[9]

According to this view, the use of nuclear weapons in implementing these political objectives falls roughly into three historical periods. During the first, which lasted at least until the mid-1950s, the U.S. enjoyed a decisive nuclear edge. The period started with American atomic monopoly, but the Soviets' first atomic explosion did not even come close to bringing this period of meaningful nuclear edge to an end, for the Soviets still lacked a sufficient number of bombs and delivery vehicles. Until 1955 or so, an all-out nuclear war would have resulted in the virtual pulverization of the Soviet Union, and, at worst, a partial pulverization of the U.S. Throughout this period, according to this view, our military policies were aimed at retaining this military advantage and thereby containing Soviet meddling in our Third World affairs.

In the second period, according to this view, we intermittently employed a more refined variant of this policy. We no longer sought raw nuclear superiority, for the Soviets by now enjoyed a credible nuclear force. Rather, America's military policies were aimed at retaining a more subtle edge over its chief adversary:

> The essence of the asymmetry in the U.S. and Soviet strategic nuclear capabilities . . . had to do with the credibility of striking first. Until 1966 or 1967, the U.S. intercontinental forces were so superior in every category . . . that it was possible to contemplate a first strike directed against the much smaller Soviet forces, using only a fraction of the U.S. arsenal, in which a large part of the Soviet retaliatory capacity would be destroyed before it could be used. The Soviet leaders would then face the choice of capitulating or launching a relatively weak retaliatory blow, with the latter course sure to result in their country's complete destruction by the sizable remaining forces of the U.S. At the same time, no such "attractive" first-strike option was open to the Soviet Union, because its forces were insufficient to destroy a suitably large fraction of the U.S. forces in an initial blow. This asymmetry—that the United States could and the Soviet Union could not credibly threaten to resort to the first use of intercontinental nuclear weapons against its adversary's homeland—gave meaning to the term "nuclear dominance."[10]

In the third phase (mid-1960s through 1991), the U.S., by and large, continued on the same course. Depending on one's perceptions of the military balance during those years, our goal, according to this view, was either the retention of this "nuclear dominance" and the political advantages it conferred, or its restoration. "The West," two influential analysts wrote in 1980, "needs to devise

ways in which it can employ strategic nuclear forces coercively . . .
If American nuclear power is to support U.S. foreign policy objectives, the United States must possess the ability to wage nuclear
war rationally."[11]

It must be noted in passing that the two components of this
view—America's alleged imperialism and nuclear brinkmanship—
are not necessarily linked. Thus, a close examination might show
that only one of these two allegations is correct, that both are
correct but that no causal relationship exists between them, or that
the Third World connection constitutes only one of the roots of
nuclear brinkmanship. An appraisal of this view must therefore
substantiate three charges: U.S. imperialism in the Third World,
nuclear brinkmanship, and a close causal link between them. Nor
can we gain much help from consulting high level senior officials.
For one thing, they might be disinclined to share the truth with the
public. For another, while practicing brinkmanship, they might
sincerely believe that they practice deterrence.

The existence of two such radically different interpretations of
American policies—and the likelihood that actual policies contained
both deterrence and brinkmanship elements throughout this period
—considerably complicate efforts of appraising the historical
record: one needs to know the aims of a policy in order to judge it.

I shall approach this methodological problem by dividing the
discussion into two parts. Brinkmanship will be taken up in
Chapter 8. In this and the next two chapters I shall assume that
universal freedom and deterrence constituted the guiding lights of
American foreign and military policies. Here there is little to argue
with the general objectives themselves, and the analysis chiefly
requires an answer to questions such as: Was deterrence the best
way of containing Soviet expansionism? Have our present and
past policies afforded the most rational route of achieving their
stated objectives of freedom and security?

To sum up. Two radically different views of America's nuclear
policies need to be explored. For methodological reasons, I shall
assume in Chapters 5-7 that the U.S. practiced deterrence. In
Chapter 8 I shall explore the claim that while the U.S. preached
deterrence, it either practiced brinkmanship or a combination of
deterrence and brinkmanship.

Victory in the 1980s?

One hysterical way of extricating oneself from a straitjacket is to deny wearing it at all. Likewise, some Western strategists have over the years tried to extricate themselves from the twin perils of totalitarianism and the arms race by asserting that victory in an all-out nuclear war was possible. Their assertion was not based on some secret weapon which would have rendered all Soviet nuclear bombs or delivery vehicles inoperative in an instant. It was based instead on the facts that we all know, including the various consequences of nuclear war described in Chapter 2.

To the extent that this position could be taken seriously, we must assume that its proponents were familiar with these consequences. They could not possibly believe, then, that we would be better off as individuals or as a nation after the war, even if its consequences turned out to be the mildest imaginable. Their assertions that victory was possible boiled down to this: both nations would have suffered much in an all-out war, but we could see to it that the Russians suffer more; that perhaps, after 30 years, we would be able to put ourselves together again and they wouldn't.

I must confess that I like Russians and would have hated to see their lives reduced to one long radioactive nightmare. But maybe these war intellectuals didn't, or maybe they didn't allow such sentiments to influence their strategic theories, so let us think only of Westerners. Let us also accept the questionable assumption that the Soviets would have suffered more, and then examine this strategic theory. To see its absurdity, we need only consider the following analogy: if two men fought a duel, and if as a result one died and the other became a quadriplegic, we could indeed say that in one sense the quadriplegic won the duel. But in another, more fundamental, sense we would say that both lost. In this case, both went to battle hoping for a better outcome, and this hope lends their actions a modicum of rationality. However, if both duelists had known the consequences of their deadly encounter in advance, and if the would-be quadriplegic decided to go ahead with it because he was going to win, most of us would have considered him mad.

This analogy suggests that a policy aimed at rendering all of us quadriplegic for the sake of killing the Russians was ill-advised. At the very least, we should have never trusted the human prospect to people who possessed such odd notions of war and politics.

Future Victory?

Those who believed in the possibility of immediate victory have always belonged to a small minority. The belief that we could become strong enough to win a future war with Russia enjoyed a much wider following and has often been used as a rationale for increased military spending. Nonetheless, history suggests that the modern quest for superiority, like the medieval quest for the elixir of life, was misguided in principle.

Though all important military inventions since 1945 have originated in the West, none has meaningfully improved the West's military or political situation. For example, the U.S. developed the technology to put multiple warheads on each missile first, and for a few years the U.S. alone could do this. As a result, we could for a while explode many more bombs in Soviet territory than they could in ours. Yet, even in the short term, this remarkable technology did not improve our military position. Likewise, we have invested enormous resources in upgrading the targeting accuracy of our warheads. As our technological competence in this area improved, we retrofitted old missiles and built new kinds of missiles precisely because we wished to increase their warheads' accuracy. Throughout the 1980s, greater accuracy provided a rationale for building new missiles. However, our lead in multiple warheads, warhead accuracy, and all other breakthroughs in the past 30 years or so, sweet as these breakthroughs were from the technological viewpoint, has not given us a decisive edge. In fact, our only reward for these efforts was this: with every successive stage, each side could be more thoroughly atomized.

It follows that (assuming deterrence as the cornerstone of our military policies) the quest for superiority has been counterproductive. As long as the Soviets maintained a sufficient number of nuclear weapons to decimate the United States after the worse imaginable American surprise attack (a minimum deterrent), and as long as we could not stop them from doing this, the quantity and accuracy of our warheads counted for little. Millions of bullets are useless in a duel, since you can only kill your opponent once. Likewise, a single weapon beyond the number of weapons needed to assure the retaliatory obliteration of Russia was useless. In a duel, a gun only need be accurate enough to kill, not to split an opponent's hairs. Similarly, as long as the bombs aimed at the Kremlin and Capitol Hill leveled them to the ground, it made no difference that one bomb came closer to target than the other.

At this point, defenders of the quest for superiority might concede the futility of devoting precious resources to such projects as the development of multiple warheads per missile and more accurate warheads. But they might still argue that we have been barking up the wrong tree since 1960 or so. After developing a minimum nuclear deterrent, we should have attempted this: acquiring a decisive edge over the Soviets by inventing and deploying something that would have removed the peril which the Soviet nuclear arsenal posed to our survival.

Unlike any senseless development project which did not remove this peril, this position made sense. It would have been nice to own something that could instantly send all their nuclear bombs to the planet Mars. Under close scrutiny, however, this position collapses. Here, I shall limit the discussion to one American military research and development project (SDI in military jargon, "star wars" in the vernacular) which was purportedly aimed at disarming the Soviets. In the mid-1980s, the strategic quest for victory stood and fell with this single project. For this reason, and because this project has been a typical component of our Cold War strategic thinking, we need to bring its blurry contours into sharper focus.

Certain powerful forms of radiation—especially chemical lasers and particle beams—might be deployed in space or on the ground to burn holes in and destroy ballistic missiles and warheads on their way to target. They could then render nuclear weapons "impotent and obsolete," as an unknown speech writer for President Reagan put it in 1983, thereby eliminating the Soviet threat to our survival.[12] In 1987, the Cold War was subsiding, but Reagan's recitations remained unchanged: "All humanity can begin to look forward to a new era of security when the burden of nuclear terror is lifted from its shoulders."[13]

From the very outset, independent experts insisted that this program constituted a mockery of truth, science, and common sense. This shield, they said, would only be able to incapacitate a fraction of all delivery vehicles. Let us leap into the year 2010 and assume that, as usual, we have succeeded in developing these weapons before the Soviets. American scientists would now inform the President that the long-waited "defensive shield in space,"[12] can be deployed. The President would inquire how effective this shield is, and the scientists would say that it can incapacitate as much as 95 percent of all delivery vehicles launched against the U.S. Assuming that this future president is not a Hollywood puppet, the only thing she might be able to do upon hearing this wonderful news is shrug her shoulders, make a few jokes about her predecessors' intelligence, and politely dismiss the scientists, for the remaining 5 percent could still demolish America.

Moreover, early opponents of this program protested, our scientists would never be able to give the system the crucial test it requires: disabling in flight thousands of missiles. They would only be able to say: "Ms. President, *most likely* 95 percent will be destroyed." "Is there any chance that none will be destroyed?" our intelligent President would ask. And the scientists will say: "Sure, every machine is fallible." "What is the probability that none would be destroyed?" she might ask. If they have done extremely well, they would be able to say, "1 percent." The President would again dismiss them; for what sane woman would risk war against the Soviets if they could pulverize her country once if her plans succeeded, and twenty times if they failed?

For argument's sake, early opponents of this project continued, let us ignore these virtually insoluble technical problems and make the unrealistic assumption that we could be absolutely certain that the new "defensive shield" would be able to destroy *all* launched Soviet missiles. Let us also ignore this program's enormous complexity and staggering costs and its violations of the spirit and the letter of a couple of then-existing arms control treaties. Either the Cold War is brought to an end (a barely conceived notion in 1983), in which case we needed spend no money on this project, or else the Cold War continued. If it continued, the Soviets would know what we were up to. Since we refused their pleas to demilitarize space, they were likely to go to great lengths to prevent us from achieving this edge. Their list of viable options was certainly long. For example, as long as they were still our equals, they might give us an ultimatum: stop, or we shall obliterate you. They might triple their nuclear forces, or increase the number of delivery vehicles (such as existing bombers and cruise missiles) which were *immune* to this "shield." They might smuggle small nuclear weapons into a few American cities and keep them there, just in case. Or, if they get really desperate, they might arm missiles with conventional weapons and use them to demolish the laboratories where this research was being conducted. What should we do then? Sink into the Dark Ages because they wished to remain in the race, or acknowledge that they had a legitimate point there and agree at long last to demilitarize space? Won't we be better off if we never have to face such decisions?

Even if we managed somehow to get through this self-inflicted *via dolorosa*, early opponents of this proposal said, we would still be faced with the question of real superiority itself. Superiority did us little good after World War II, and no sound plan exists for deriving from it meaningful political gains in the future. Suppose we acquired the ability to protect our country from nuclear destruction while still retaining the ability to atomize Russia. Suppose, moreover, that we could somehow know in advance that we could raze Russia without bringing upon ourselves and the world an unparalleled environmental catastrophe. Suppose we presented them with an ultimatum on some international issue like South Africa or Indonesia and they refused to budge. Would we demonstrate our resolve by obliterating Moscow? As long as the U.S. remains a democracy (which allegedly is what the fighting is all about in the first place), this was unlikely.

Thus, early opponents of this program argued, in a few years the Russians would catch up with us, as they always have in the past. Now, for the first time, you might say, we need no longer dread their nuclear weapons, nor they ours. Unfortunately, this is not so, and not only because 100 percent effectiveness and certainty are not given to man. For, especially if they were, we would be in the gravest danger imaginable. Long before either side acquires anything resembling a "defensive shield," it would acquire the capacity to disable satellites. So by the time the "shield" is in the sky, both sides would only need to knock out a few dozen satellites in a surprise attack in order to achieve immediate superiority. Now, each side in this make-believe world would be apprehensive that the other might put its satellites out of commission. So scared in fact, if we were to believe our mid-1980s' war intellectuals, as to be tempted to launch a preemptive strike and knock the other's satellites out. If we were lucky, both sides would have either overcome this temptation or confined the reply to space. If we were not lucky, this game could have unleashed an unthinkable disaster here on earth.

Five years after this costly program was launched, even the Congressional Office of Technology Assessment joined the ranks of its opponents. After a two-year study, it concluded that the proposed missile-defense system would probably "suffer a catastrophic failure" as soon as it was needed.[14] By late 1989, even President Bush's Defense Secretary conceded that this project had been "oversold" and that its chances of success were "extremely remote."[15] Consequently, in 1990 the USA spent a *mere* $3 billion on this project. Were our politicians, then, only caught up in starry-eyed nonsense, or were they pork-barreling our future?

We may safely conclude that the quest for decisive military superiority in the nuclear age has been based on a delusion. Short of magic wands or some spectacular scientific developments, we could never acquire it. We had nothing to gain and much to lose, then, from our decision to turn this quest into a key component of our military policies.

New Nuclear Weapons?

A seemingly more reasonable school of thought urged us to improve our nuclear arsenal not for victory's sake, but for the sake of keeping up with the Russians. In this context, we may wish to remind ourselves first that we have always been at least one step ahead of them (see Chapters 6, 7). However, we still need to dispose of the argument that the next time around they might be ahead, and therefore that we could take no chances and had to continue to develop new weapons and improve the old.

What would have happened, for instance, if we had not developed multiple warheads? To begin with, we could have reached an agreement with the Soviets that neither side deploys such warheads, and they almost certainly would have agreed—if for no other reason than they were lagging behind us. But for argument's sake, let us say that the Soviets had agreed to negotiate them out of existence and then cheated, or that they refused to sign a fair agreement and we then decided, unilaterally, not to go ahead. In either case, they would not have been able to rely on spies and open publications to see how we actually did it, so it would have taken them much longer to develop multiple warheads.[16] Let us be generous and say that they would have started their deployment by 1980 and completed it in 1995. The only result: we would have been in the same position they were in just a few years earlier. Because the Soviets retained a credible nuclear deterrent, multiple warheads did little to improve our military or political situation.

The drive for more sophisticated nuclear weapons and delivery vehicles was misguided in principle. To be relevant to the military equation in the nuclear age, a new weapon had to eliminate the Soviet nuclear threat. No such weapon was in sight. Therefore, our alleged struggle against totalitarianism would have benefited from diverting elsewhere the resources which nuclear weapons and their delivery vehicles purposelessly blotted up.

Some proponents of weapons development conceded that the fraction of our nuclear arsenal which was sure to survive the worst imaginable surprise attack was enough to deter rational men from attacking us in the first place. But they still urged us to develop new weapons on the grounds that, as former Secretary of Defense Harold Brown put it, "perceptions can be as important as realities in the international arena. . . . Indeed, in some sense, the political advantages of being seen as the superior strategic power are more real and more usable than the military advantages of in fact being superior in one measure or another."[17]

By this, I conjecture, Mr. Brown meant that, in any confrontation, the comparatively greater atomization his side could wreak in a first strike against military targets, his side's more thoroughgoing potential of razing the other, or his side's ability to do so with more sophisticated weapons,[18] would have given America a psychological advantage. That is, when we came eyeball-to-eyeball again, they would have backed off, or better still, they would have treated us with greater respect so that we wouldn't come eyeball-to-eyeball at all.

We need only point to the difference between deceptions and appearances to see the weakness of this argument. In the case of deceptions, the enemy's mistaken appraisal of the situation often contributes to his defeat. Indeed, many military victories had been won by inferior forces through the brilliant use of guile. But I know of no victory that has ever been won by keeping appearances, for in the case of appearances, the enemy knows that a naked emperor wears no clothes.

Now, the Soviets, like anyone else, could be taken in by guile, but they were not simple-minded enough to treat us with greater respect because of appearances. The elementary fact, which remained regardless of our action, was this: the launching of a war by either side would have led to the destruction of both sides, and beyond that point there was nothing that either side could do to the other.[19]

Seeing the types of arguments our policy makers resorted to in order to justify nuclear weapons development, one cannot help wondering: Over whose eyes were they trying to pull the wool, the Soviets' or ours?

A Window of Vulnerability?

This popular and recurring strategic theory (the name kept changing but the illogic stayed the same) went something like this. The Soviets were trailing close behind us in the production of multiple, and accurate, warheads. Missiles were expensive, warheads were cheap. Therefore, the Soviets could strike all our land-based missiles with only a fraction of theirs. They would, after such a sneaky attack, be left with more missiles than we would, so we would not dare retaliate. They would then proceed to blackmail us in all kinds of ways, the end result of all this being a gruesome totalitarian takeover.

This contention, like the fictitious missile gap of the late 1950s, was evidently strong enough to carry a man to the White House. It was not, however, likely to sweep informed people off their feet.

In the first place, this argument ignores the obvious survivability of our strategic arsenal. Even if the Soviets could wreck 90 percent of our land-based missiles in a surprise attack, we would have had enough to flatten the Soviet Union at least four times.[20] A high-level government commission,[21] set up in 1983 by Mr. Reagan to review his Administration's war preparation program, concurred with this conclusion. Although the commission dutifully endorsed most aspects of his program, it rejected the window argument on strictly technical grounds. The Soviets, it pointed out, could not simultaneously destroy American land-based missiles and strategic bombers. There would have been, in other words, enough strategic bombers *or* land-based missiles left after the worst imaginary surprise attack to undo the Soviet Union. Add to this the invincible missile submarines we had at sea, and you get a *zero* probability that rational heads of state would have ever contemplated the impossible task of forcibly disarming America (see Chapter 6 for a discussion of the survivability issue).

This perennial contention also ignored the many uncertainties which surround the actual use of missiles and bombs. Anyone contemplating such an attack had to consider potential problems with accuracy, reliability, and the coordination of such a large-scale operation. One independent American expert examined the technical aspects of this program in 1984 and concluded that "calculated outcomes of counter-silo attacks in which only 30 per cent of the attacked silos are destroyed by all-out attack are at least as probable as the calculated outcomes, usually quoted by US officials in congressional testimony, that anticipate 90 per cent destruction of US silos in an all-out Soviet attack."[22a]

If they were rational, Soviet rulers had to reckon, besides, with the remote possibility that we would launch our land-based missiles before these missiles were hit. In that case, we would be in a "better" position right after they attacked than they would.[21]

Proponents of this argument also forgot that we would be

shocked and outraged. Consider, for example, the reminiscences of a nuclear explosion's survivor. The scene is a hospital ward in the outskirts of Hiroshima a couple of days after the city was atomized:

> A man came in . . . with the incredible story that Japan had the same mysterious weapon . . . and . . . had now used the bomb on the mainland of America. . . . At last Japan was retaliating! The whole atmosphere in the ward changed, and for the first time since Hiroshima was bombed, everyone became cheerful and bright. Those who had been hurt the most were the happiest.[23]

Now, we must assume that the Soviets know some psychology. Would they risk everything on a desperate gamble that we would not avenge the deaths of ten million Americans (give or take eight million) and the partial despoliation of our land? How could they be reasonably certain that, at the very least, we would resist the temptation of giving them a bit of their own radioactive medicine?

The Stockholm International Peace Research Institute is certainly not given to hyperbole. Yet, it concluded that the fears upon which the window argument was based were "unfounded and unduly pessimistic, if not contrived . . . it is simply unwarranted and injudicious to make firm predictions about the outcome of a counter-silo attack. To base defence policy or weapon procurement and planning on such predictions approaches the irresponsible."[22b]

In short, the inveterate window of vulnerability projection was humbug. It failed to see the folly of the entire situation and it ignored the fact that our survival hinged upon the Soviets' good judgment. What if they suddenly became insane? In that case, both nations were lost and there was *nothing* we could do about it. The suggested remedies—building more missiles of all kinds, more sophisticated bombers, or quieter submarines—had absolutely nothing to do with this basic vulnerability and with our absolute dependence on their rationality. It follows that our problem was not a window, but a whole sky, of vulnerability, and that the only sure way of removing it was not racing, but negotiating, with the Soviets.

After decades of continuous allegations in the alternative media and presses that first-strike projections bordered on intellectual fraud, cracks were beginning to appear in the mass media as well. In 1990, for instance, one mass circulation magazine opined:

> A madman bent on self-destruction is, almost by definition, impossible to deter. It has always required a suspension of disbelief to imagine a sane Soviet leadership, no matter how cold-blooded, calculating that it could, in any meaningful sense, get away with an attack on the U.S. nuclear deterrent.[24]

The futility of attempting to shut a window through an arms buildup, instead of closing a whole sky of vulnerability through multilateral disarmament, can also be seen by carrying the window argument one step farther. Suppose Seattle's mayor scoffed at the Soviets' Lenin-worship rituals. Suppose they got mad and craterized Seattle. Now, while we are still debating our response, the Soviets warn us that their entire nuclear force is on hair-trigger alert and offer an armistice. Clearly, the balance of power is totally unchanged. In fact, nothing has changed except that Seattle is now gone. What should we do? We have already lost Seattle, but if we go to war with those raving maniacs, we would lose everything! The point of this contrived balderdash? It makes just as much sense as the window argument. As long as the Soviets remained sane, they were not going to raze Seattle or pulverize American missiles in a surprise attack. If they went out of their minds, all bets were off, regardless of how many more trillions we chose to spend on weapon research and development. We were indeed vulnerable, but in a deeper sense of depending on their rationality for our survival. Setting out to replace an imaginary leaky shingle on an utterly roofless house is not the best way of preparing for a downpour.

Launch Under Attack?

Here is another intellectual gem from the strategic jewelry box of that period. The Soviet Union might strike first, disable our nuclear weapons and delivery vehicles, and run us over. We could not possibly take such a risk, so we had to empty our silos as soon as we had good reasons to suspect that our land-based missiles were under attack.

This theory's underlying premise is incorrect. We have always had enough deliverable weapons to roundly decimate the USSR after a no-holds-barred surprise attack. In fact, it is hard to see, from a strictly nuclear point of view, that we would have suffered much from a successful first strike against us (see Chapter 6). We must also bear in mind the very real possibility of false alarms. Bombers on their way to St. Petersburg can be recalled, so it made sense to have them take off when a supposed attack was in progress. Ballistic missiles could be destroyed on their way to target by fitting them with remote control devices. The proposed devices could only be activated by the country that launched the missiles in the first place. Hence, such devices would reduce the chances of catastrophic accidents without weakening a country's retaliatory potential. Such devices may have been present in Soviet missiles but not in American missiles.[25] Consequently, once America's missiles were in the air, they could not be recalled.

Let us now add to these facts the highly conservative assumption that the chance of a false alarm leading us to empty our silos in the last twenty years was one in a thousand. Should this small probability be ignored? Consider the alternatives: if it were a false alarm, and if we emptied our silos just in case, the USA, USSR, perhaps even civilization itself, would be in ruins for no reason at all. If it were not a false alarm, we would have had enough left to undo the Soviets after they had wrecked as much of our nuclear weapons and delivery vehicles as they could. So on one hand, we had everything to lose, on the other, nothing to gain, from adopting a "launch-on-warning" policy. It is not clear whether the USA or the USSR have ever adopted this policy.[26] But although many of our so-called strategists urged us to adopt this policy, it us transparently obvious that we should have ignored their advice.

Nuclear Retaliation?

Our avowed strategy was based on deterrence. To deter, we had to say that we would retaliate. But, if they actually launched an all-out attack, should we have kept our word? Clearly, we would have lost everything by then, and so the question was: Should we have made them lose everything too?

The morality and wisdom of automatic retaliation were not as immediately obvious as our government and mass media supposed. The attack could be accidental or the brainchild of a deranged individual. Even if deliberate, the decision to attack us would have been made by a few men, not by the billions of men, women, and children that our weapons would have killed or harmed. We would be wise to assume that nuclear war would precipitate the worst environmental disaster and therefore that by retaliating we might increase all humankind's suffering and peril. And, if the main issue that set us apart was indeed freedom or slavery, would not democracy be vindicated by exercising this supreme act of self-control? Before Gorbachev's seven years in power, we could also present the Kremlin with an ultimatum: "Now that you have committed this genocide, even if by accident, you must either dismantle your nuclear arsenal and totalitarian form of government under our strict supervision, or else suffer total destruction." (We could do this because by then we would have little to lose, and they might still have a country to lose—this, ironically, was the one way our quest for superiority could succeed).

Obviously, the USA and the USSR felt it necessary to say that they would pay back in kind. Each side had to make the other believe that it was not bluffing. In the heat of the moment, either side might have retaliated. Each side had to take into account the outside chance of environmental collapse after the war. So each side had to assume that the other side, or *nature*, would revenge and this was deterrence enough. However, the considerations given above suggest that the wisdom of retaliation should have not been taken for granted even after the most treacherous and cold-blooded surprise attack.

Concluding Remarks

This chapter's treatment of Cold War America's military strategy is obviously incomplete.[27] It omits in particular many debates, moot issues, and heated controversies. Throughout the Cold War seemingly intelligent Westerners in position of power were setting their brains to work on such profound questions as: Should we act as if we were slightly out of our minds in order to convince the Soviets that, if they stepped too far out of line, we would blow them and ourselves up? If war breaks out, should we blow up their command, control, and communication centers?

But we can safely assume that these and similar questions were as senseless as the ones we have already discussed. Hence, strategic thinking in the United States utterly failed to provide a rationale for our military and foreign policies. Moreover, if we ever faced the puzzles which so intrigued our war intellectuals, our choice would have made little difference because by then all might have been lost. So, although these never-ending puzzles may have been serviceable as tactical exercises in war academies, although they reportedly propped up a *two billion dollar a year* think tank industry,[28] in the final analysis they cloaked a fundamentally mad exercise with an air of rationality, and they diverted our attention from consequential issues.

The real and significant questions were not "Should we have acted a bit crazy to deter the Soviets from attacking?" but "Were we courageous enough to stop this race to oblivion?" Not "Should we have destroyed their command, control, and communication centers in time of war?," but "Were we really mad enough to needlessly risk self-destruction?"

Summary

Modern scholarship offers two radically different interpretations of American military and foreign policies. Deterrence emphasizes the defensive nature of these policies in face of a harsh and ruthless adversary, these policies' overriding preoccupation with freedom and democracy at home and abroad, their essentially peaceful intentions, and their humanitarian interest in the well-being of the world's people. Brinkmanship insists that, like any other empire in history, the United States was primarily concerned with furthering the interests of its ruling class. The U.S. is alleged to have done so by portraying the Soviet Union as inherently evil and warlike, building a sufficiently large war machine to enrich its upper class and to persuade Soviet rulers that it might, if provoked, destroy their nuclear weapons in a surprise attack. It did so by propping up compassionless and subservient dictators in the Third World and by brutally helping them to suppress their communist and democratic opponents. By striving hard to retain an apparent nuclear edge, the U.S. has deliberately projected a willingness to risk total destruction in order to achieve its aims. It thereby kept Soviet encroachments on its highly profitable Third World operations to a minimum. This book does not try to resolve the deterrence/brinkmanship controversy. Instead, it examines American policies under either premise and shows that, in either case, these policies can only be viewed as heartless and unwise.

This chapter highlights a few representative specimens of strategic thinking in Cold War America, including the (1) belief that the U.S. could win a nuclear war with the Soviet Union, (2) view that it might have been able to do so through such projects as space militarization, (3) rationales offered for construction of new nuclear weapons and the maintenance of tens of thousands of nuclear weapons, (4) window of vulnerability strategic theory, (5) theory that ballistic missiles must be launched if they are believed to be under attack, and (6) commitment to retaliate an all-out nuclear attack. Not a single one of these strategic theories is congruent with the deterrence interpretation of American policies, with rationality, or truth. Their widespread use could be viewed as one more illustration of the belief that simplemindedness is not a handicap in the competition of social ideas, or as a left-handed and eminently successful attempt to disguise their real aims—a smokescreen for brinkmanship. In a properly working democracy, such misconceptions and fallacies could not be successfully used to justify America's military and foreign policies.

Chapter 6

THE MILITARY BALANCE

Today, in virtually every measure of military power, the Soviet Union enjoys a decided advantage.

Ronald Reagan[1], 1983
(40th President of the U.S.)

The United States is the most powerful country in the world. . . . I believe those who mistakenly claim that the United States is weak or that the Soviet Union is strong enough to run all over us are not only playing fast and loose with the truth, they are playing fast and loose with U.S. security.

Harold Brown[2a], 1978
(President Carter's Secretary of Defense)

But the lie about the Soviet "military superiority" . . . is not just the biggest but also the most dangerous lie of our time. . . . It is the biggest lie not only because it is often based on exaggerations, false figures, and pure concoctions, but also because it ignores some major politicogeographic realities. . . . [It] is . . . also . . . the most dangerous lie of our time . . . for at present it is virtually the only rationale for the arms race. This lie is also dangerous because it poisons the political atmosphere and sows fears, hostility, and distrust. . . . Thus, since this real situation is so rudely and persistently distorted, the motives can be only sinister. Is it not logical to assume so?

Georgy Arbatov[2b], 1982
(A Soviet strategist)

Overkill

Overkill has been briefly discussed in Chapter 5. The problem, you will recall, is: How much was enough? According to one

123

view, there was no such thing as enough: we had to have at least as many nuclear bombs and delivery vehicles as the Soviets, if only for nuclear blackmail or psychological reasons.

A second view holds that we only needed the capacity to atomize the Soviet Union once after it had launched the worst imaginable surprise attack against our nuclear forces. Beyond this point of minimum deterrence, any further expenditures on enlarging and modernizing our nuclear forces were wasteful and purposeless. "The very least we can say is that, looking ten years ahead, it is likely to be small comfort that the Soviet Union is four years behind us," Robert Oppenheimer observed in 1953. "The very least we can conclude is that our twenty thousandth bomb . . . will not in any deep strategic sense offset their two thousandth."[3] In the world we live in today, Gorbachev observed 35 years later, "striving for military superiority means chasing one's own tail. It can't be used in real politics."[4] This second view does not assume that Soviet leaders were civilized, moral, or incapable of the worst crimes. It only assumes a modicum of rationality which we had to grant them in view of their past record and in view of the paradoxical quality of nuclear deterrence. Assuming for the moment that this second view is correct, what kind of damage would ruthless but rational men be unwilling to accept?

They would probably consider unacceptable anything that would have put the survival of the Soviet Union as an organized, modern society at a grave risk, deprived them of power, reduced everything they had worked for to rubble, and jeopardized their lives and the lives of their relatives and friends. Note that I have deliberately made them out to be worse human beings than they were. I am assuming, for argument's sake, that they were totally indifferent to the plight of their people and to their ideals, that there was no special place, say, in Moscow, so dear to their hearts that they would not risk it for anything in the world. I am only granting them one human quality—a minimal degree of rationality.

Relating the number of bombs exploded to the damage they inflict is not an easy matter, so the figure which will be cited here could be on the high or low side by a factor of two. In the late 1980s, about 4 percent of the explosive power in America's total nuclear arsenal would have inflicted a rather *unacceptable damage*:

the annihilation of 125 million Soviets, the cities they lived in, and much of their country's industry.[5a]

Now, this 4 percent is not the figure we seek. We are interested, rather, in our nuclear firepower after the worst imaginable sneaky Soviet attack. Following such an attack, what percentage of our surviving nuclear power could have inflicted unacceptable damage on the Soviet Union? To be on the conservative side, and to give our hawks the benefit of the doubt, let us ignore the massive American arsenal in places like Europe and aboard aircraft carriers. Let us also ignore the arsenals of our French and British allies. Let us look only at American-based land missiles, missile submarines, and bombers. By the late 1980s, we had some 36 submarines, of which at least 20 were at sea at any given time (and hence invulnerable); just 7 could inflict unacceptable damage.[6] Over 300 large bombers were based in the U.S., at least 150 of which were expected to survive a Soviet first strike and at least 75 were expected to reach their destination;[7] just 20 could inflict unacceptable damage. Well over 1,000 land missiles make their home in the continental U.S.; even the worst pessimists conceded that 150 would have survived a direct attack, and 150 could take care of this job too. It follows that even if the Soviets destroyed as much of our nuclear arsenal as they possibly could, we would still be able to kill half their people and raze most of their industry 7 times over. It might still be argued that we want to have a large margin of safety. This has already been provided several times in our calculations, but let's play it safe and reduce the estimate by a factor of 2. We are still left with the awkward conclusion that, throughout the 1980s, we possessed at least 3 times the number of nuclear weapons needed to deter a nuclear attack.

Thus, it makes little sense for upholders of deterrence (as opposed to upholders of brinkmanship) to log every bomb, missile, and submarine. If the Soviets could decimate us once over regardless of what we did, would it mattered to them that we could decimate them 3, 30, or 300 times? If any attempt to decimate them just once could have brought an unparalleled environmental disaster upon us even if they did not retaliate, what was the point in putting ourselves at an even greater risk by preparing to triply decimate them?

Throughout the Cold War, this bit of simple logic was controversial. Some people insisted that we were better off with overkill, if only for political and psychological reasons. Others refused to believe that a great nation has based its policies for years and years on either reckless brinkmanship (see Chapter 8) or an atavistic notion of military superiority. Given such objections, I would hate to base my indictment of American policies on such a controversial point, especially since I can comfortably make my case on the accepted facts alone. So let us assume for now that, with nuclear weapons, the more you have, the better off you are. Let us also assume that other meaningless technical aspects like pinpoint warhead accuracy really matter. Let us then ask: Who's stronger? To do this, we must take out our balance sheets, outmoded texts on strategic theory, and start counting.

A Note on the Reliability of Data

Before we start the actual counting, we need to examine our sources of information. Until 1985, the Soviets were not given to the habit of disclosing facts about their military machine. Their spy-mania was so deeply rooted that they did not even teach their soldiers how to read topographic maps, let alone issue them such maps.[8a] Almost all the facts about the military balance originated therefore from official American sources.

Modern governments know all too well the close link between information and political power and they do not hesitate to color the truth when they believe it is in their interests to do so.[9] We must examine what bias, if any, each side introduces to the information it disseminates about the military balance. As far as the Soviets were concerned, their conduct accorded with common sense, history, and Harold Brown's theory of appearances (Chapter 5). The few facts about the military balance which they used to divulge, and the general picture they tried to portray, downplayed American strength (the Chinese Paper Tiger Tactic) and inflated their own.[10a] Summarizing the postwar record, one historian explains that Moscow compensated for American superiority through policies of deliberate deception. It did not reveal the extent of postwar demobilizations. To the contrary . . . it encouraged its adversaries to believe that there remained forces that could be unleashed, yet farther afield if necessary. . . . Stalin belittled the importance of the atom while directing a top priority effort to unlocking its secrets. The first longer-range bombers . . . would make flypasses . . . in front of assembled foreign dignitaries, double back, and fly past again to give the appearance of greater numbers. When the first few missiles were developed . . . Soviet leaders made fantastic claims as to their effectiveness . . . long after it was realized that they were in fact so primitive and so faulty that few if any were likely to reach their targets.[11]

Now, here is a strange thing. The U.S. government—the world's chief supplier of military data—also warped the balance by understating our power and overstating the Soviets'. This consistent bias ran counter to our supposed doctrine of appearances. It ran counter to our general aversion to cooperating with the Soviets in military affairs. It ran counter to our avowed respect for the truth. Above all, it ran counter to our national interest. Nonetheless, our government deliberately *distorted* the military balance in favor of the Soviet Union.

It would take too much space to recount here our government's lack of candor, or to even marshal the opinions of many independent observers.[12] Instead, I shall only quote and comment upon the views of a former Assistant to the Deputy Secretary of Defense:

National security studies almost inevitably . . . tend to cease concentrating on the evidence . . . cease to examine the facts, and concentrate on organizing them to prove something . . . their resulting assessment of the balance . . . is tailored to 'sell,' rather than measure each side's capability.[13a]

This candid appraisal of the situation appeared in a highly regarded, semi-official analysis of the military balance. Among other things, this publication included forewords by two conservative, high-ranking, Republican senators. The institutionalized falsification of data this publication divulges is critically important to any appraisal of the military balance. The views of this high-ranking official merit therefore close scrutiny:

I. Every estimate of the balance was ultimately derived from the U.S. government. Within the government, one agency, the Defense Intelligence Agency (DIA) was the "key link in shaping all free world estimates of Soviet force strength."

II. This "often leads to an exaggeration of Soviet capabilities."

III. DIA experts knew what was expected of them and what was likely to satisfy their superiors. "Both military and civilian bureaucracies need high estimates of the threat to justify force levels, new weapons, and defense research."

IV. Intelligence officers were "usually prevented from comparing U.S. and foreign [read: Soviet] systems by informal pressures" from their superiors.

V. The hardliners' cause was helped by portraying our allies as weak. "Informal pressures" accounted for the tendency to "underestimate Allied capabilities."

VI. Intelligence officers were forced to offer estimates in areas where they could not conceivably know what was going on, thus making falsification easier for their, and everyone else's, consciences. This allowed them to "make guesses which maximize threat capabilities."

VII. Most of their superiors did not seek objectivity, but demanded estimates that would help them "meet their policies and needs."

VIII. These "bureaucratic and career pressures" could be explained by "a long tradition that intelligence is a servant and not a partner." In other words, they were traceable to a long tradition of distorting the truth, intimidating people whose duty it is to tell the plain truth, and of subverting the democratic process and our national security in favor of personal and organizational needs.[13a]

This prevarication, Soviet reticence, and the de facto Soviet-American collusion in presenting the same one-sided view of the military balance, constrain all attempts to arrive at an objective assessment. Thus, the USA has been almost certainly far stronger, and the USSR weaker, than the open literature suggests.

Before we take out our score sheets, let me restate the position we have just reached. I am trying to show that the link between deterrence and American military policies is tenuous. The overkill quality of nuclear weapons, I believe, makes my case conclusive.

But this being a moot point, I have, for argument's sake, conceded it to the opposition. Another popular argument for the arms race invokes Soviet superiority. To be evaluated, this argument calls for a factual analysis of the military balance. We need the true and relevant facts. But the facts which the Soviet and American governments chose to divulge—and these are virtually the only facts we have to go on—twist the military balance in favor of the Soviets. And again, for argument's sake, I shall totally ignore this bias. In other words, I am quite willing to meet the arms racers on their chosen battleground, on their own terms, and with their own prevaricated data. Despite these self-imposed handicaps, I am going to prove now that what they said about the military balance was incorrect: even if we were misinformed enough to think that "a decided advantage" could be enjoyed in the nuclear age, this advantage was enjoyed by the United States of America.

The Nuclear Balance

Number of Deliverable Nuclear Bombs

Some analysts view the number of warheads each side owned "as the single best, if oversimplified, 'figure of merit' in an overall comparison" of nuclear forces.[14a] The exact numbers throughout the last 46 years are uncertain.[5b,c,13-20] One 1988 source attributed 23,400 warheads[5d] to the USA and 33,000 to the USSR.[5e] A more meaningful "figure of merit," in my opinion, involved the number of warheads each country could fire at the other in a first strike. In this measure, the U.S. commanded, at the very least, a 40 percent edge. However, our government insisted that only bombs based in one "superpower" and capable of reaching the other should be counted. In this case, by 1990 the American government probably commanded over 12,000 bombs and the Soviet some 11,000, giving the U.S. a 9 percent advantage.[21]

We must be a bit more realistic, however. In 1983, for example, the USSR could also be razed by some 700 fighter-bombers and a few dozen ground-launched cruise missiles stationed in Europe, South Korea, and on aircraft carriers.[14b] No comparable Soviet forces were capable of razing the U.S. These American bombers and cruise missiles were equipped with nuclear bombs, they were assigned the task of attacking the Soviet Union, and they alone could decimate the Soviet Union. If we add them, the American advantage in deliverable warheads and bombs exceeded 50 percent.[20a]

American war plans also called for the use of low-yield nuclear weapons as ordinary bombs, cannonballs, or mines, in anti-submarine warfare, and for other limited objectives. In this category of "tactical" weapons, the U.S. was probably ahead too (by 25 percent to 300 percent, depending on your source).

Given this numerical superiority, one would expect our war intellectuals to have felt secure about this aspect of the nuclear balance. But they didn't. It turned out that, in the early 1980s, for every warhead placed on an American, British, or French missile located in Western Europe and marked for delivery to the Soviet Union, the Soviets may have had about three marked for Western Europe. These feelings of insecurity, and the measures that were taken in the early 1980s to alleviate them by placing all sorts of missiles on European soil, rested on the allegation that we had to be equal or superior to the Soviets in every single aspect of the military balance. This premise is strictly analogous to a basketball team worrying that the average height of the opposing, and emphatically inferior, team is a bit greater. They then recruit a 7'1'' guard for $10 million, just to make sure that even in this single aspect in which the inferior team is ahead—average height—superiority, or the appearance thereof, is achieved.

In conclusion, all through the 1980s Washington could deliver considerably more bombs to Soviet soil than Moscow could deliver to American soil. In Europe and elsewhere the U.S. had an edge in tactical weapons. Through fighter-bombers stationed in Europe, the U.S. enjoyed decisive edge in weapons which could be delivered to the Soviet Union from European soil (compared to weapons that could be delivered to Western Europe from Soviet soil). In the early 1980s, this edge in bombers stationed in Europe and elsewhere outside the United States was offset only in part by Soviet missiles targeted on Europe; by 1988, these missiles were negotiated out of existence. So, in the supposedly critical measure of deliverable nuclear warheads, we were ahead.

Explosive Yield

There is some uncertainty regarding the total explosive yield of the two arsenals in the 1980s. Estimates ranged from rough equality to Soviet superiority by a factor of two. The safest bet might give the Soviets a 50 percent edge.

When long-term radiation and environmental effects are considered, the greater explosive yield of the Soviet arsenal is of some value. But this figure is not as important to the overall destructive balance as it might first appear. A few warheads can cause much more damage than a single weapon whose explosive yield is equal to the sum of their yields, and the U.S. had more warheads. Moreover, a bomb that explodes closer to target causes more damage than a bomb that explodes farther away, and American warheads were more accurate. In fact, American planners made a deliberate choice, precisely because of such military considerations, to gradually reduce the explosive power of the average warhead in their arsenal to one-third of its 1960 levels.[5f,22] McGeorge Bundy, President Kennedy's special assistant for national security affairs, cites the "misuse" of the sharp reduction in the total yield of America's nuclear weapons, as a "remarkably clear example of the way" Reagan's Pentagon "engaged in strategic flimflam; the reduction in megatonnage it so proudly cited was the incidental consequence of a military decision to multiply the real destructive power of the bomber force."[23]

Taking into account now both measures—number of deliverable warheads and explosive power—we can still say that the U.S. had a marked edge in the overall destructive balance, or, if the most favorable assumptions about Soviet power, and least favorable about American, are made, that they were equal.

Survivability of Nuclear Weapons

This aspect of the nuclear balance is more directly related to deterrence and politics than other aspects, so it is a far better candidate, I believe, for the title of single best "figure of merit" in the overall nuclear balance. We wish to compare here the nuclear positions of the two antagonists following a massive surprise attack which was aimed at destroying as many of their nuclear weapons as possible. This subject can be approached by comparing the vulnerability of each of the three legs—land-based missiles, bombers, and missile submarines—which made up the strategic triads of both nations, and then summing up these separate figures to compare the survivability of both nations' nuclear arsenals.

Let us begin with land-based missiles. These missiles carried less than 25 percent of the United States' strategic nuclear warheads, but almost 75 percent of the Soviet Union's. This was unfortunate for the Soviets. Over-reliance on land-based missiles was considered unsafe because such missiles were more susceptible than other delivery vehicles to direct attack. Soviet missiles and warheads were less reliable and accurate, so a greater fraction of American land-based missiles would survive a surprise attack. Throughout the 1980s, most American missiles were propelled by solid fuel and could be launched within seconds.[24] In contrast, even in the late 1980s, over 80 percent of Soviet missiles were propelled by liquid fuel[25a] and would have taken minutes to launch. Knowing that American missile silos could be emptied before they were hit, a Soviet planner would have been reluctant to launch a surprise attack. An American planner, on the other hand, hoping that Soviet missiles could be hit before they took off, might have been more tempted to launch a surprise attack.

Missile submarines were the most survivable nuclear weapons system. About 25 percent of Soviet warheads aimed at the U.S. were placed in nuclear submarines, compared to about 50 percent of American warheads. Moreover, Soviet submarines could spend much less time at sea. They were noisier and thus easier to detect. They required longer and more frequent maintenance. Unlike Soviet submarines, each American missile submarine had two alternate crews, allowing it to spend more than half its working life at sea.[26] Despite the Soviet Union's long coastline, Soviet submarines encountered more difficulties in going out from homeport to sea. Owing to this limited access and to the technological lead the U.S. commanded in anti-submarine warfare, Soviet submarines at sea were much more vulnerable to direct attack than American submarines. According to one source,[27] the USA (but not the USSR) deployed a vast network of sensors spread on the ocean floor, several hundred airplanes, and more than 80 special submarines to follow and destroy missile submarines.

These advantages enabled the USA to keep some 60 percent of its nuclear submarines at sea, while the USSR kept only 15 percent. Moreover, America's 60 percent were virtually invincible; the USSR's 15 percent were vulnerable.[5g] Conservative Soviet planners had to assume then that they would have comparatively little nuclear firepower left at sea following an American first strike; their American counterparts knew that they would have a lot left.

In the 1980s, about 25 percent of America's nuclear warheads were to be delivered by bombers. The Soviets had fewer bombers which could carry fewer bombs, so bombers would deliver less than one-tenth of their warheads. More than one-third of the American force, and probably zero of the Soviet, was on continuous alert. Overall, American bombers were superior to Soviet bombers. So here too, the Soviets had to assume that none of their bombers would survive an American first strike, Americans could safely assume that a sizable fraction of theirs would.

In all these calculations I've ignored cruise missiles, British, French, and Israeli nuclear forces, and the 700 or so American fighter-bombers which carried nuclear bombs and which were stationed at the time in Europe, Korea, and on aircraft carriers.[28] These weapons undeniably added to the West's survivability advantage, but, in deference to the Western position that they need not be counted, they will be omitted from the following estimate.

Despite the Soviets' many handicaps, it is still probably true that both sides had a secure second strike. If we accept the claim that quantities are important, the foregoing suggests that the U.S. had a considerable survivability edge. To arrive at a highly conservative estimate of this edge, let us suppose that one-third of the bomber force of each side survived a first strike and that one-sixth reached its targets. Let us further suppose that all submarines at sea survive and that some 15 percent of each side's land-based missiles survived. Finally, let us suppose that American fighter-bombers and missiles in Europe and elsewhere were not used in retaliation and that our allies stayed out of the exchange.

After a surprise attack against them, the Soviets might have been left with over 1,400 warheads, the Americans with over 4,000—an almost one to three ratio. This, as I have said, is a highly generous estimate (one to nine would be a far more realistic estimate[20b]), but many will take exception even to this. So let us not quibble and just conclude that more American warheads were likely to survive a Soviet surprise attack than vice versa. Therefore, in this critical measure of the nuclear and political balance— the power to deter (or to credibly threaten a first strike)—the United States enjoyed a decided advantage.

Defensive Measures

Before rounding out the 1980s' nuclear equation, let us consider defensive measures which could be brought to bear against nuclear weapons.

At present, there is no way of effectively defending one's country against modern ballistic missiles. Already in the 1960s, our hawks assured us that anti-ballistic missiles made such defense possible, but the project they urged upon us never got off the ground in either country for many valid technical, tactical, logical, and political reasons. (In the 1990s, they may try to revive this debate by overstating the performance of anti-ballistic missiles during the Persian Gulf War.) In the 1980s, the same hawks wrongly assured us (Chapter 5) that laser devices could do the job. For whatever these devices were worth, by 1991 the U.S. was light-years ahead.

Some bombers, unlike ballistic missiles, can be stopped with an adequate air defense system. The Soviet Union had only about 150 antiquated bombers able to reach the U.S. The U.S. had some 1,000 modern bombers, and they carried a much larger percentage of America's total number of warheads. The Soviets had to worry, in addition to their concerns about the United States' nuclear arsenal, about the arsenals of China, Britain, France, and Israel.[29] For these and other reasons, the Soviet Union invested much more than the U.S. in its air defense system. Consequently, this system, which included thousands of interceptor aircraft and surface-to-air missiles, was several times larger than ours.

For the most part, however, the Soviet massive air defense system was a gigantic mistake. It was ineffective against ballistic missiles. At best, it might have stopped only about 50 percent of U.S. bombers. It was costly. It could be easily crippled if a bomber attack was preceded by destruction of the main radar and command posts with a few submarine-launched ballistic missiles. It was quickly approaching obsolescence—many U.S. bombers, as well as some ground and naval forces, carried cruise missiles. These missiles could be launched a safe distance from target, were harder to stop than airplanes, and were far cheaper to produce than the air defense system that would have been needed to stop them. A publication of the U.S. National Academy of Sciences politely summed up the situation:

> The U.S. military remains confident that its strategic aircraft . . . can effectively penetrate Soviet defenses. Moreover, by upgrading the bomber force it is believed that this penetration capability can be maintained into the foreseeable future. Given this assessment of the limited effectiveness of Soviet air defense and the complete vulnerability of the Soviet Union to ballistic missile attack, continued Soviet emphasis on air defense remains something of a puzzle.[30]

Having been taught that the world of politics is a rational place, we find it hard to believe that dinosaurs like the Soviet air defense and the American spaced-based "initiative" (Chapter 5) are either meaningless or self-damaging. A little reflection, however, should convince anyone that this textbook dogma of rationality and patriotism is a myth (see Chapter 9).

Another defensive measure is evacuation of cities. The Soviets, we were told, invested much money on this measure; we spent almost nothing. From time to time, this led some sheepish Western strategists to conclude that Soviet evacuation plans gave them a tremendous edge—that, thanks to their awe-inspiring plans, the Soviets had no reason to fear us. To close this frightening civil defense gap, we were urged to hastily invest the needed billions.[13b]

Surely, we would have known when mass evacuation was afoot and could warn the Soviets to stop it or else. We could re-target our warheads in a few minutes to these new evacuation sites. We might have decided to re-target them to new heights (surface bursts increase radiation damage). What, pray, will happen to the Soviet economy if war did not materialize? What are all these good people going to eat? What about those freezing Russian winters, how will those city people survive in open trenches for weeks if we hit them at Christmastime? And what about that chilling forecast of nuclear winter?

This rhetorical list could be prolonged, but enough has been said to make it clear that evacuation of millions in an all-out nuclear war is a joke. We stopped our politicians from going ahead with such tomfoolery. If they could, Soviet citizens would have stopped their politicians too. Since they couldn't, their rulers betrayed their national interest by spending untold sums on yet another white elephant, while our politicians and their well-paid tacticians betrayed our national interest by claiming that this white elephant was a tiger.

The case of fallout shelters is altogether different. An extensive network of well-built and well-stocked shelters able to accommodate and sustain most people for about one month could considerably raise the fraction of survivors. If, to take an extreme example, we could put all Americans underground within ten minutes after a general alert has been sounded and keep them there for a month, our chances as individuals and as a nation of pulling through would have improved. The Soviets could have countered such a network by building and exploding more bombs, raising the number of surface bursts, or intermittently exploding their bombs for months. Fallout shelters were therefore just one part of a complex equation. As such, they need to be considered in working out the overall nuclear balance.

The USSR was reportedly spending much more on its program than the USA; in the 1980s, it had enough fallout shelters to accommodate about 10 percent of residents of cities whose population exceeded 25,000.[31a] More important, perhaps, most Soviet citizens knew what to do in times of emergency (walk slowly to the cemetery so as not to create panic, according to a once-popular Russian joke). To be on the safe side, we might conclude that the Soviets had an edge in the fallout shelter portion of their civil defense preparations. But even if it existed, this edge was not decisive in the overall 1980s' nuclear equation, and claims of a "civil defense gap" seriously misperceived reality. As one Secretary of Defense, writing *ex cathedra*, put it, the effectiveness of the entire Soviet civil defense program was "highly questionable."[31a]

The Overall Nuclear Balance

By 1991, the broad picture remained unchanged. The USA had more deliverable warheads, more accurate warheads, more reliable delivery vehicles and other equipment, and a more survivable nuclear force. The USSR had greater explosive yield, and, allegedly, a more adequate civil defense program. For all practical purposes a parity—which was unlikely to be altered by any conceivable technical development—prevailed. If we insist on ignoring overkill and on taking all components of the nuclear balance into consideration, measure for measure, we can still say that the U.S. had superior nuclear forces. The claim that the Soviet Union commanded nuclear superiority for a single day from 1945 to 1991, or that it was likely to command it in the next twenty years or so, was without foundation.

The Conventional Balance

A comprehensive review of the military balance must compare conventional forces. For one thing, American and Soviet non-nuclear forces frequently influenced the conduct of small nations. Throughout the 1980s, Nicaraguan domestic and foreign policies were shaped in part by the United States' potential and actual military presence in Central America; French and Hungarian policies took into consideration the Red Army's conventional strength. Moreover, some analysts argued that a strictly non-nuclear Soviet/American war could take place. In 1987, for instance, one influential Pentagon consultant used a variant of this argument to justify the nuclear arms race. This consultant readily conceded the United States' nuclear edge but averred that this edge had to be retained to offset Soviet conventional superiority. Without this edge, he implied, Western Europe and the Middle East would have been run over long ago by the vastly superior Warsaw Pact's non-nuclear forces.[32a] By 1990, even *Time* was dismissing such influential "thinkers:" "Scenarios for a Soviet invasion of Western Europe have always had a touch of paranoid fantasy about them."[33] But let us, for argument sake, grant the plausibility of such an invasion and examine the East/West 1980s' conventional balance of forces.

Throughout the Cold War, most Western strategists insisted that the Soviet Union could fight conventional wars better than the United States. They could not possibly mean that the Soviets were superior to us in conflicts far away from the Soviet Union's land mass. It is generally agreed that if a conventional war between the Western alliance and the USSR broke out in Africa or Latin America, if no proxies or guerrillas were involved, and if both sides were willing to push themselves to their limits, that the West would have prevailed.[34] According to one American analyst, in 1982 the Soviets were not even up to British standards: "The USSR, had it been in Britain's position, might not have been able to mount an operation to retake the Falklands; the Soviets had very limited naval infantry, no aircraft carriers comparable to the two used by the British, and no island bases in the South Atlantic."[25b] This Western advantage was underscored by an even greater disparity in the number of reliable Third World military bases—in 1988, 111 for the USA, a mere handful for the USSR.[25c] The popular claim about Soviet conventional superiority only made sense in connection with areas that could receive supplies and reinforcements via land routes from the Soviet Union—China, other poor countries on the Soviet Union's southern border (like Iran), and Western Europe. As far as China and other southern neighbors were concerned, this claim was perhaps true. Taken by themselves, American conventional forces may have not been able to prevent a Soviet conquest of Iran. However, the Soviet Union's military superiority over its southern neighbors did not tilt the conventional military balance in its favor, because this balance was, at the very least, offset by American ability to invade, blockade, or ostracize countries like Mexico or Cuba.

Putting aside areas where either the Americans or the Soviets were clearly superior, and the overall superior interventionary capacity of the U.S. in conflicts far away from either country's shores, we must still deal with the overall conventional balance, and with the important case of the conventional balance in Europe.

Here, our war party placed inordinate emphasis on static indicators of strength. It forgot that history teaches us precisely the opposite lesson—that the fortunes of non-nuclear wars between roughly equal opponents are determined by intangibles like superior strategy, morale, social cohesion, economy, technology, and flexibility.[35] In the Persian Gulf War, for example, many forecasts and strategic decisions were flawed precisely because they overrated the importance of static indicators. In Finland's Winter War (Chapter 3), a little David was fighting an oversized Goliath but the little David was more efficient and knew that justice was on his side, and withstood the giant's onslaught for months against all odds. During the Nazi invasion of the Soviet Union,[14c] the Nazis had fewer men and weapons than the Soviets (e.g., 2,434 Nazi for 24,000 Soviet tanks; less than 3,000 Nazi for 10,000 Soviet airplanes). Yet they were clearly winning at first (e.g., after just three months, the Nazis were deep inside Soviet territory and had lost 550 tanks to the Soviets' 17,500).

It is also difficult to share our strategists' grave worries about a deliberate Soviet invasion of Western Europe, loaded as it was with an amazing variety of nuclear weapons, and possessing, as we shall see, so many advantages over the Soviet Union. But let us, for argument's sake, accept the claims that static numbers are critically important and that the Soviets were mad enough to contemplate war in the European "theater," and inquire into the static balance of power in Europe and the world.

Standing Armies and Ground Forces

This subject will be approached through a brief examination of three historical points.

In 1976, NATO outspent the Warsaw Pact, had more soldiers, and (if a commonsense definition of reservists is used) had more reservists.[36]

In 1982, the U.S. and NATO countries had some 5 million people in uniform,[15a] the Warsaw "Pact" 4.8 million. The Soviets themselves had only 3.7 million people in uniform, of which one million were stationed on their long border with China. In Europe, NATO had 2.1 million, the "Pact" 1.6 million, and the Soviets less than one million. The respective figures for ready reserves were 5, 7.1, and 5.2 million. So, even if the Warsaw Pact had been a bona fide military alliance, the West had enjoyed ground forces superiority in Europe and the world.

In 1987, NATO had a total of three million active ground

forces, of which 2.4 million were stationed in Europe and 0.8 million in the alleged immediate area of conflict (Central Europe). For the Warsaw Pact, the respective figures were 3, 2.4, and 1 million. The numbers of active reservists were also roughly comparable.

There is still another static element which must be introduced into the total equation and which concerns the question: What is a soldier? Their definition was broader than ours, so more support personnel on their side were included in the overall numerical comparisons.[13c] Thus, even before the massive 1989 withdrawal of Soviet troops began, the actual numerical balance was more in our favor than a reading of official statistics suggests.

At the very least, a rough East/West parity in standing armies in both Europe and the world has prevailed in the 1980s. Combined with nuclear overkill and Soviet comparative rationality (Chapters 1, 7) in nuclear and foreign affairs (and not taking into consideration recent pullbacks of Soviet troops from Eastern Europe and the recent breakup of the Soviet Union itself), this parity suggests that aggression in Europe was "a high-risk option with unpredictable consequences."[15b] In other words, and contrary to most official pronouncements on the subject, it would have been insane for either side to launch a non-nuclear attack against the other.[37]

Airplanes

According to former Defense Secretary Brown, in 1980 we had air superiority "because our airplanes and pilots are superior to those of the Soviets, although their numbers are somewhat greater." By the mid-1980s, however, the qualitative gap was expected to be narrowed and not to be "sufficient to compensate for the quantitative advantage the Soviets will have by then."[31b] The issue is still controversial, and perhaps the Soviets were our equals by 1991. But it is likelier that our war intellectuals underestimated the importance of quality and that the skies would have been ours in conventional wars by 1991 too. Thus, in one engagement, the Syrians probably had the best equipment and training the Soviets were capable of giving, the Israelis the best the Americans were capable of giving. The final score: some 92 Syrian airplanes and 23 surface-to-air missile sites destroyed for 2 or 3 Israeli airplanes[38a] and one or two helicopters.[39] Similarly, the Persian Gulf War's score sheet suggests a qualitative gap between American and Soviet flying machines.

Tanks

In central Europe, the Warsaw Pact had many more tanks.[40a] But this edge was probably offset by NATO's superiority in the air (airplanes can destroy tanks), by the higher quality of its tanks, and by the greater number and superior quality of its anti-tank weapons.

In fact, Soviet over-reliance on tanks could have been a handicap. Former Secretary Brown asserted that anti-tank weapons might have "a revolutionary impact by the mid-1980s."[31b] Another expert stated that "both technical and cost considerations seem to point to a stronger position for anti-tank weapons in relation to tanks."[38b] To be sure, these appraisals could be mistaken and the tank might be as important in the future as it had been in the past. All the same, one thing is clear enough: we shall be ill-advised to defer resolution of this aspect of the military balance to mainstream Western pundits.[32] In all probability, if the Soviets had more cavalry divisions, our analysts would have lost much sleep over a "cavalry gap."

Navies

Despite the Soviet Union's long coastline, it had limited access to the oceans, especially in winter. Owing to geographic limitations, the Soviet Navy has been actually divided into four separate fleets with little ability to provide mutual support.[13d] Furthermore, the Soviet Union hasn't yet fully developed the traditions of a seafaring nation and its efforts to develop a navy like our own often began from scratch. Many other factors must be considered in working out the overall naval balance, some of course favorable to the Soviets. But I shall not go into details here since most independent analysts share the view that the "navies of the United States and her Allies have more and better warships and remain more capable than the Soviet Navy."[40b]

Interventionary Forces

In this century's volatile international climate, a nation's ability to conduct wars far away from its shores is considered important. The U.S. had the logistical network to do this, as shown by its massive interventions in Vietnam and Kuwait. The Soviets were behind.[41,42] Moreover, loyal troops were hard to come by in a police state. Soviet troops away from home could be fought with bullets, but they could perhaps also be fought with a standing offer of immigration visas to a country freer than their own. Thus, Soviet foreign adventures entailed higher risks of defection and the consequent blow to both Soviet interventionary effort and international image.

Other Factors Affecting the Military Balance

Technology

Recent wars (e.g., the Persian Gulf War) suggest that, under most circumstances, technological competence would have strongly influenced the outcome of Soviet/American conventional engagements. Similarly, the Soviet-American nuclear arms race has not involved a competition among soldiers, but among scientists, engineers, technologists, and industrialists. In all these professions, the USA far outshone the USSR. As a result, from 1945 through 1991, practically *every new military innovation* originated in the West.[10b,25d,38a]

National Economies

According to Marx and Lenin, military power hinges on economic strength. President Carter's Defense Secretary concurred: "Historically, victory in a long war goes to the side with the greater economic potential."[31c] Despite a 30 percent larger labor force, the Soviet economy was roughly half the size of ours.[43a] This does not even begin to tell the story, for the Soviet economy was also far more backward and inefficient (Chapter 1). Peacetime shortages of basic consumer goods were common. The Soviet transportation network was primitive by Western standards. In 1980, for example, the entire stock of Soviet passenger cars was smaller than the number produced in one year in Japan. Despite the Soviet Union's enormous size, total length of paved roads was a bit shorter than it was in the state of Texas alone.[43b] As we have seen, the USSR's agricultural sector employed 25 percent of the workforce (compared to our 3 percent) but could hardly meet domestic needs. We could raise defense expenditures sevenfold for a few years and keep better living standards than they kept in 1980. Their system, on the other hand, would have collapsed long before it reached such spending levels. Given these economic considerations, their chances of emerging victorious in a protracted conventional war against the U.S. were close to zero.

Moreover, we were not the only ones to dislike the Kremlin. The Western Europeans, whose combined economy was at least twice as large as the Soviets', bore them a grudge. Japan, with an economy roughly the size of theirs and short a few islands, was a potential enemy too. Everything that has been said in comparing the Soviet economy to the American could be said in regard to Western Europe, and to a certain extent, Japan. So, when we look at the combined economic force of all these nations, the Soviet Union emerges as a bantam cock. One then begin to wonder: Was the claim of a Soviet menace based on objective reality, or was it the cleverest deception of the twentieth century?

Democracy

Though the American system of government is a far cry from a genuine democracy (Chapters 3, 9), throughout the Cold War it came nearer to this ideal than the Soviet system. Hence, over the long term the U.S. commanded a more effective decision-making process (Chapter 1). This advantage is less obvious, and less consistent with the historical record, than a larger and more efficient national economy. Nevertheless, under some circumstances it could be just as important.

Appreciation for the bond between democracy and military might goes at least as far back as Herodotus:

> Thus did the Athenians increase in strength. And it is plain enough not from this instance only, but from many everywhere, that freedom is an excellent thing; since even the Athenians, who,

while they continued under the rule of tyrants, were not a whit more valiant than any of their neighbors, no sooner shook off the yoke that they became decidedly the first of all.[44]

Allies

The Soviets had no friends to speak of, even if one were naive enough to take the Warsaw Pact seriously. In fact, all of the strongest nations on earth were neutral or on our side. Germany alone came close to defeating the Soviets in 1941, and might have done so had it not been fighting on two fronts, had its occupation policies been less heinous, and had the U.S. not been there to help the Soviets. Japan held its own warring with old Russia, as did France. Nothing, as far as I can tell, has conferred a "superpower" status on Russia since its losing war with Japan.

True, the Soviets possessed more nuclear weapons and delivery vehicles than our allies. But France and Britain had already, in my opinion, a credible nuclear deterrent.[45] It would have taken a reckless Soviet leader to apply nuclear blackmail to either one, even if that country were to face this blackmail completely alone. Moreover, many of our allies were thoroughly capable of developing a respectable nuclear deterrent of their own within a few years. So the limited French and British nuclear arsenals, and the nonexistent arsenals of a few other American allies, may reflect nothing more than a deliberate decision to rely in whole or in part on our "nuclear umbrella," instead of going to the trouble and expense of creating one of their own.

To illustrate this point, let us imagine that by 1985 the U.S. sank into the sea and that American nuclear forces stationed in Western Europe came under European command. Imagine also that the Europeans were willing to defend themselves, and that they decided to completely integrate their military into a single functional unit. Who would be ahead now, they or the Soviets? For a while the Soviets might have enjoyed numerical superiority in nuclear weapons. But this superiority doesn't mean much, for the Europeans would have more than enough to pulverize the Soviet Union in a retaliatory strike. As far as conventional forces are concerned, if the morale of troops, technological lead, democratic efficiency, and like factors are taken into consideration, it is, to say the least, an open question as to who would have been ahead (see below). The Soviets would still have China, Japan, Australia, and Canada to worry about. Couple this with the Europeans' superior economy and other elements in the overall military balance, and in the long run, I'd say, they would have been considerably superior, with or without the Americans.

Another myth which the Soviets invented, and which some of our politicians were all too eager to accept, was the Warsaw Pact. In the event of a conventional war, we were told, soldiers from the then satellite nations of Eastern Europe would have fought along their Soviet comrades. Could anyone ever be reasonably confident that most Czechs, Germans, or Poles would have bravely fought and died in the cause of the nation that trampled their national independence and individual freedoms under foot?[46]

Internal Dissension

The Warsaw Pact was not the only myth. Long before 1992, objective analysts insisted that the Soviet Union itself was, in some ways, a myth too. Would the non-Russian half of the population have fought in the Soviet Union's cause against the West if the most likely outcome of defeat would be greater national independence? Would the Estonians, Ukrainians, or Abkhasians have fought us or deserted to our side? And what about the oppressed Russians themselves? Some observers believed that, "if war with the West should break out, Soviet soldiers would surrender by the million. . . . And the politburo has no illusions about this."[8b]

This view is strongly supported by the historical record. The Nazis were received with open arms when they first invaded the Soviet Union,[8c] and could have had most of the population on their side. Foolishly and heartlessly, however, they treated the people in the occupied lands even more savagely than the communists did, arousing their hatred and patriotism. Even so, many Soviet citizens fought in Nazi ranks. "This was a phenomenon totally unheard of in all world history: that several hundred thousand young men . . . took up arms against their Fatherland as allies of its most evil enemy."[47a]

Yet some of our warpath intellectuals ignored this question of morale in working out the military balance. They would have had us believe that, say, in 1983, Hungarians would have fought for the Soviet State just as well as Georgians, Georgians as well as Russians, and Russians as well as Germans or Frenchmen defending their own soil, national independence, and individual freedoms.

Homeland Invasion

Given the Cold War's military and political realities, it was unrealistic to suppose that American territory could be invaded. No one was about to invade Soviet territory either, but this was something that Soviet rulers had to be worried about because their lands had often been invaded, and because many powerful nations (including China, Japan, and Germany) had territorial claims against them.

Organizational Inefficiencies

One analyst argues that organizational inefficiencies within the American Armed forces constituted the "root cause of America's military decline."[48a] Other analysts might disagree with this sweeping generalization, but most would probably concur that comparative efficiencies must be considered in any meaningful discussion of the military balance.

Military organizations are perceived in some quarters as models of efficiency. Historians often speak admiringly of Alexander the "Great's" army, or about the awesome Nazi war "machine." Yet some students of the military and other organizations, as well as people who had the dubious pleasure of wasting a few years of their lives inside a typical military unit, know that such organizations are scandalously inept.

My own experiences strongly supports this dim view of military prowess. Years ago, I informally interviewed dozens of active paratroopers of the Israeli Defense Forces—members of an elite combat unit in one of the world's best armies. Yet they were perplexed by the rigidity, inefficiency, and foolishness that afflicted every facet of their unit's operations. They traced their country's swift victories to factors such as superior morale and technology. At the same time, they often felt that these factors would have amounted to very little if the military organizations facing them had not been even more incompetent than their own.

According to one writer, the U.S. Department of Defense is characterized by a state of organized anarchy and institutional drift which inhibit efficiency and increase "the likelihood of failure. Parochial service interests still dominate defense decision making . . . . the services are led to pursue weapons development programs that serve more to protect their share of the pie than to guarantee the nation's security." Bureaucratic politics in an organized anarchy provide "startling insights" into the 1980 failure to rescue U.S. hostages held in Iran. "Logic and efficiency demand that a complex operation be undertaken by a small, tightly organized force; organized anarchy demands 'a piece of the action' by all services."[49] Needless to say, all four services were involved in the abortive operation. According to another Western analyst, "although much of the defence debate is cast in terms of meeting the threat from the Soviet Union, in fact the military services are often more concerned with the threats they pose to each other."[50]

Another analyst traces the poor performance of the U.S. military in places like Vietnam, Grenada, and Lebanon to "fundamental maladies of our defense establishment." To students of organizational logic, the structural problems this noted analyst sees in the U.S. military are strongly reminiscent of Parkinson's classical description of such decaying organizations as the British Colonial Office.[51] For instance, this analyst concludes that the U.S. military defense system is "quite incapable of self-reform." The armed forces also mimic the classical British case with the disproportionate growth in the number of senior officials. On June 30, 1945, there were 2,068 flag-rank officers (senior officers, starting from one-star brigadier general and Navy commodores and going all the way to four-star generals and admirals) in the American Armed Forces. "A good many of them were employed in direct command . . . The supporting organizations . . . accounted for only a small part of the flag-rank total. . . . the ratio of flag-rank officers to enlisted men was 1.9 per 10,000. . . . By 1980 . . . the ratio had increased . . . to 6.4 . . . or more than three times the 1945 level." This analyst goes on to argue that "the increased ratio encompasses the root cause of America's military decline."

A summary of the resultant problems again parallels the British case. "An overhead of greatly disproportionate size had found employment for itself in the systematic overcomplication of every aspect of peacetime defense and of whatever warfare we have had. . . . In the peacetime workings of the defense establishment, the combination of civilian and military overmanagement systematically rejects any simple, direct, and economical solution. . . . When there is fighting to be done . . . bureaucratic compromises displace the tactical ingenuity, operational art, and sharp choices that strategy always demands."[48b]

Though the point of military efficiency is rarely raised in discussions of the military balance, it contributes to threat inflation. Seeing the all-too-familiar inefficiencies that permeate his side, the typical analyst (who is rarely a student of organizational logic) tends to dismiss evidence that they also afflict the other's military machine. Thus, even independent American analysts were inclined to view the Soviet defense establishment as vastly more efficient and rational than their own.

The Soviets were more secretive. As we have seen, they were also, unlike Americans, strongly committed to portraying their military and civilian organizations in the rosiest possible terms. However, the little evidence that is available about the Soviet military establishment suggests that in this critical measure of the military balance—comparative inefficiency—the Soviet Union was not ahead of the United States.

According to one observer, "a detailed look at the real state of the armies of the two military blocs leads inescapably to the conclusion that neither army is particularly prepared for . . . serious warfare, and that the military men who control their respective machines are not . . . very interested in changing this state of affairs."[52] The picture this observer portrays of the Soviet armed forces is, if anything, grimmer than the American picture. Soviet soldiers were chronically underfed and malnourished. Diseases caused by vitamin deficiencies were common. Racial discord, lack of discipline, and physical intimidation were customary. Alcoholism and theft of military supplies were rampant. "The unofficial organization of Soviet units, in which at any time half . . . is being brutalized and exploited by the other half, is hardly likely to foster the trust and mutual confidence that makes for cohesion." At the upper levels, corruption, intrigue, and favoritism were endemic.

Officers were usually promoted on the basis of loyalty and connections, not competence. Compared to their Western counterparts, Soviet soldiers, pilots, and seamen on active duty and in reserve units were insufficiently trained. As in agriculture, initiative and decentralization—so critical to successful military performance —were discouraged, and for similar reasons. Though these problems seriously detracted from combat efficiency and readiness of most units, little was done to curb them.

As in the U.S., weapons production suffered from "bureaucratic stagnation." Soviet production would often start and continue for bureaucratic reasons, not to fill a genuine military need. Operational performance of Soviet tanks, airplanes, missiles, and other weapon systems was usually inferior to Western performance. The costly and impractical Soviet civilian defense (evacuating and sheltering civilians from nuclear attack) had "little or nothing to do with actual warfare and everything to do with internal military politics, as is so often true with Soviet (or U.S.) military affairs."

To sum up. Scandalous as the situation within the American armed forces has been, we may safely conclude that, on this critical measure of the military balance (organizational inefficiencies), Americans have not been worse off than the Soviets.

Additional Soviet Advantages

A few Soviet advantages bore directly on the overall military balance:

I. Being more used to privations and hardships, Soviet citizens might have adjusted more readily to war conditions.

II. Soviet leaders were often willing and able to sacrifice countless lives. They could begin and end a war at will. They could increase military spending and starve a fraction of the people with impunity. In politics and war, savagery has its rewards. According to one account,

> More than a million Soviet soldiers were killed during the last two weeks of the war for the sake of being the first in Berlin—a priority which was unnecessary for final victory, which was about to be achieved anyway. . . . During the last few weeks of fighting, the Soviet army lost more soldiers and officers than the British and American armies lost during the whole war.[53]

In the "Great Patriotic War," trouble-makers of all sorts, supposed cowards, and others were assigned to penal units. Of these units, the largest were the penal battalions. Each penal battalion was made up of three penal companies, a guard company, and an administrative group. Just prior to an attack, the penal companies were brought to the front and given weapons. The guards lined up behind them with machine guns and the men were ordered to attack. If they stayed put, they were mowed down by the guards; if they attacked, they were mowed down by the Nazis. The few survivors of one such engagement were routinely given another, so wartime assignment to a penal battalion was only marginally superior to outright execution. Some observers believe that these battalions made notable contributions to Soviet victory in World War II and that they could continue to play a key role in future conflicts.[8d,47b]

III. The Soviet Union's economic and military machine was less dependent than the West's on imports of raw materials (but more dependent on high technology goods).

IV. In 1946, Stalin said in an "election" speech: "the Soviet social order is a form of organization, a society superior to any non-Soviet social order."[10c] He said this about a social order that came close to defeat at the hands of a much smaller Germany fighting simultaneously on two fronts; an order that was based on terror, the like of which had rarely been recorded in the annals of our weary planet; an order that was spared disastrous defeat, as he himself acknowledged at one point, in part through the massive support it received from "inferior" democracies. He said this about a country that might have been, without the help of the Bolsheviks, at the forefront of civilization and culture by 1946, but that, thanks to them, was a pathetic backwater. He said all this when the U.S. could have run him and his superior order to the ground with either conventional or nuclear weapons, as he would have probably done, unprovoked, if he could.

The point here is not what this shrewd villain (whose successor would one day describe as "a criminal, an assassin, a mass murderer"[54]) had to say, but that we took his tiresome boasts seriously. Despite the obvious and observable contradictions, we still listened to propaganda East and West. This Western myopia constituted a major military and political advantage for the Soviet Union. When NATO's Supreme Commanders, one after another, complained for years about Western inferiority, they compromised Western security. When American Presidents, one after another, sang weekly praises of Soviet might and the wonders of totalitarian efficiency, Westerners might have believed them, with cool reason giving way to panic. This curious and consistent lack of objectivity in Western perceptions of Soviet military prowess was an important Soviet asset in the overall military balance.

V. We have seen that the Nazis were unable to make use of the low morale of Soviet troops. Though they realized the nature of the penal battalions, they were unable to adjust their strategy to fit the new circumstances (for example, by letting those unwilling kamikazes through their lines, disarming them without firing a single shot, and treating them well). Likewise, our generals and politicians frequently failed to take advantage of the low morale of our adversaries' troops. This myopia partially offset the lower morale of their troops.

VI. From the military standpoint, the Soviet Union was a monolith. Its equipment was standardized and its rigid command structure went all the way to Moscow. In comparison to this, the West was a veritable motley crew. Owing to national rivalries, NATO's military equipment was not standardized and its command structure relied on semi-voluntary cooperation among all member countries. On some occasions, diversity could prove a handicap. (On others, however, diversity could be a blessing. It permits, for instance, greater initiative to commanders more familiar with actual field conditions, and it entails fewer adverse consequences when a particular weapon turns out to be a dud.)

VII. Top Soviet leaders tended to stay longer in power than American leaders. They were thus, ironically, in a better position to learn from their mistakes. They possessed more varied professional backgrounds than the lawyers and businessmen who made up the bulk of America's political elite. They owed their rise to power to something other than eloquence, youthful looks, a full head of hair, or a firm handshake. They had to go through a far more grueling process of getting to the top and staying there. They had virtually a free hand in foreign and military affairs and could consistently pursue long-term goals. Because they "refer to much broader trends and take a longer perspective than is usual for most Western statesmen,"[43c] their policies enjoyed greater tenacity and coherence. Considering the gains this consistent edge made possible throughout the Cold War, it could perhaps be viewed as their strongest suit in the overall military balance.

Concluding Remarks

The chief conclusion from the foregoing account is that, at the very least, the United States has been the military equal of the Soviet Union. This conclusion being so clear and irrefutable, it compels the subsidiary conclusion that anyone voicing a different opinion was either misinformed or insincere.[55] The following curious anecdote, taken out of hundreds, vividly illustrates the confusion surrounding this subject. In August 1983, *Armed Forces Journal International* awarded one of its symbolic darts (a slap on the wrist) to the then Secretary of Defense for his "appalling track record in telling Congress and the American public about the strategic balance." "Americans know," the *Journal* went on, that "there is something wrong with the strategic balance, and so far have supported the President's efforts to fix it. But . . . the day has arrived when the Secretary of Defense must appeal to reason, not just rest on authority."[56]

I hope that this chapter explains such evasions: from August 6, 1945 to December 25, 1991; from the atomic destruction of Hiroshima to the breakup of the Soviet Union, an appeal to reason would have made a mockery of our government's version of the military balance.

Summary

In view of the United States' and the Soviet Union's enormous nuclear arsenals, and in view of the fact that either side could destroy the other after the worst imaginable surprise attack, minute comparisons of their military machines are futile. Moreover, such historical comparisons are still handicapped because they rely on the information both governments wished to share with the world's people, an information which has been consistently distorted in the same direction: both governments massively overstated Soviet power and understated American power. Nevertheless, since claims of Soviet superiority, or near-superiority, fueled the arms race since its inception, they must be examined.

On the nuclear front, the USA had more deliverable warheads, more accurate warheads, more reliable equipment, and a far more survivable nuclear force. The USSR was said to possess a greater explosive yield and a more adequate civil defense system. If the overkill quality of the nuclear arsenals is ignored, a nuclear advantage must be conceded to the United States.

American push for nuclear superiority has been sometimes explained as an effort to counterbalance Soviet advantage in conventional warfare and the consequent Soviet ability to run over Western Europe in a matter of weeks. From 1945 through 1991, such claims had an air of unreality about them. Even in central Europe, roughly equal numbers of troops faced each other throughout most of the Cold War. The Soviets had more airplanes, but the West had better pilots and its airplanes were far more advanced; the West would have probably controlled the European skies in the event of war. The Soviets had more tanks, but the West had better tanks and more and better anti-tank weapons. The U.S. enjoyed decisive superiority at sea, had greater access to many more reliable military bases throughout the world, and a far greater capacity for overseas military intervention. The U.S. was far superior in science and technology, economic performance, efficiency of its political system, strong and reliable allies, cohesion of populace and troops, and invulnerability to homeland invasion. Although the armed forces of both nations suffered from scandalous inefficiencies, the Soviets seemed to fare slightly less well on this critical aspect of the overall military balance. The Soviet people seemed better poised for the privations and hardships of war. The Soviet Union could more easily sacrifice the lives of its citizens for political and military objectives. The USSR benefited from the West's exaggerated portrayal of Soviet power and from the West's reluctance to make internal dissension in the Soviet Union a consistent feature of Western wartime strategy. The USSR derived some benefits from the centralized control of its military machine. In particular, it had a more competent and experienced top leadership and hence, more tenacious and coherent policies.

Thus, even if nuclear overkill and institutionalized biases are ignored, from 1945 through 1991 the USA emerges as militarily stronger than the USSR. Under the deterrence premise, the frequent claims to the contrary make no sense; under brinkmanship, they make perfect sense.

Chapter 7

HISTORY OF THE COLD WAR

There can be peace without appeasement. The attitude of almost the entire American people has been warped by a partial presentation of facts. . . . It is my belief that reactionary elements in both Britain and the United States are strengthening and hastening the development of the forces which they fear. . . . Depending on our decision, we shall become the most beloved or the worst hated nation of all history.

Henry A. Wallace,[1] 1948
(Vice-President of the U.S., 1941-45)

I have indeed the impression that our nation has gone mad and is no longer receptive to reasonable suggestions. Its whole development reminds me of the events in Germany since the time of Emperor William II: through many victories to final disaster.

Albert Einstein,[2] 1950

The invocation to historians to suppress even the minimal degree of moral or psychological evaluation which is necessarily involved in viewing human beings as creatures with purposes and motives . . . seems to me to rest upon a confusion of the aims and methods of the humane studies with those of natural science. It is one of the greatest and most destructive fallacies of the last hundred years.

Isaiah Berlin,[3] 1954

The last two chapters have been forced to conclude that official explanations for American military policies in the 1980s had been based on irrelevant or disingenuous strategic considerations and on false claims about the military balance. The history of the arms race, this chapter will try to show, clinches the case against Cold War America.

155

This is not the place to present a comprehensive history of the arms race. Rather, I shall merely discuss bits and pieces of this history, not necessarily in chronological order, and draw from them some general conclusions. But, from our standpoint here, the brevity of this rough sketch detracts little from the general picture to which it gives rise, for this picture fits well with the entire history of the Cold War. There is, moreover, every reason to believe that this tragic picture does not merely apply to the past and present, but also—barring a cataclysm, lack of barely credible enemies, or a sharp break from past practices—to the future.

Peace or War?

Before evaluating the past, we must resolve a controversial issue which confronted policy makers and the public throughout the Cold War: Should the West pursue, if given a choice, peaceful coexistence with Russia, or should it pursue an indefinite continuation of the arms race? I shall begin by considering arguments against coexistence:

I. To keep its economy going, the West had to import raw materials from the vast underdeveloped regions of the Third World. It had to purchase these materials at reasonable prices and it had to keep open the investment opportunities and markets that these underdeveloped regions provided. To guarantee these economic objectives, and its consequent long-term survival and freedom, the West had to retain its predominant position in that part of the Third World which is already under its influence. To retain its position, it had to close out the hostile Soviet Union. This, in turn, could only be accomplished by keeping the arms race going and by retaining or regaining a favorable asymmetry in the nuclear balance of terror. Although the West paid a high price for this policy (Chapters 2, 3), it was a price it could afford. In contrast, coexistence might have entailed loss of profits and economic decline.

This argument—which has rarely been stated so starkly but which is believed by some observers to account for the nuclear arms race (Chapter 5)—will be appraised in Chapter 8.

II. If we want to preserve peace, we must be prepared for war by continuing the arms race.

This argument ignores nuclear realities. We could abandon the race, substantially diminish its various costs and risks, and still prevent aggression against us and our allies by retaining a minimum deterrent.

This argument only applies to unreasonable aggressors. In the 1930s, Czechoslovakia could not dissuade Nazi Germany from attack. So, small as it was, Czechoslovakia would have done well to be prepared for war, as would Britain, the Soviet Union, and other victims of unprovoked Nazi aggression. But history suggests that if both sides are reasonable and if both are willing to seriously consider bilateral disarmament and the gradual phasing out of the military option, then the best way of preserving peace is by *not* preparing for war. We consider war between the United States and Canada unthinkable, but things were not always that way. We have a lasting peace because Britain and the United States were far-sighted enough to gradually give up the military option. So, even if the overkill argument is rejected, our response to the perceived totalitarian threat should have depended on the totalitarians' interest in mutual disarmament. If they were interested, we could best safeguard peace not by racing with them, but by putting an end to the arms race.

III. The Soviets harbored imperialistic ambitions which could only be contained by force.

During the greater part of the Cold War, Soviet imperialism is undeniable. Likewise, many people point to our record of intervention in the internal affairs of many countries, often against genuine democrats and for bloodthirsty tyrants, and claim that American imperialism is undeniable. But disarmament, not imperialism, is the issue. Again, the question is not what anyone's wish is, but whether the Soviets were rational enough to see that their self-interest required acquiescence to a modus vivendi with the democratic West.

IV. "Why," asked one hardliner, "should they act honorably and nobly towards you when they crush their own people?"[4]

To begin with, neither Khrushchev nor Gorbachev crushed their people. But let us grant the likelihood of Boris Yeltsin being replaced by a hardliner; or let us recall the times when brutality reigned. What, then, should one do if one's fundamental interests, or even one's life, are tied to those of a knave?

If the knave is rational enough to see that a compromise can serve his interests, earnest negotiations are in order. At the same time, the negotiated agreement should bar the knave from gaining an advantage. Likewise, we should have negotiated, assumed that the Soviets would cheat if cheating served their interests, and put as many safeguards in place as were needed to make sure that it did not. To paraphrase Adam Smith, it is not from the benevolence of powerful knaves that we ought to expect our security, but from their regard for their own interests.

This leaves us with the question: were the requisite safeguards in existence? As a perennial feature of Cold War sophistry, verification deserves a close look. First, a consensus which emerged in a gathering of American experts: "Our verification abilities . . . permit confidence that . . . violations of agreements . . . [cannot] become dangerous to our security."[5]   Second, the search for absolute certainty about every detail of Soviet military activities (which verification "concerns" often presupposed), like the search for many other absolutes, was misguided in principle. Until 1987, we only needed to strive for "a workable verification system" able to detect "*militarily significant* violations in time to make an appropriate response."[6] Opponents of peaceful coexistence have never been able to describe or *imagine* a single credible instance of cheating which would have violated this eminently reasonable criterion of verification adequacy. And, from 1987 to 1991, verification disputes lost any shred of relevance to the real world, for by then the Soviets learned to live with intrusive on-site verification measures.

Take, for instance, the endless Cold War disputes regarding a treaty to ban all nuclear test explosions. Leaving aside contrived allegations that only the American stockpile of weapons needed to be tested, that only American weapon makers would suffer declining morale and performance,[7a] and that the Soviets would conduct clandestine nuclear explosions on the moon,[7b] verification emerged as the only credible bone of contention. Yet this concern, which appealed to reasonable suspicions of Bolshevism, was just as dissembling as the others. In 1985, according to a U.S. government geologist, it was "clear that political considerations have stood in the way of . . . [the] treaty all along, and verifications problems have been used as an excuse."[8] The price for this was not only peace and justice, but national security in its most traditional, hardline sense. Looking back on America's refusal to conclude a comprehensive test ban treaty in 1963, our one-time chief negotiator in the Moscow talks observed: "When you stop to think of what the advantages were to us of stopping all testing in the early 1960s when we were still ahead of the Soviets it's really appalling to realize what a missed opportunity we had."[9a]

V. The international system is based on anarchy and on the rule that might is right. We cannot, under any circumstance, relax or entertain the notion that peace is possible. We must convince ourselves instead that victory is possible or at least convince the Soviets that we are crazy enough to think so.

This argument is similar to the above. Sadly, its anarchic premise is correct. But, as I have said, this is not an argument against all negotiations, only against careless and naive concessions.

Also, history suggests that this jaundiced view of human nature, which ignores the plasticity of human behavior and its dependence on cultural and social influences, is mistaken. Cannibalism and slavery were probably seen once as uncontrollable sides of human nature. The ancient Scythians used enemy scalps as napkins and enemy skulls as drinking cups. They most likely derided, or scalped and turned into drinking vessels, reform-minded fellow tribesmen wishing to discontinue this practice. Dueling is the subject of historical novels, not TV news. Not so long ago, it was fashionable to ascribe poverty and infectious diseases to bad genes. Our descendants may one day consider the hardliners' belief that wars and nation states are in the nature of things in a similar light. Without unduly risking our individual freedoms, we ought to ease this transition into a better world, not stand in its way.

VI. Totalitarianism is far more efficient than democracy. We must double our efforts and keep up with these efficient monsters, or else we shall become slaves.

Among other things, this argument persistently ignored overkill, the futility of the quest for superiority in the nuclear age (Chapters 5, 6), and totalitarian backwardness (Chapter 1).

VII. Totalitarianism is terribly inefficient: everything they could do we could do better. In the end the West would have achieved a decisive edge, liberated the Kremlin's long-suffering subjects, and made the world safe for democracy.

The premise of this argument is defensible (Chapter 1), its goals commendable, but its application placed civilization at a grave risk. It was too late by the mid-1960s, short of an unforeseeable and extremely improbable scientific breakthrough, to gain a decisive edge (Chapter 5). We would have been wiser to abandon the illusory quest for a successful military showdown and find other means of advancing the cause of freedom. The problem with this approach then (seen from my own anti-totalitarian perspective) was not its goals but its failure to assimilate nuclear realities, its disregard for the enormous costs and hazards of the arms race, its dismissal of evidence which suggested that cooperation was more likely to bring about democratization of the USSR, the short shrift it gave to the observable realities of our common humanity and interdependence, and its presumption that the USA stood for freedom in the Third World (Chapter 8).

VIII. Even if we succeeded in turning our swords into plowshares and preserving our freedom, what could we do with the millions of Westerners who would have been thrown out of work? Could the free world's economy survive peace? Was not a Cold War, and a small chance of a diabolically Hot War, better than the economic chaos that would have surely come in the aftermath of peace?

We could, if we wished, have peace *and* greater prosperity, more leisure, and less unemployment than we had. History tells us that much: the end of World War II brought massive conversion of our economy from military to civilian footing, and greater prosperity. There is no reason to believe that this historical precedent could not be repeated. Common sense tells us as much: After all, from the consumer's standpoint, the military is useless. Soldiers do not put food on our tables nor can tanks get us anyplace in a hurry. If nothing else, we could convert our tanks to bicycles or go on paying these millions of people the same salaries for producing tractors, fighting pollution, teaching in our crowded classrooms, or sunbathing.

We could also overcome some of the challenges of peace by reducing the workweek and sharing the shrinking work and expanding leisure more equally, as some Scandinavian countries have been doing.[10] Simple devices like negative income tax could minimize the real costs of peace by setting a floor to the standard of living below which no person's income is allowed to fall.[11] Fairly slight increases in corporate taxes could also help us meet the economic challenges of peace.[12]

Most independent experts would probably agree that although the obstacles to conversion from military to civilian spending in the West are real, they "would not form a serious barrier to disarmament if political conditions were suitable. . . . Cutbacks in the scale likely to be caused by any arms control agreement could be easily absorbed through compensatory policies directed at the industries most affected. . . . While economic considerations play a part in the opposition in the United States towards any policy of disarmament, the most serious obstacles lie elsewhere."[13a] Similarly, in the Soviet Union, "the difficulties of conversion, although considerable, are not insuperable. They could be overcome if the appropriate political conditions prevailed, and the political will existed to surmount them."[13b]

IX. The Soviets, according to a former American President, "cannot vastly increase their military productivity. . . . But they know our potential capacity industrially, and they can't match it."[14] Because they were poorer than us, we could bring them to their knees by increasing military spending to a point where they could no longer keep up. For decades, their economy has already been wobbly and short on such vital commodities as grain and computer parts. With the added pressure of a revved up military competition, the Soviet Union was bound to either lose this competition or else collapse. A variant of this argument suggests that, by forcing them to spend enormous sums on arms, we prevented them from using the money in ways which could be even more damaging to our interests than their military spending.

Some people go on to suggest that this argument has been vindicated by history. From 1980 to 1985, they say, the U.S.

military budget rose by some 53 percent (in real terms). Consequently, in the seven years that followed, both the Soviet empire and its military machine suffered severe setbacks.

It would have taken decades to achieve the point of economic attrition or of meaningful political gains. Was it wise, in the admittedly long intervening period, to undertake the enormous costs of the arms race (Chapters 2, 3)? This argument ignores overkill, for even if they stopped racing and kept their existing arsenal, they would have remained unbeatable. Before they reached the point of economic collapse, they might have acknowledged overkill, and all our lost trillions of dollars would have amounted to nothing. Through a policy of economic attrition, we merely robbed their helpless subjects of leisure and consumer goods. The rulers, no matter what we did, lived comfortably. This, and the entire historical record, strongly suggest that their system was unlikely to perish by whatever level of military spending we saddled it with.

Although the attribution of Soviet setbacks and the breakup of the Soviet Union itself to Reagan's military spending cannot be as readily dismissed, the record is open to other, no less plausible, interpretations. These setbacks can be reasonably ascribed to internal developments in the USSR and to Gorbachev's personality, not to Western pressures. Stalin responded to economic and military pressure through growing intransigence and by speeding up his own Manhattan Project; Khrushchev through a combination of disarmament proposals, the erection of the Berlin Wall, and setting the stage for the Cuban Missile Crisis; Brezhnev through a massive missile buildup. It thus could be argued that Gorbachev's program took place *despite* Reagan's buildup. Indeed, with more cooperative American policies, a similar revolution might have transpired earlier. According to *Time*:

> Gorbachev is responding primarily to internal pressures, not external ones. The Soviet system has gone into meltdown because of inadequacies and defects at its core, not because of anything the outside world has done or not done or threatened to do. Gorbachev has been far more appalled by what he has seen out his limousine window and in reports brought to him by long-faced ministers than by satellite photographs of American missiles aimed at Moscow. He has been discouraged and radicalized by

what he has heard from his own constituents during his walk-abouts in Krasnodar, Sverdlovsk and Leningrad—not by the exhortations, remonstrations or sanctions of foreigners.[15a]

As we have already seen, he has also been radicalized by what he has heard from his ecologists about the fate of the earth and from his economists about global interdependence. Memories of life under Stalin, of Khrushchev's brief thaw, and a seemingly extraordinary (for a politician) humanitarian streak must have also played a part.

The 1985-1991 Soviet twilight period shows that proponents of this economic argument against peace were insincere. Now that they have "succeeded," one would expect them to help Russian democratization. Yet, by early 1992, President Yeltsin's repeated warnings that he was feeling "the breath of the redshirts and brownshirts" on his neck were still falling on deaf ears. Proponents of this argument avowed delight in what they saw, but their reluctance to cut "defense" spending and to provide substantial economic assistance to the new Commonwealth betrayed a wish to bring back the days when an enemy was ready at hand. After all, wars against Columbian drug dealers, Japanese car makers, and home-grown flag burners provided too transient a substitute.

So while the argument about economic attrition cannot be dismissed out of hand, it could be utterly mistaken or irrelevant. Hence, it could not by itself justify the arms race.[16a]

X. By far the most convincing argument against negotiations and disarmament invoked inflexible linkage. This argument stated that we could not conclude any agreement with the Soviets because of the great political differences between the two societies, because of their ruthless behavior towards their subjects, or because of their repugnant foreign policies. Thus, irreconcilability was used to explain our refusal to accept their comprehensive disarmament proposal of May 1955 and their more moderate proposals in the May 1988 Moscow summit; the ban on Jewish emigration explained our opposition to one treaty (SALT I) and to the lifting of trade restrictions (Washington 1990 summit); the invasion of Afghanistan explained our refusal to ratify another treaty (SALT II; see below for details); and the temporary suppression of secessionist movements in the Baltic republics served to justify American conservatism in the disarmament sphere and niggardliness in the economic sphere (1990).

We can begin refuting this argument by observing that although the Soviets viewed some of our actions with aversion and contempt, they rarely let these emotions guide their disarmament policies. One might surmise that our role in subverting an elected democratic government in Guatemala and a popularly elected socialist government in Chile, or our support for the bloodthirsty regimes that took their places, appeared just as contemptible to them as their brutal suppression of the Prague Spring appeared to us. Yet, they have rarely—and then only half-heartedly—let inflexible linkage determine their policies (one possible exception involved the U-2 spy mission episode, see below). According to a former Secretary of Defense:

> The SALT I negotiations were concluded despite Soviet concerns about the U.S. mining of Haiphong harbor . . . In the United States, on the other hand, even favorable arms limitation agreements can be derailed by popular and congressional concern about Soviet behavior in other areas, as happened to SALT II when the Soviets invaded Afghanistan.[17]

The historical record strongly suggests that a policy of inflexible linkage tended to undermine its stated objectives.[18] In the early 1970s and late 1980s, we were negotiating with the Soviets on disarmament, trade, foreign policy, and internal repression in the Soviet Union, behaving all the while as if we believed that peaceful coexistence was possible. This was accompanied by unprecedented cooperation on their part. For example, under strong pressure from the United States Congress, the Kremlin allowed some 100,000 Soviet Jews and a few thousand ethnic Germans to leave the Soviet Union in the early 1970s. According to one observer of the Soviet scene: "Given the Kremlin's acute sensitivity to the proud image of the Soviet Union abroad as the promised land of socialism, permitting such an exodus was an unprecedented concession."[19] In a similar vein, most observers would probably agree that democratic reforms in former Soviet republics were likelier to flourish in the clear air of East-West rapprochement.

Some Soviet dissidents urged us to assume an uncompromising stand on linkage. Unfortunately, the corporate media gave their views the widest coverage and ignored the diverging views of many other dissidents. Unfortunately too, some influential Westerners took these various warnings to the West and speeches to the Americans as the New Gospel. Insofar as these dissidents alerted us to the dangers of totalitarianism, their insights merited close attention. Insofar as they took a stand against a repressive system, they deserved our gratitude. But their first-hand familiarity with Leninism and their principled stand should have not prompted us to adopt their tunnel vision as our own. Inflexible linkage satisfied an understandable emotional need to avenge repression, but there are no reasons to believe that it has brought more justice to the Soviet Union and the world.

Inflexible linkage also dimmed the prospects of international cooperation. To survive in the long run, to prevent the militarization of our societies, to avoid the corrosion of the moral fiber that holds them together, to stop the enormous diversion of resources to unproductive military purposes, the two nations had to cooperate. They also had to work together on global issues which concerned them both, including nuclear proliferation, environmental pollution, depletion of the ozone layer, global warming, and rapid population growth. Their common humanity manifestly superseded the conflicts which set them apart. It is inexcusable to sacrifice such goals for a policy which gave vent to feelings of moral indignation but which otherwise aggravated the condition it sought to cure.

Before leaving the subject, I wish to make it clear that it is not the concept of linkage itself which I oppose, but its rigid application. In the long run, only a comprehensive settlement which went far beyond disarmament issues would have safeguarded peace. Such things as human rights in the Soviet Union or widespread unemployment in the United States could have been brought to the negotiation table and both sides should have been willing to make great sacrifices to remedy them. The future of humanity, however, needed not be among them.

No matter what we think of the previous arguments against peaceful coexistence and for the arms race, on balance, the case for peaceful coexistence and against the arms race was overwhelmingly stronger.

Moderate advocates of peaceful coexistence did not deny the irreconcilability of Soviet socialism and Western plutodemocracies, and they conceded either side's wish to dismantle the other's institutions. They believed that the U.S. had to remain strong enough to defend itself, its allies, and its vital interests, and that continued competition between the two sides in non-military fields (e.g., curbing poverty in the Third World) was likely to linger. But they were also convinced that rivals can remain rivals and yet work toward common goals which benefit both. After all, this is exactly what both sides did during World War II, when they entered into an alliance against the Nazis. There were good reasons to believe that cooperation was even more urgent in the 1980s than it was during World War II, or, for that matter, than it was in any other historical epoch:

I. The threat of total war which hung over both nations (Chapter 2) would have receded with peaceful coexistence. Similarly, the two nations could jointly curb the ominous worldwide proliferation of nuclear weapons.

II. Besides nuclear war, the world's people paid an enormous price for the arms race, including trillions of dollars, growing militarism, damaged national security, adverse environmental effects, and nuclear proliferation (Chapter 3).

III. Owing to scientific and technological advances, both sides, and humanity, faced other perils besides nuclear weapons (e.g., depletion of the ozone layer, global warming, acid rain, the new biology, massive extinction of wild species). These perils could be best minimized through effective international cooperation. Similarly, both sides could benefit from cooperation in areas such as space exploration.

IV. Peaceful coexistence would have allowed us to retain our freedom, and would only concede to the Soviets what they already had: control over their own empire. Suppression of the Prague Spring and many other instances of American non-intervention in the internal affairs of the Soviet Empire show that we were likely to make this concession in any event. The early 1990s suggest that only internal developments were likely to cause the dissolution of this empire.

V. Peaceful coexistence could have improved our international position by advancing our reputation as a peace-loving nation and allowing us to divert enormous resources to enhance living standards, educational levels, and the quality of life in this country and planet.

VI. As we have seen, both common sense and history strongly suggest that successful democratization of Soviet society was more probable with peaceful coexistence than with the arms race. Increased Soviet-Western contacts and the consequent easing of the Soviets' perennial obsession with invasions and conspiracies were likely to strengthen the democratic faction in the Soviet Union.

It is a sad commentary on the Cold War years that, even now, peace and relaxation of tensions must be defended at such great length. However, as the frequently heard arguments against negotiations and disarmament (above) suggest, and the actual history of the Cold War (below) indisputably shows, militarism in America cannot be overkilled.

Atomic Secrecy

Unlike some farseeing scientists, our leaders failed to grasp the futility of trying to conceal the large-scale Manhattan Project from the Soviets. In 1944, for example, physicist Niels Bohr was granted separate interviews with both Roosevelt and Churchill, at which he implored them to inform Stalin about this project and to try to reach an agreement on the international control of atomic weapons.[20a] Unfortunately, both the distinguished scientist and his wise counsel were summarily dismissed (Bohr narrowly escaped prolonged security surveillance following this "subversive" act).[21]

The only real secret about the bomb, Bohr knew, was its producibility. Given the temporary nature of atomic monopoly, there was little to lose from cooperation. Moreover, any attempt by a society as open and diverse as ours to hide from view anything as gigantic as the Manhattan Project was inherently futile. We know

now, and we could have surmised then, that the Soviets had spies in Los Alamos and elsewhere; that they knew about the Project; and that they were familiar with many of its scientific details.[22] Openness would have helped to dispel the Soviets' deep suspicions of us and mitigate the Cold War and the ever-present prospects of a Sizzling War. As one thoughtful observer put it: "If Russia had been formally consulted about the bomb during the war . . . it might have made no difference. The fact that she was not, guaranteed that the attempts made just after the war to establish international control, which might have failed anyway, were doomed."[20b]

One typical incident from this era involved an invitation from the Soviet Academy of Sciences to a number of American and British scientists to a celebration of its 220th anniversary. On the eve of their departure, American scientists working on the Manhattan Project were forbidden to go. Similarly, owing to American pressure, eight British physicists who were already at the airport were forced to return home.

> The English newspapers gave great publicity to the cancellation . . . All this, of course, was known in Russia, although it was never mentioned in the American press. It is inconceivable that the Russians could have misunderstood these last minute cancellations and the total absence of any American scientist who had anything remotely to do with atomic energy. . . . Russian diplomats could not have misinterpreted so clear a statement of mistrust by their wartime allies.[23a]

There was another chance for candor in 1945, when Stalin, Churchill, and Truman met at the Berlin suburb of Potsdam to discuss the postwar settlement. What took place there really belongs in a comedy of manners, not at such a momentous crossroads. Though the policy of secrecy failed with the Soviets, it worked wonders with Vice-President Harry Truman, who learned of the bomb's existence only when he became President (a few months before the Potsdam Conference). In contrast, Stalin, thanks to his spies, had reportedly launched a miniature Manhattan Project of his own by 1943. At Potsdam, Truman and Churchill fancied that Stalin knew nothing about the Manhattan Project and that they were facing a quandary: if they tell Stalin about the Project he might ask to get involved; if they don't, he might, upon discovering their secret later, reasonably interpret their silence as bad faith towards an ally.

Their solution to this self-created quandary? After a formal conference Truman approached Stalin, with Churchill intently looking at the proceedings some distance away, and told him (casually, of course), that the U.S. possessed a "new weapon of unusual destructive force."[24a] Historians still debate Stalin's response. Some believe that he failed to grasp Truman's allusion. Others believe that poker-faced Stalin expected a remark of this sort and pretended not to care less. Stalin, in their view, understood the nature of the new weapon and its implications better than Truman but fooled his English-speaking cohorts into believing that he was unimpressed.[25a]

The policy of secrecy, attempted monopoly, and beating around the bush was a serious blunder. What exactly was the point of keeping the atom secret two weeks before Hiroshima? By strengthening the Soviets' resolve to speed their nuclear program and to distrust the West, this policy contributed to the growing polarization of the world. In the opinion of one observer, this misstep marks the beginning of the arms race. "Although much is clouded in secrecy," he says, "the beginning of the nuclear arms race can be pinpointed precisely: It was 10:00 P.M. Potsdam time, July 24, 1945."[22a]

The Baruch Plan

Another opportunity came shortly after the war. Some scientists continued to tell the politicians that the Soviets were likely to acquire the bomb in four years or so, and that it was therefore in America's long-term interest to reach an agreement on the abolition of all nuclear weapons. In 1946, a few of these insights were incorporated into a high-level proposal, the so-called Acheson-Lilienthal Report. But sharing the nuclear "secret" was a bit too much for the press, the public, the politicians, and especially the hardliners. Our folksy president thought that if other nations wanted to catch up with us they would "have to do it on their own hook, just as we did."[22b]   We had the bomb, the Soviets didn't. And besides, some distinguished American generals were saying, it would take the Soviets twenty years to develop a bomb of their own, or they might never develop it at all (the Soviets being, you see, either psychologically or racially unprepared for such a task).

The Acheson-Lilienthal Report was handed over to Bernard Baruch, an astute stock market speculator and politician, who saw his task in terms of "preparing the American people for a refusal by Russia."[23b]   Baruch renamed this report the Baruch Plan, and changed its contents enough to guarantee its palatability to the Western public and its rejection by the Soviets.   As Baruch explained the situation to contemporary critics of his provocative plan: "Anyway, we've got the bomb!"[24b]

To be a bit more specific, the Baruch Plan would have left the United States with decisive nuclear superiority until the details of the Plan could be worked out. It would have nipped the Soviet nuclear program in the bud. And it would have left the U.S. with a monopoly of nuclear know-how, a monopoly that could have easily been converted into a decisive military edge any time the agreement broke down.[9b]   According to one historian, "the Baruch plan did not differ in substance from an ultimatum the United States might have given Russia to forswear nuclear weapons or be destroyed."[26] This plan could therefore be reasonably interpreted by the Soviets as a ploy to secure American dominance,[27a] especially since they knew that a less inequitable plan had been seriously considered at first.

The Soviets rejected the Baruch Plan, proposed an unrealistic plan of their own, and the negotiations came to a halt. Seventeen days after Baruch presented his plan to the United Nations, on July 1, 1946, the United States conducted the world's first postwar nuclear test.[27a]

The Soviets under Stalin would have most likely rejected the Acheson-Lilienthal Plan, but this plan could have served as a basis for negotiations. In contrast, the Baruch Plan, as most insiders then knew, couldn't. This missed opportunity and its foreboding implications were summed up by one patient observer:

The opportunity to bring nuclear weapons under international control had been lost from the beginning. Knowing now the course of history in the decades to follow, we must deem this a tragedy, the enormity of which cannot be exaggerated. . . . The pattern of the superpowers' game of disarmament had been set: both sides would present proposals for disarmament agreement, of often wholesale dimensions, but would be careful to see to it that these would contain conditions which the opposite side could not accept.[27b]

Developing the H-Bomb

Years passed. The first Soviet explosion of an atomic bomb triggered a heated controversy in the U.S. One school of thinking urged, on strategic and moral grounds, that the U.S. desist from developing the hydrogen bomb, regardless of what the Soviets chose to do. Another path[24c,28a,29] was urged by Enrico Fermi and a few other distinguished scientists: develop the bomb, but only after failing to negotiate it out of existence. In this case, verification would be easy, since a test anywhere on earth could be readily detected. An additional safeguard against Soviet cheating would have been provided by the growing American stockpile of Atomic weapons (some two hundred by 1949[25b]). A third path—the one actually taken by the USA and the USSR—urged development without negotiations.

It must be stressed again that, owing to our lead and to the overkill quality of nuclear bombs, no risk was involved in heeding the moderates' advice and making the bomb only after failure of disarmament negotiations. Indeed, Dean Acheson, then Secretary of State, thought the new H-bomb had little to do with the military standoff, and much to do with the domestic standoff between the hawkish Mr. Truman's and his even more militant critics. He didn't see, Acheson reportedly said, "how the President could survive a policy of not making the H-bomb."[28b]

"Had restraint been practised," one historian summed up this episode "the opportunity might conceivably have emerged . . . for political moves to restrain Soviet-American nuclear arms competition. In the event, the competition . . . continued unabated."[20c]

The Moment of Hope:
May 10, 1955[30a]

This tale begins with a comprehensive set of disarmament proposals which were put forward by the major Western powers from 1952 to 1955. As Soviet attitudes began to thaw following Stalin's death, Canada, France, Great Britain, and the United States advanced a modified joint proposal which met the Soviets' objections half-way. On May 10, 1955 the Soviets dropped a bombshell: a counterproposal which incorporated key components of the joint Western proposal.

Had it been accepted, the Soviet proposal would have led to the elimination of all nuclear weapons everywhere on earth, a comprehensive ban on the testing of all such weapons, a system of verification measures carried out by an international control agency with extensive inspection powers and unimpeded access to all military installations in Soviet and Western territories, dismantling of foreign military bases, and massive reductions in conventional armaments and armed forces.

After three years of trying to convince the Soviets to accept their comprehensive proposals, the Western negotiators could not believe their ears. They knew that the Soviet proposal only marked the beginning of a long and tortuous road, that many details needed to be ironed out, and that the Soviets could be bluffing. All the same, for the first time peace was conceivable. The French delegate's immediate response was that "the whole thing looks too good to be true." After 48 hours of consultation with their governments, his English-speaking counterparts took a similar stand. The American delegate, for instance, said: "We have been gratified . . . that the concepts which we have put forward over a considerable length of time . . . have been accepted in a large measure by the Soviet Union."[30b]

There are good reasons to suppose that the Soviet proposal was sincere and that Soviet foreign policies after Stalin's death were undergoing radical improvements. The military conflicts in Korea and Vietnam ended in a truce. In May 1955, a Soviet-American accord to end ten years of joint occupation of Austria and permitting it to become a neutral, independent democracy was signed.[31a] The Soviets voluntarily gave up Finnish naval bases which they had appropriated in 1945. Later, the Soviets made drastic unilateral reductions in the size of their standing army. In short, winds of change were unmistakably blowing over the Kremlin.

However, by August of 1955 it turned out that the United States was uninterested in working with the Soviets or its own allies toward peace. It placed a "reservation"[30] on its earlier disarmament proposal, and put forward a limited, unfair, irrelevant, and meaningless counterproposal. The Soviet delegate kept reminding us of the larger issues of war and peace, but we were no longer interested. America's counterproposal—Eisenhower's bombastic "open skies" proposal—is still taken seriously by some American historians, so it is important to dispel any doubts by seeing what Eisenhower himself had to say about it: "We knew the Soviets wouldn't accept it. We were sure of that."[31b]

I must say that when I first read about this brief moment of hope, I simply could not believe my eyes. I still find it hard to admit that what I've just related happened. We had a chance to work toward peace but we, not the Soviets, chose the Cold War instead. Perhaps Dwight Eisenhower was reflecting on this shameful episode of American history and of his own life when he said: "I think people want peace so much that one of these days governments had better get out of their way and let them have it."[32] Perhaps he had something else in mind (such as the 1954 overthrow of Guatemalan democracy), but there is little doubt that in 1955 our government stood in the way of peace. One knowledgeable friend of the open society summarized this episode:

> Time is showing that the United States' rejection of the Russian offer of May 10, 1955, may have been a terrible mistake. It may take time before the United States Government comes round again to the belief that equal and balanced armament reductions, under an adequate system of control, do not diminish, but increase, the national security of the signatory States."[30c]

As we shall see, by 1991, the U.S. had still not come round.[33]

The Comprehensive Test Ban

The next item is not a brief historical episode but a sequence of events which originated on or before 1954, and which continued through 1991. It concerns efforts to work out a comprehensive test ban treaty: a mutual agreement to stop all nuclear test explosions.

Following the 1954 Bikini incident (Chapter 2), protests against atmospheric testing spread. Despite the undeniable health risks, it was unthinkable for a United States President to make a major peace initiative on his own. Our government and media tried to allay reasonable public fears with the usual denials, misrepresentations, trumpeting the views of respectable but sadly misinformed or compromised scientists willing to publicly endorse atmospheric tests, and muffling the small brave voices of their independent antagonists. It fell to the Soviets to make the first move. The same Soviets who were, we must remember, definitely behind us in the mad race to nowhere and who, according to conventional military wisdom, had more to lose from a test ban (because such a ban would have frozen their relative inferiority).

In 1957, the Soviets proposed a testing moratorium of two to three years. Reportedly, Eisenhower was favorably disposed towards the Soviet move, but was dissuaded by the hardliners. With continued testing, our war party argued, scientists would be able to solve the fallout problem by creating "clean" nuclear weapons in five to seven years. Even now, this promise has yet to be kept. The hardliners were also worried about clandestine tests, of which worries enough had been said earlier. On such grounds, the U.S. decided to turn down the Soviet proposal. But a flat refusal would have made for bad public relations, so we put forward another of our left-handed counterproposals which was inequitable enough to make it totally unacceptable to the Soviets,[9c] and ambiguous and high-sounding enough to deceive the trusting American people. End round one.

Time passed again in fruitless talks, and one can only wonder at the tenacity of the communists in pursuing peace despite the apparent ill faith of the Americans. Recall too that in those days the Soviets were not only talking but concretely demonstrating a genuine interest in peaceful coexistence. From 1955 to 1958, for instance, they unilaterally reduced their standing army from over 5.5 to 3.5 million men. In 1958 Khrushchev was planning again, against considerable domestic opposition, a further reduction of more than one million.[34a]

It is against this background that the Soviet Union's 1958 announcement that it would stop testing, provided other nations followed suit, must be judged. Given mounting public opposition at home and abroad, Britain and the United States followed the Soviet lead. Thus, owing to *Soviet* initiative and the indignation of Western voters, American, British, and Soviet tests ceased for three years.

Nineteen sixty. While the moratorium was still in place, a total test ban was almost agreed upon. American hardliners were scandalized by these feeble rays of hope and appeared eminently capable of dimming them. According to one British official, genuine negotiations were allowed to continue only thanks to a last ditch effort at personal diplomacy by Conservative British Prime Minister Harold Macmillan, who managed to convince President Eisenhower to respond favorably to the new Soviet plan.

For the first time since the war, the hardliners appeared close to defeat. Two weeks before the conference, Eisenhower personally authorized a U-2 plane spying mission over Soviet territory.[35] He approved this flight even though, in the words of one American historian, "the President considered violating the airspace of an unfriendly nation tantamount to an act of war," and even though he understood the risks. "If one of these planes is shot down . . ." Eisenhower said, "the world will be in a mess."[36] Some cynics suspect that this entire episode was staged and that American hardliners were quite willing to sacrifice a plane and a pilot in order to wreck the talks. Others wonder what on earth could justify, just before such a historic moment, taking this risk. Some suspect hardliners on the Soviet side for the fateful timing of this incident. But maybe these skeptics are going too far, and maybe it was an honest mistake which just happened, as far as the hardliners on both sides were concerned, at the right time.

Imagine, at any rate, our reaction if we shot down *their* reconnaissance plane over *our* land just before a summit conference. But Khrushchev wanted detente, understood the madness of the arms race, and staked his reputation at home on Eisenhower's credibility.[34] Right after the incident he showed restraint and left the door open for Eisenhower to say that it was an unauthorized mission. Eisenhower, however, took full responsibility for the affair. Two weeks later, in May 1960, the two met at a summit conference. Khrushchev demanded an apology, Eisenhower refused, and Khrushchev stormed out.[34b] These events probably contributed to the Soviets' resumption of tests in 1961, to be followed in about two weeks by American tests. There are good reasons to believe that, at this point, each side was more interested in testing its adversary and public opinion than in testing nuclear weapons.

Nineteen sixty-three. Both Kennedy and Khrushchev had been deeply shaken by the Cuban Missile Crisis of the year before. The negotiators reached an impasse on the issue of on-site inspections, an issue on which the U.S. stood firm. Bear in mind our earlier conclusion that American insistence on such inspections was not traceable to the fear that the Soviets would cheat and go undetected, but to the fear that the hardliners would use this issue to wreck the talks; not, as is frequently alleged, that the risks in rejecting a total ban were greater than the risks of accepting it, but that there were no risks at all. Note also that our national security, even in the narrow sense in which the hardliners define it, would have been immensely improved with the ban. Opponents of the total ban, according to President Eisenhower's science advisor, "concocted elaborate scenarios on the feasibility of clandestine Soviet tests, befogging the central issue that a comprehensive ban would have been to our advantage, in view of our technological lead."[37a] Still, the U.S. would not budge from its demand of seven on-site annual inspections, each encompassing an area of some 150 square miles.

In the 1960s, the Soviets were unlikely to accept this demand, for theirs was a closed police state well known for the iron curtain which surrounded it, its penchant for secrecy, and its pervasive spy-mania.[19,38] Moreover, most independent scientists believed that on-site inspections were unnecessary, so the Soviets could legitimately regard American insistence on such inspections as a thinly disguised attempt to gain military intelligence. Yet, against all odds, Khrushchev agreed to three annual inspections. Although some thorny details remained to be worked out,[39a] the prospects for a total ban appeared brighter than ever before. It was, one might say, another moment of hope. With so much on the balance, it seemed inconceivable that we would falter over the question of three or seven *superfluous* inspections.

But falter we did. A total ban required Senate ratification. Despite Kennedy's efforts, a poll taken in the Senate in May 1963 showed that a ban would have fallen ten votes short of the needed two-thirds majority.[22c]

In this way, another opportunity was missed. Both sides settled for a partial treaty that banned tests in the atmosphere, underwater, and space, but allowed underground tests to continue. This treaty was thus a modest victory for the biosphere, not for peace. Environmentalists would now tackle other critical issues, the coalition for total ban would dissolve, and nuclear tests would continue happily thereafter—underground. And even for this limited treaty Kennedy had to give a pound of flesh. To get Senate ratification for the partial test ban, Kennedy needed the Joint Chiefs' endorsement. To get this endorsement, he had to consent to *more* tests than before.

Many years passed and nothing substantive happened. Like Kennedy, Carter wanted a total ban. During his tenure, serious negotiations were again under way. Both sides made concessions and an agreement was within sight.[40] Seeing, however, no prospects of Senate ratification, Carter let the treaty languish.

The years-long hopeful negotiations were still going on when Carter's successor took office. Here the record is even clearer than before. In 1981, the United States withdrew from the talks because of "verification" difficulties.[41] In 1982 the U.S. formally announced that it was no longer interested in negotiating a total ban, on the grounds that a total ban could no longer serve a useful purpose.[42a] Also in 1982, a call in the United Nations for a test moratorium was accepted by the Soviets and rejected by the Americans and the British.[42b] Similarly, in December 1982 the U.S. was the only nation (out of 147) to cast a nay vote against the initiation of "substantive negotiations" by the U.N. Committee on Disarmament.[39b]

In 1985, the USSR unilaterally suspended its nuclear tests,

stating that this moratorium will last forever if "the United States refrains from conducting nuclear explosions." But this unilateral action was, according to our government and mass media, merely a propaganda ploy, for, in Mr. Reagan's words, the Soviet Union was "ahead of us in the development and the modernization of nuclear weapons." Besides, Mr. Reagan recited, it was a ploy because the Soviets, unlike the Americans, "just finished their tests," and had nothing to lose from a temporary moratorium.[43] Reagan's first charge has been put to rest in Chapter 6. His second is put to rest by the military insignificance of all nuclear tests (Chapters 5, 6) by America's technological lead, and by the fact that, in the seven months before the Soviet unilateral suspension of tests, the USSR conducted fewer tests than the USA (six to nine).

Nineteen months after their unilateral moratorium began, following America's first nuclear test in 1987, the Soviets resumed testing. Throughout these nineteen months, the Reagan Administration clung to the view that a comprehensive ban treaty would harm the national security of the United States. Even by the close of 1991, more than four years after the Soviets proved their willingness to accept Western demands for intrusive verification measures, no substantial progress has been made.

As a result of this Cold War saga, our lives were still in the balance and, by mid-1980s, our military advantage over the Russians, for whatever it was worth in the nuclear age, has narrowed. Evidently, we Americans are a strange people, occasionally putting men who are marginally guilty of compromising our national security behind bars, or, when we really get mad at them, frying them in the electric chair; but always putting in charge of our ship of state men who are indisputably guilty of recklessly imperiling its very existence.

The 1980s

As we have seen, the Soviets were interested in a test moratorium and a lasting treaty, but we weren't. So throughout the decade (with the exception of the nineteen-month-long one-sided Soviet moratorium of 1985-1987), both sides continued to test nuclear weapons. In 1982, the USA conducted eighteen tests (the highest number since 1975), the USSR thirty-one (the highest since 1962). In 1989, the USA conducted eleven tests, the USSR seven.[42c]

In 1982, the Soviets announced that they would not be the first to use nuclear weapons. This unilateral commitment, they said, would be reviewed if it was not followed by reciprocal announcements from other nuclear-weapon states. The United States, however, refused to renounce the first use of nuclear weapons,[42d] stating that it might deploy them first for defensive purposes.

In the 1980s, a total test ban would have been a mere drop in the bucket. A slightly more meaningful proposal concerned a bilateral freeze on the testing, development, production, and deployment of nuclear weapons and their means of delivery, and on the production of all fissionable materials which could be used to make nuclear bombs. Given the rough parity that existed between the two sides, it is clear that a freeze would have placed neither side's national security at risk and that it would have served the interests of both. The USSR, a few Western governments, and many American Congressmen, expressed interest in the idea. The Reagan and Bush administrations, however, were uninterested.

Generalizations about political decisions often fail to capture some of the flavor and real motives behind them. A Committee of the U.S. National Academy of Sciences captures them through a brief description of a typical episode:

> The Soviet Union had formally submitted a freeze resolution at the United Nations in October 4, 1983. Soviet Foreign Minister Andrei Gromyko stated in his speech, which was read in absentia because his plane had not been permitted to land in New York, that the Soviet Union proposed to cease, under effective verification, the buildup of all components of nuclear arsenals, including all kinds of delivery vehicles and nuclear weapons; to renounce the deployment of new kinds and types of such arms; to establish a moratorium on all tests of nuclear weapons and new kinds and types of nuclear weapon delivery vehicles; and to stop the production of fissionable materials for the purpose of creating arms. Gromyko added that the freeze could initially apply to the Soviet Union and the United States on a bilateral basis, by way of example to other nuclear states. The Soviet proposal received little attention in the United States.[39c]

The United States was opposed to a freeze, because, it said, it would have frozen its relative inferiority. It had to catch up first. During Mr. Reagan's first five years in office, this catching up was implemented on a colossal scale. In real terms, the overall annual defense budget went up by nearly 53 percent, while military purchases rose by a staggering 112 percent. In contrast, during that period Soviet spending was rising far more slowly or not at all.[44] Our submarines were far better than theirs, but we have been catching up by building larger submarines whose missiles could level Soviet land-based missiles and cities some fifteen minutes after a war began. Notwithstanding the "huge" lead the U.S. enjoyed in biological weapons, spending in this area underwent "dramatic" increases from 1981 to 1985.[45a] We were far ahead of them in the supposedly critical area of cruise missiles, but we have been catching up by deploying these missiles, a few years ahead of the Soviets, practically everywhere and on everything. We always had a much greater interventionary capacity in conflicts far away from either country's shores, but we were set on catching up with them on this score too.

Long before the conclusion of the race to the moon, and despite some unfortunate setbacks, we have had a more promising space program. All the same, we have been catching up with the Soviets in the presumably critical area of space militarization, instead of taking them up on their proposals to demilitarize space. Space militarization continued through 1991, despite years of virtually unanimous assessments by independent experts that the key component of this project was likely to "suffer a catastrophic failure."[46]

After many years of haggling, American and Soviet negotiators worked out a treaty (SALT II) which had, for whatever it was worth, somewhat improved America's comparative military position vis-a-vis the Soviet Union.[37b,47,48] President Carter's valiant efforts to get it ratified failed (owing in part to false allegations about a new Soviet combat brigade in Cuba[49a]). The Reagan Administration claimed that this treaty was "fatally flawed" because this treaty accepted the nuclear status quo and created a "window of vulnerability."[50a] Until late 1987, this apparently was a matter of faith—any treaty with the Soviets, even if it left them with only hammers and sickles, was "fatally flawed." This discrepancy between fact and fiction had strange consequences. According to a former Deputy Assistant Secretary of Defense and his co-author, in 1982 both sides continued to observe this "fatally flawed" treaty, "with the result that only the Soviets appeared to benefit from American failure to ratify: they would have been required to dismantle several hundred of their weapons on ratification, and the United States would not have been required to dismantle any."[51] This anti-American impasse ceased in 1986, when the U.S. broke this treaty.

In the early 1980s, the Reagan administration put forward a new plan, which, it said, was going to better achieve the goals of SALT II and the freeze. But this plan did not come close to a bilateral freeze in its scope, and can only be regarded as a left-handed public relations effort. As Mr. Reagan himself recited in a candid moment: "Any controversy now would be over which weapons the United States should produce and not whether it should forsake weaponry for treaties and agreements."[52] Former Senator Fulbright put it better: "this President's not serious about arms control. The negotiations . . . are a charade, a cover-up while he builds more weapons."[53]

These quotations speak for themselves, but let me cite one more observation in favor of Mr. Fulbright's conclusion. As we have seen, the USA was deploying long-range cruise missiles by the thousands and the USSR was considerably behind in this area. So, naturally, American 1980s' proposals simply *defined* these missiles out of the talks and insisted, despite strenuous Soviet opposition, that they were irrelevant. When these missiles are taken into consideration, it turns out that these proposals did not, as alleged, signal a fresh start. Rather, they continued the time-honored American game of putting forward vacuous and unfair proposals. In this case, our bombastic proposal was this: if you agree to reduce your total nuclear arsenal, we shall agree to enlarge ours.[54] In other words, heads you lose, tails we win.

In a 1986 meeting in Reykjavik, according to the *New York Times'* Washington bureau chief, the Soviets made "significant concessions."[50b] "Reagan needed a gambit to match Gorbachev's call for a halt to nuclear testing and for the elimination of all strategic weapons by the year 2000." Reagan proposed the elimination of all strategic missiles (missiles based at one country and aimed at the other) from the two countries' arsenals. Characteristically, Reagan's speechwriters had him hail this package as "perhaps the most sweeping and important arms-reduction proposal in the history of the world."[50c]   In reality, this proposal "cut the heart of the Soviet nuclear arsenal (ninety percent of Soviet nuclear warheads are on ballistic missiles), but it left us with a big advantage in nuclear bombers and cruise missiles."[50b] All the same, by now the U.S. had learned from bitter experience that the Soviet Union might accept ludicrous proposals. So, to be on the safe side, Reagan's proposal was backed with a "safety catch"—it was "deliberately vague" and it included "no actual commitment to get rid" of ballistic missiles.[50d]

In the 1987 negotiations on European missiles, the West again took a stand which, by conventional standards, gave it a 400-mile head start in the Indianapolis 500. It put forward a proposal which "many Reagan Administration officials were convinced that Moscow would never accept." In fact, many Western commentators "proved" that Moscow would reject this proposal because it gave the West nuclear "superiority" in Europe. But the Soviets would not play the game of disarmament by the old rules and caught the West "off guard" by their "accommodating policy."[49b] In addition to numerical asymmetries, the Soviets gave up the eminently reasonable idea that European missiles should be viewed in the larger context of the nuclear balance. (As we have seen, the U.S. would have had to give up a great many nuclear toys for the two sides to approach parity.) The Soviets also accepted unprecedented verification measures, even though they had good reasons to regard them as superfluous. They made a few other surprising concessions, while the West did not substantially revise its negotiating position on a single point. As a result, the USA and USSR agreed to destroy some land-based European missiles and to remove 1600 Soviet, and 450 American, nuclear warheads.[55a] It is to the great credit of the Reagan Administration, perhaps its single achievement in eight years, that it did not back away at this point. To be sure, at America's insistence, this treaty did not eliminate nuclear bombs from either side's arsenal.[56] Nor did it change by one iota the meaningful balance of terror. It did however accomplish the first physical destruction of a functional part of humanity's means of delivering nuclear weapons. It thereby held up the hope that, despite the obstacles, America might one day stop living by its sword.

In late 1988, the USSR announced plans to reduce Soviet troops by 500,000 and cut conventional weapons by a substantial amount, thereby lowering their nation's military expenditures by over 14 percent. In June 1990, the U.S. announced that by *1995* it planned to cut its troops by 442,000[57] and its expenditures by 0 percent.

Once ballistic missiles are launched, they cannot be recalled. Hence, an accidental or unauthorized firing of nuclear missiles, or the firing of missiles which are wrongly believed to be under attack, could have disastrous, unintended, consequences. It is critically important therefore to provide such missiles with remote control devices which would enable the country which launched such missiles to destroy them in flight. By 1989, the U.S. showed no interest in retrofitting its missiles with such devices even though this would have not degraded their destructive potential or operational readiness. Soviet missiles, in contrast, may possess such devices.[16b]

In 1989, the Soviets' peace offensive continued apace. Among other things, they announced a 5 percent unilateral cut in their country's arsenal of short-range nuclear missiles in Europe. They also proposed massive reductions in both sides' conventional forces in Europe. President Bush's speechwriters conceded that "a new breeze is blowing across the steppes and cities of the Soviet Union" and promised to match "their steps with steps of our own." One step: a revived version of Eisenhower's meaningless "Open Skies" proposal. Another step: increased trade, *provided* the Soviet Union changed its emigration laws to allow its citizens to emigrate at will.

By 1990, the USSR granted genuine national independence to its Eastern European satellites, recognized Finnish neutrality, allowed massive Jewish immigration despite protests from its Arab allies, and continued to implement far-reaching democratic reforms. In contrast, China reverted to a more ruthless authoritarianism. Yet the Bush Administration insisted on retaining relaxed barriers on trade with China (according to *Time*, this policy "dishonored the martyrs of Tiananmen"[15b]), while adding a new condition before even considering granting similar status to the Soviet Union. Granting such status, Bush implied, hinged on the Soviets' favorable response to secession moves by the three Baltic republics.

Moreover, the Bush administration remained committed to a nuclear program which, according to *Time*, amounted to "expensive, redundant, and provocative . . . monuments to old thinking."[15c] This was all the more surprising in view of the Pentagon's opinion that the Soviets' planned cutback would virtually eliminate the possibility of a surprise conventional Soviet attack on Western Europe.[15d]

By 1988, even prestigious institutions within the American war establishment were saying that something like 70 percent reduction of the strategic nuclear weapons of both sides would reduce the chances of nuclear war without diminishing the "strong existent deterrent effect" of nuclear weapons.[58] Hence, bilateral massive reductions—which the Soviets had been vigorously pursuing for years—could improve U.S. security. All the same, in 1990 the U.S. was only considering 11 percent reductions in its strategic stockpile.[59] If one day such reductions are carried out, they would leave the United States with *more* nuclear weapons than it had when President Reagan first announced his plans for radical reductions of these same weapons.

Throughout Gorbachev's term in office, Soviet concrete disarmament proposals encountered stiff American resistance. According to President Bush's National Security Adviser, Gorbachev's overtures were not aimed at peace, but at creating dissension within the Western alliance. Also, conventional reductions posed a problem for they could reduce forces "below the point at which effective defense can be maintained." To be sure, in 1990 some people in the Bush administration admitted that the Soviet Union under Gorbachev did not pose a threat to Western security. Mr. Bush, however, chose to side with those who averred that U.S. military spending "must remain high to assure the United States can defend itself against any threat posed by a Soviet Union reverting to its pre-Gorbachev role."[60] While this explanation may puzzle logicians, it came as no surprise to Gorbachev, who had earlier observed: For "the U.S. ruling class and the military-industrial complex . . . disarmament spells out a loss of profits and a political risk; for us it is a blessing in all respects, economically, politically and morally."[61] "What more," he asked elsewhere, "can one do when all one hears is the same stereotyped, cheerless 'No.'"[60]

One can wait and hope for the best. If Russian, Ukrainian, and other reformers manage to hang on to power for a few more years, American policies may change. Beyond a certain point, even the average voter may perceive the absence of one enemy and the presence of another.

General Characteristics of the Arms Race

The history of the arms race is strikingly repetitive: weapons changed but the policies didn't. This repetitiveness was already clear by the late 1940s. One prominent participant remarked in connection with the H-bomb debate that "this whole discussion makes me feel I was seeing the same film . . . for the second time."[63] This repetitiveness continued, unabated, in the 1980s. In 1986 another observer remarked: "For those who have followed the evolution of the arms race, President Reagan's Strategic Defense Initiative has a sense of deja vu about it. The late 1960s also witnessed a preoccupation with strategic defense and, with it, strong pressure from many quarters to build an antiballistic missile (ABM) defense."[64] Thus, popular perceptions[65] that American policies in the 1980s constituted a sharp break from the past are incorrect: American policies have been remarkably consistent from 1945 to 1991. This consistency enables us to move from individual episodes and case histories to more abstract generalizations:

I. Since 1955, the Soviet Union has been more interested in disarmament than the United States. By now, this observation is conceded by many mainstream analysts: "Of the two countries," says one, "it is the Soviet Union that seems to have made more numerous and more substantial concessions."[66] At times the Soviets made unprecedented concessions and even agreed to terms that would have left them (by conventional wisdom) at an inferior position. In contrast, most disarmament controversies in the U.S.

ended in victory for the hardliners and in rejection of treaties which would have improved America's military position.

II. In the making of American foreign policies, some scholars believe, Presidents command more power than the original framers of the Constitution intended them to have. This belief is backed up by recent history. For example, from its very beginning in 1950, American involvement in Vietnam was decided upon almost exclusively within the executive branch. Sometimes, as with the infamous Tonkin Gulf resolution, Congress was deliberately manipulated to give the President an almost blank check in committing American troops to that country.[67,68] Subsequent events, including Bush's decision in 1990 to deploy hundreds of thousands of troops in Saudi Arabia (biggest deployment since Vietnam), followed the same pattern. These same scholars then go on to trace our deficient foreign policies to this imbalance of power. They go on to suggest that these policies could be considerably improved by restoring a more proper balance between the legislative and executive.

This is not the place to refute this naive perception of our foreign policies. We need, however, take up the related question: Could our disarmament policies be improved by merely restoring the balance of power between the two branches of government?

Historical evidence presented in this chapter conclusively shows that they could not: you can't cure dehydration with a single drop of water. Kennedy, Macmillan, and Khrushchev wanted a total test ban, but all three were thwarted by the American Congress. A similar situation prevailed with Carter, Brezhnev, the total test ban, and SALT II. In American politics, it seems, there is nothing safer than advocating a hard line on disarmament issues.

A more correct generalization would be: in most policy disputes, the militaristic faction prevails. The problem with our disarmament policies is not Imperial Presidency, but Hardline Supremacy.[69] Restoring the balance between the executive and legislative branches of government might not be a bad idea on Constitutional and other grounds, but it will definitely not restore sanity to our disarmament policies. To eliminate the needless threat of war, we must do much more than place limits on Presidential power.

III. The West has been the pace setter in the arms race; practically every new military gadget was developed here and only then adopted by the Soviets.[70] In 1991 this was clearly the case with anti-submarine warfare, cruise missiles, lasers, space technology, and biological weapons, as it has been in the past with nuclear bombs, heavy bombers, guidance systems, hardened missile silos, multiple warheads, and missile submarines. Even during the 1957 Sputnik launch the U.S. had apparently enjoyed "a substantial lead . . . in almost every area of missile and rocket technology."[55b] By 1956, according to one historian, the United States could launch a more advanced satellite than Sputnik but refrained from doing so for political reasons.

It is even possible that without our help the Russians would have never been able to develop many weapons they now possess. Through our semi-open political process and publications, and through their extensive spy network, the Russians could often put their hands not only on the kinds of new weapons that could be built, but their exact blueprints. Moreover, until 1985 they conducted this catch-up exercise as if their lives depended on its outcome; no sacrifice, they seemed to believe, was too great. The five years or so lag time between America and Russia can be interpreted then as the time it took the Russians to gain hold of our blueprints and apply their newly acquired knowledge to the development of the new weapon.

At any rate, though it could perhaps be reasonably argued that the Russians would have been able to develop all these weapons without us, it is inarguably true that we have always been ahead, and that they have always managed, by hook or by crook, to trail along.

IV. Curiously, it is often our old ex-officials who show the courage, civic responsibility, and patriotism which are apparently needed to take the hardliners to task. Their ranks include retired presidents, congressmen, ambassadors, generals, weapon scientists, and other senior officials. This can be explained by assuming that retirement gives powerful people a better perspective on history, or, as appears more likely, that the penalties for taking the hardliners to task when one's political career is over are more bearable.

The fact itself—outspokenness of retired officials—is widely acknowledged. For instance, after carefully documenting the need for fundamental military reforms, one hardliner[71] remarks that when the time comes for the preliminary hearings,

> no help can be expected from military officers on active duty. Any number of retired generals and admirals will readily . . . [denounce] the present system, but it is idle to expect confirmation from the inmates of the present service-dominated structure. With their careers at stake, on the ground of service loyalty, they cannot criticize the system unless they are totally certain that it will be changed, and very soon.

V. The West's economic and technological primacy and the respective strengths of the peace and war parties in the Soviet and Western blocks throw some light on another curious generalization: The fate of every international disarmament debate has been almost exclusively determined by internal political developments in the U.S. That is, in virtually every case in which a strictly domestic controversy was decided in favor of disarmament, the Soviets went along. This suggests that, as long as the former Soviet republics remain rational (and God knows that we were doing little to strengthen the peace factions in these republics), comprehensive disarmament only required a radical change in American policies.

VI. Contrary to popular perceptions, the arms race has continued practically unabated throughout the Cold War. All the so-called treaties and successes, despite the fanfare with which they have been announced by decision-makers and the enthusiasm with which they have been greeted by some war-weary people, have amounted to little more than the institutionalization of the arms race. Even by 1991, not a single weapon, technical improvement, or new military development has been given up. SALT I, the defunct SALT II, the threshold test ban treaty, the non-binding non-proliferation treaty, the treaty on intermediate-range missiles, the ban on chemical weapons, held the hope of meaningful cooperation in the future and reduced prospects of a fatal confrontation, but were militarily trivial.

The atmospheric test ban treaty was an important environmental victory,[72] but not a victory for peace on earth. By the time this treaty was signed, all important tests could be performed underground. To be sure, this treaty ruled out tests of near-simultaneous explosions in the same area, thereby further reducing the chances of a deliberate preemptive strike against military targets. But given the magnitude of the overall threat, such treaties resemble the crow's diligent efforts to drain the ocean by removing its contents one drop at time: "When negotiated agreements have managed to close off certain avenues of the arms race, the result usually has been simply to divert the efforts of the weaponeers into the other channels still available."[73]

VII. Throughout the Cold War, hardliners have been opposed to any settlement whatsoever. The atmospheric test ban and SALT I, according to them, posed the gravest risks imaginable to our freedom, our republic, and the world. The ten foot tall Soviets, we were told, would not sign a fair agreement, they would cheat, or, in general, they would have something devious up their sleeve.

On the few occasions when the hardliners were overruled, their dire prophecies failed: the hardliners' crystal gazing record is unsurpassably dismal. The claim that Sputnik was "a greater defeat for America than Pearl Harbor,"[55b] and the national hysteria the Sputnik launch caused, were as grounded in objective reality as the panic which followed the broadcast of H. G. Wells' *War of the Worlds*. The 1963 atmospheric test ban treaty was concluded despite the hardliners' vehement opposition, and has been in force ever since. Observably, it did not lead to our subjugation, as they prophesied. In fact, even some in their ranks now admit that its passage only prevented needless deterioration of public health. Precisely the same can be said about anti-ballistic missiles, an antennae farm that would have covered a significant portion of Wisconsin, the biological weapons treaty, or the ban on chemical weapons.

VIII. Taken together with Hardline Supremacy, this dismal record strongly suggests that the arms race has been a strikingly irrational enterprise. This irrationality is also evident from the repetitiveness of every debate, the enormous costs whose only official rationale is not preparation for war but its prevention, the net decline in the national security of both sides, the near-exclusive preoccupation with Russia in an obviously multipolar and multifaceted world, and the steep decline in America's meaningful military edge over Russia and other potential adversaries.

IX. Like the nuclear chain reactions that made it possible, the nuclear arms race tended to fuel itself.

This self-perpetuating tendency is evident in each side's fears of what the other side might be up to. Assuming the worst about the other's intentions and capabilities, an old-fashioned military planner typically braced himself for every contingency. It is just possible that the Soviets will beat us in the race to develop an H-bomb, therefore we must produce an H-bomb in all possible haste. It is just possible that the ineffective (or even bogus[38]) ring of anti-ballistic missiles around Moscow can really, somehow, defend it, and therefore we must be prepared to meet this peril to our nuclear deterrent through the manufacture of "smarter" weapons.

The new technologies often perpetuated the arms race by fueling anxieties. For example, during the 1960s, the Soviets showed an interest in developing anti-ballistic missiles. This prompted the following (and familiar) hardliners' projection. The Soviets may be able to destroy our missiles in a surprise attack. We shall be unable to retaliate because many of our remaining missiles will be destroyed on their way to target by the Soviets' new anti-ballistic missiles; and the few that could reach target will not suffice as a deterrent. Consequently, the Soviets will run us over. One way of overcoming this threat involved fitting our missiles with multiple warheads capable of saturating any conceivable anti-ballistic missile defense the Soviet Union could deploy. We promptly developed this new technology. The Soviets naturally followed suit, and their multiple warheads, along with increased warhead accuracy, were used in turn to raise the unrealistic "window of vulnerability" projection (Chapter 5). And this self-created window, in its own turn, was the chief official justification for the 1980s huge arms buildup.

The arms race is self-perpetuating in the psychological and political sense too. Psychologically, we have come to consider it as a normal, perhaps inevitable, part of life. Politically, as the arms race flourishes, its constituencies in military, industrial, political, academic, and other sectors of our society become more powerful. So, as we divert more resources to the arms race, and as it becomes institutionalized in the fabric of our lives, the task of bringing it to a nonviolent end becomes increasingly harder.

Given this self-perpetuating attribute and the Russians' growing distaste for the "arms control" game, some cynics suggest that Western elites would love to see Russian hardliners back in power. Our steadfast refusal to give Russian and other ex-Soviet democrats a helping hand lends a measure of support to this claim. But lack of evidence for covert actions against Russian and other reformers, as well as subdued expressions of delight with their actions, suggest a more ambivalent attitude among Western power elites.

X. Each successive wave of this repetitive, irrational, and self-perpetuating race has led to the erosion of American, Russian, and world security. Despite the hardliners' claims (e.g., anti-ballistic missiles, evacuation plans, space militarization), there has never been an effective defense against nuclear weapons. Barring spectacular and unforeseeable scientific advances, we do not have the faintest idea how such a defense could be developed in the future. Instead, the arms race amounts to a series of improvements and amplifications in either side's ability to destroy the other. The most likely outcome of this absurd situation is greater insecurity for all.

XI. To prop up their view that our policies provide the only appropriate response to the twin perils of totalitarianism and the arms race, the hardliners were willing at times to put veracity and reason aside and to employ an assortment of effective but intellectually dishonest tactics. Only a few recurring variations of these tactics need to be described here.

The Tactic of the Imaginary Gap employed phony claims about Soviet superiority—overall or in a specific area—as excuses for speeding up the arms race. This tactic has a long history. It contributed, among other things, to the election of Kennedy (missile gap) and Reagan (overall gap).[74] From 1945 to 1990 we have had the conventional war gap; in the mid-1950s the bomber gap; from 1959 to 1961 the missile gap; in 1960 the chemical and biological weapons gap;[45b] in the early 1980s a gap in the capacity for military interventions in the Third World was well on its way.[75] Naturally, in all these cases there had been a gap all right—in our favor.

Sometimes the gap was alleged in areas where the Soviets were in fact superior, but in which this superiority meant little. It is in this light that their evacuation plans, air defense, tanks, intermediate-range missiles in Europe, and total yield of nuclear explosives should be viewed. In each case, the alleged superiority amounted to little, either because it overlooked the overall balance or because it signaled unwise resource allocation. But time is short and no one can become an expert in everything. So, as a public relations exercise, in order to gain political office, or as a means of speeding up the arms race, the Tactic of the Imaginary Gap has been unquestionably effective.[76]

The Tactic of the Irrelevant Argument can be illustrated with the following episode. Even if we choose to ignore overkill and dynamic military indicators, we might expect all arguments about the military balance to be concerned with the respective strengths of both nations. But this logical requirement presents a problem for the hardliners, for the USA was, at the very least, equal to the USSR. It is, however, much harder to compare the military expenditures of both nations, so here a lively controversy can be stirred up to make us forget that the issue is not spending, but the military balance.

This tactic assumed macabre proportions one day in 1976 when the CIA revised its estimates upward and concluded that the Soviets have been squandering all along, not 6 percent of their gross national product on defense (roughly the fraction we were squandering), as was believed for a long time, but 12 percent[77] (a more recent estimate puts it as high as 20 percent[78]). This revelation was followed by the usual alarms and admonitions. The hardliners, of course, failed to realize that the 6 percent figure simply made no sense—if the Soviet economy was half as large as ours, if it was less efficient, and if the Soviets' military was as large as ours, than the fraction the Soviets spent on their military machine was at least twice as large as the fraction we spent on ours. (For our war party, it seems, a braying ass in a lion's skin is a lion.) They forgot that this spending was irrelevant, because the important thing is not how much money you spend, but what you get for your money. They also forgot that this revision, as the CIA report which contained it clearly indicated, had no significance to the military balance except in showing that the Soviets were far less efficient than official dogma asserted. As one retired CIA analyst put it, "what should have been cause for jubilation became the inspiration for misguided alarm."[77]

The Tactic of the Wolf in Sheep's Clothing employs a peace-loving facade to cover up a bias in favor of the arms race. Here you attend meaningless "summit" conferences (e.g., Washington, 1990); or you put forward proposals which are likely to be rejected (e.g., Baruch, START). If you make a miscalculation and the other side accepts your proposal (May 1955), you retract it and then put forward irrelevant or unacceptable proposals. You might portray yourself as a peacemaker by heralding a virtually worthless treaty as a great leap forward (e.g., the 1987 treaty on European missiles); or as a peacekeeper by arguing that weapons which slightly raise the prospects of a final confrontation, and which undermine your country's well-being, safeguard the peace (e.g., space militarization).

The Tactic of the Wolf in Sheep's Clothing, history shows, is handiest in bringing about a virtual dissolution of the peace party. Mistakenly believing that their leaders are beyond cynical demagoguery or self-destructive folly, that small beginnings are bound to usher in great events, that a partial victory is better than none, that a compromising attitude is always a virtue, that "thinking globally and acting locally" can get them someplace other than the village green, and that hard work and dedication ought to be rewarded with immediate results, peace activists have traditionally walked straight into the hardliners' jaws by endorsing, or even fighting for, meaningless "arms control" treaties. From Potsdam to Moscow, from 1945 to 1991, the verdict of history is unequivocal: the cause of peace gained precious little from their valiant, well-meaning—but manifestly futile—efforts.

Summary

All things being equal and when given a choice, peaceful coexistence with the Soviet Union would have been compellingly superior to the arms race. Early episodes at the dawn of the Cold War, including attempts to keep Stalin in the dark about the Manhattan Project, a marked disinclination to negotiate atomic and hydrogen weapons out of existence, and rejections of genuine Soviet disarmament proposals, suggest that the United States was not interested in "equal and balanced armament reductions, under an adequate system of control." Later events, including the decades-long aborted search for a ban on nuclear tests, and every single occurrence of the 1980s decade, similarly suggest that the United States preferred the arms race to peaceful coexistence.

Throughout the Cold War, American military and foreign policies have been amazingly consistent—politicians came and went, but the policies remained. This repetitiveness eases the historian's task of distilling regularities from the myriad of available details: (1) From 1955 through 1991, the Soviets have been more interested in peaceful coexistence than the Americans. (2) The American President's power is often overrated; the correct historical extrapolation is not imperial presidency but hardline supremacy. (3) The West has been the exclusive pace setter of the arms race. (4) Senior retired officials and executives are far more likely to tell the public the truth than their employed counterparts in government, industry, and the armed forces. (5) The fate of every disarmament issue has been determined by internal political developments in the U.S. (6) All meaningful disarmament efforts have failed; all "arms control" treaties merely institutionalized the arms race, created the false impression of movement towards peace, and led to diversion of resources to other warlike channels. (7) The hardliners were even opposed to these cosmetic treaties, wrongly prophesying dire consequences if they were signed. (8) Several military, political, psychological, and economic features of the arms race conferred upon it a self-perpetuating and irrational character. (9) Each successive phase of the arms race eroded the security of all Western nations. (10) To prop up its view that American policies provided the only appropriate response to the twin perils of totalitarianism and the arms race, the Western establishment employed an assortment of effective but intellectually dishonest tactics, including the concoction of imaginary gaps, irrelevant arguments, and peace loving slogans aimed at covering up warring proclivities.

If American policy makers attempted to practice deterrence throughout the Cold War, the historical record could only be regarded as the handiwork of ignoramuses, morons, or lunatics. If they practiced brinkmanship, it acquires a certain degree of coherence.

Chapter 8

BRINKMANSHIP AND IMPERIALISM?

I call it the Madman Theory, Bob. I want the North Vietnamese to believe I've reached the point where I might do anything to stop the war. We'll just slip the word to them that, "for God's sake, you know Nixon is obsessed about Communism. We can't restrain him when he's angry—and he has his hand on the nuclear button"—and Ho Chi Minh himself will be in Paris in two days begging for peace.

Richard Nixon,[1] 1968

The madmen are planning the end of the world. What they call continued progress in atomic warfare means universal extermination, and what they call national security is organized suicide.

Lewis Mumford,[2] 1946

The earth will probably sink and drown; but at least it will be the result of generally acknowledged political and economic ideas, at least it will be accomplished with the help of science, industry, and public opinion, with the application of all human ingenuity! No cosmic catastrophe, nothing but state, official, economic, and other causes.

Karel Capek,[3] 1936

Nuclear Diplomacy

The notion of brinkmanship (Chapter 5) is counterintuitive. Given the enormously destructive power of nuclear bombs, their potentially devastating environmental impact, and the 12,000 nuclear bombs the Soviets could fire at the continental United States, any attempt to use these weapons in any role other than deterrence

195

appears insane. Ordinary people might be familiar with something like the oft-cited advice to American policy makers at the dawn of the nuclear age: "Thus far the chief purpose of our military establishment has been to win wars. From now on its chief purpose must be to avert them. It can have almost no other useful purpose."[4a] From cradle to grave Americans been have assured that their country subscribed to this notion. Even when the U.S. enjoyed a decisive nuclear edge, American leaders often embraced this view in public. As early as 1954, for instance, President Eisenhower said: "We have arrived at that point, my friends, where war does not present the possibility of victory or defeat. War would present to us only the alternative of degrees of destruction. There can be no truly successful outcome."[5]

All the same, we need more than apparent implausibility to reject, or accept, the brinkmanship interpretation. The best clue to its verisimilitude does not lie in intuition, avowals, and *a priori* reasoning, but in the historical record.

Truthfulness and objectivity seem to be the exception in politics, not the rule. The power elite in nineteenth century America said little about dispossession and economic exploitation of Native Americans, and a great deal about manifest destiny. European colonialists said little about profits, balance of payments, or national power and prestige, and much about civilizing missions, Christianity, and the white man's burden. Iosif Stalin declared—and the majority of Soviets and Eastern Europeans probably believed—that his policies sought peace and justice. During their long war with the Spartans, the ancient Athenians had to be reminded: "Do not imagine that you are fighting about a simple issue, freedom or slavery; you have an empire to lose, and there is the danger to which the hatred of your imperial rule has exposed you."[6] Such historical precedents show that a nation's actual policies can sharply differ from its stated policies, and that a great number of citizens often confuse avowals with facts. It remains to be seen whether this applies to Cold War America.

For the most part, the discussion in the last three chapters was anchored on the assumption that our actual policies have been chiefly aimed at safeguarding freedom and deterring nuclear attack. Virtually none of our strategies and decisions, we saw, served this purpose. From the insincere Baruch plan to the proposed militarization of space; from the mid-1940s' claims of Soviet conventional superiority to 1989 claims of Soviet superiority in laser technology, from the strategy of massive retaliation to that of nuclear war fighting, from Eisenhower's to Bush's "Open Skies" proposals, we had to conclude that our military policies could not be interpreted, by any stretch of the imagination, as serving the cause of deterrence. Occasional irrelevancies between policy objectives and the means used to achieve them are to be expected in human affairs, but a consistent divergence between ends and observed means raises serious questions. In particular, the possibility exists that the divergence is not between means and ends, but between the stated and actual ends of America's nuclear policies.

How does the brinkmanship interpretation fare with the same facts? To answer this question, we need to re-examine our Cold War policies, this time under the new premise that these policies were neither essentially defensive nor aimed at deterrence, but offensive and aimed at retaining or regaining a politically meaningful nuclear edge. I shall not attempt a detailed re-interpretation of the strategies, claims, and events discussed in the last three chapters, for the evidence seems to be conclusive—the brinkmanship hypothesis throws more light on American policies than its deterrence rival. Time and again, policies that can only be judged as astoundingly irrational or misinformed under the deterrence premise suddenly acquire a meaning.

The case being so clear, I shall merely place a few facets of our policies under this new magnifying glass.

The brinkmanship interpretation is not, by a long shot, the imaginary hallucinations of some wild-eyed radicals. Apparently, it has been taken for granted by some of our most influential decision makers. A former Secretary of State wrote in 1982 that the loss of American nuclear superiority in the early 1970s "was a strategic revolution even if the Soviets did not achieve a superiority of their own. For that, to some extent, freed the Soviet capacity for regional intervention."[7] This view is shared by other mainstream analysts: "American superiority in nuclear weapons . . . was an important element in inducing Soviet caution."[8] Another observer attributes "the surrender of Soviet pretensions over West Berlin,

. . . the [favorable] outcome of the Cuban missile crisis, and . . . the prudent Soviet stance in the 1967 Arab-Israeli war" to the diplomatic leverage the United States obtained from the nuclear edge it still enjoyed in the 1960s.[9a]

Some observers believe that the bombing of Hiroshima and Nagasaki "may well have been intended as much to impress and intimidate the Soviet Union as to bring the war with Japan to a prompt conclusion."[10a] Mainstream American historians scoff at this "revisionist" charge. Still others take an intermediate position. For instance, after expressing uncertainty about Hiroshima, President Kennedy's special assistant for national security affairs wrote in 1988 that "it is hard to see that much could have been lost if there had been more time between the two bombs."[11a] But regardless of one's views on this controversial matter, it is certain that the first peacetime tests of nuclear weapons were carried out by the U.S. and that "the idea that nuclear bombs are actually usable as military weapons and as instruments of coercion in international affairs is an invention of the Western powers."[10b]

That the U.S. was the first to test and use nuclear weapons is well known, but we must explore the point about coercion. "In addition to the abstract notions of deterrence ostensibly conferred on the US and USSR by their mutual nuclear weapons capabilities held in readiness against the other, these weapon systems have been utilised in crises far more often than people—including political scientists—are aware of. We have been fortunate that this level of use has not yet led to actual use in wartime, but that has perhaps been due to more complex factors than the restraint with which we ordinarily assume nuclear weapons are handled."[12a] "U.S. leaders have run calculated nuclear risks not for self-defense, high moral principles, or the protection of weak countries from the Soviets, but to further U.S. power."[13a]

The first quotation might have raised some eyebrows in 1980, when it was published. By now the facts it describes are either acknowledged or ignored—but not to my knowledge denied—in all Western scholarly and official publications. At the very least, the U.S. employed nuclear coercion in nineteen separate incidents.[12b] It certainly did not take much to trigger this tactic. For instance, Guatemala's acceptance of "Soviet block support" (see below) in

May 1954 led to an implicit nuclear threat against the Soviet Union.[14] Similarly, according to President Eisenhower, veiled nuclear threats were decisive in ending the Korean War in 1953 and the conflict over the tiny Taiwanese islands of Quemoy and Matsu in 1955 and 1958.[11b] President Carter made it clear in 1980 that "an attempt by any outside force to gain control of the Persian Gulf region will be regarded as an assault on the vital interests of the United States of America, and such an assault will be repelled by any means necessary, including military force."[13b] Administration officials explained that Carter was referring to nuclear weapons: "The Soviets," said one, "know that this terrible weapon has been dropped on human beings twice in history and it was an American president who dropped it both times. Therefore, they have to take this into consideration in their calculus."[13c]

Psychologically, brinkmanship throws some light on the everlasting gaps, windows, and alleged Soviet plans to win nuclear wars. It is far easier to attribute one's own intentions and capabilities to an implacable enemy than to figure out what the other side thinks and does. Also, real motives and intentions—regardless of who actually holds them—are as a rule far more credible than imaginary ones.

The recurring theme in influential political and military circles in the U.S. "that the use of nuclear weapons must be regarded as absolutely normal, natural, and right" and the efforts to attack "emotional resistances to using nuclear weapons"[4b] are utterly incomprehensible under deterrence theory; practitioners of deterrence are expected to daily sing the horrors of nuclear war, not its praises. But the West's proclivity to normalize the unthinkable is entirely consistent with brinkmanship. Even in 1992, high-ranking American officials are not in the habit of admitting in public—as their Russian counterparts have been freely doing for decades—that a nuclear war would be an unparalleled catastrophe.

A few quotations will suffice to give the flavor of this line of thinking. An American Secretary of State (1954): "It should be our agreed policy in case of war, to use atomic weapons as conventional weapons against the military assets of the enemy whenever and wherever it would be of advantage to do so."[4c] A former commander of our nuclear forces (1968): "A war fought from . . .

a base of nuclear superiority would leave the United States sorely wounded, but viable and victorious."[4d]   An influential analyst (1979): "There is a role for . . . the sensible, politically directed application of military power in thermonuclear war."[4e]   George Bush felt that a nuclear war could be won (1979): "You have a survivability of command and control, survivability of industrial potential, protection of a percentage of your citizens, and you have a capability that inflicts more damage on the opposition than it can inflict on you. That's the way you can have a winner."[13d]

The United States has never disavowed the first use of nuclear weapons. On the contrary, it has been explicitly committed to deploy such weapons first "to repel a Soviet invasion of Western Europe."[10b] This commitment is also implicit in America's declaratory policies, dating from 1979, to use any means necessary to protect its interests in the Middle East.

In the late 1980s, the USSR presented the deterrence/brinkmanship dispute with a crucial test. Practitioners of deterrence and democracy would have greeted Soviet reforms with open arms. They would have agreed, as early as 1985, to massive bilateral military cutbacks. They would have responded to the Soviet testing moratorium with gestures of their own. They would have gasped with disbelief and joy at Soviet disengagement from Eastern Europe, though they may have been somewhat wary about the re-unification of Germany and the chaos, bloodshed, nationalist hysteria, ethnic feuds, and religious fanaticism that the breakup of the Soviet Union itself might unfold. Their suspicions that the Soviets were still playing war and politics by the old rules would have been largely dissolved once they noticed Soviet willingness to accept unfair disarmament proposals. They would have realized that Soviet humanitarians faced formidable reactionary opposition (especially from communists and nationalists), that they faced severe economic challenges, and that their fate hinged in part on Western cooperation and help. Although Russian, Ukrainian, and other reformers may succeed despite America's wait-and-see attitude, American policies raised the probability of reversion to the authoritarian past and renewal of the Cold War. Even though American policy makers understood that much, they seemed unduly reluctant to let go of the "enemy" which so faithfully justified their domestic, foreign, and military policies. Needless to say, their actions accord with the brinkmanship interpretation, not its deterrence rival.

Proponents of the deterrence interpretation fail to account for America's pursuit of overkill. In contrast, brinkmanship theory demands it, as one Pentagon consultant put it:

> One hears it said endlessly that the competition between American and Soviet . . . nuclear forces is . . . futile, because each side can already destroy the population of the other "many times over." That . . . is a vulgar misunderstanding. It is not to destroy the few hundred cities and larger towns of each side—easy targets neither protected nor concealed—that . . . nuclear forces continue to be developed. The purpose is not to threaten cities and towns already abundantly threatened, to "overkill" populations, but rather to threaten the . . . nuclear forces themselves. . . . Thus there are several thousand targets, as opposed to a few hundred cities and towns, and many of those targets can be destroyed only by very accurate warheads.[9b]

Though there is no attempt to trace the origins of the "vulgar misunderstanding" in this analyst's writings, the point itself is well taken and explains much that otherwise defies explanation. It is consistent with the brinkmanship theory's basic postulate of the strive for asymmetry (Chapter 5). It puts the perennial obsession with warhead accuracy in a new light. It tells us why we developed the H-bomb, multiple warheads, killer submarines, and the like. It explains our resolve to militarize space: it is not the technically impossible absolute shield that we are after, but a shield which might appear strong enough to continue playing Russian roulette. It tells us why the U.S. targeted 10 percent of its strategic weapons at Soviet population centers and some 90 percent at the Soviet Union's military forces.[15] It explains why, even under Secretary of Defense McNamara, the shift to assured destruction was at the declaratory level, while the actual targeting policy remained unchanged.[16] Indeed, how else could the reported 1983 existence of more than 40,000 potential targets be explained?[4f] It elucidates otherwise inexplicable utterances about thinking the unthinkable, acceptable casualty levels, limited nuclear exchanges, controlled nuclear salvos, escalation dominance, nuclear victories, and well-managed nuclear conflicts.

American Intervention in the Third World

I have documented earlier the sharp contrast between (1) American domestic policies, which have been, taken as a whole, more humane and rational than pre-1985 Soviet policies, and (2) American disarmament policies, which have been, for the most part, less humane and rational than the Soviets.' The same sharp contrast can unfortunately be observed between the two nations' domestic and Third World policies. Here is a 1980 appraisal:

> The Soviet regime is without doubt the bloodiest and most deceptive caricature in modern history, a cruel parody of the ideas that supposedly inspire it. . . . And yet in Africa, Asia, and Latin America, national liberation movements . . . generally find that the Soviet Union is on their side, while the liberal democracies of the West have almost always during the past three decades been on the side of oppression in the Third World.[17]

In public, American policy makers and their academic underlings usually explained this strange situation in something like the following terms. We faced, they said, an unpleasant dilemma. Sure, many of the Third World's peoples have been ruled by cynical, heartless, and greedy tyrants. We did not like these tyrants, but we kept them in power because the alternative was even worse: if we abandoned these tyrants, they would have been replaced by even more ruthless communists, who would then pose a grave threat to their people and to our security and freedom.

Convincing as this argument may sound, many proponents of the brinkmanship interpretation persuasively argue that it has nothing to do with the real world. The choices we faced in Greece, Turkey, Cuba, South Vietnam and scores of other places were not between dictators and totalitarians, but, they say, among dictators, totalitarians, and New Deal *democrats*. To be sure, unlike the dictators but like genuine democrats everywhere, these democrats have been more concerned with the plight of their peoples and less concerned with the profit margins of American corporations; their foreign policies were more independent of ours; and they believed that the best way of fighting totalitarianism was not jailing, killing, or torturing communists, but bringing greater freedom to their peoples.

In view of this issue's controversial nature and vast scope, the following account subserves a modest goal: showing that allegations of American preference for Third World dictators over both communists and democrats are not as far-fetched as a casual reading of our newspapers and semi-official histories might suggest. To do this, the narrative is limited to just one country—Guatemala— chosen at random from among a score of countries which readily present themselves. It is largely confined to one period in that country's history: *The Guatemalan Spring*, 1945-1954. It avoids questionable occurrences and moot theoretical points, sticking instead to accepted facts. I shall then argue that this sad tale provides a reasonable approximation of not only U.S.-Guatemalan relations but of America's Third World policies as a whole.[18] From this I shall conclude that, at the very least, brinkmanship and imperialism—despite their untextbookish nature—are more plausible than the competing interpretations of deterrence and of American commitment to a democratic Third World.

In 1944, the order which prevailed in Guatemala can be best described as feudalism, twentieth century style. Hunger and malnutrition were widespread. The death rate was one of the highest in the world,[19a] which meant, for example, that one out of every two Guatemalan children never made it beyond the age of five.[20a] Only three out of ten Guatemalans could read.[21a] Some 2 percent of the people owned more than 70 percent of the land, and 75 percent owned less than 10 percent of the land. Annual per capita income was $180 overall, and for the poorest two-thirds, $70. More than half of all Guatemalans lived in one-room shacks with no running water, windows, or cooking facilities. More than half could not afford to buy a single pair of shoes.

In some ways, these numbers portray an unrealistically bleak sketch. They ignore, for example, the rewards of economic self-sufficiency; the beauty of semi-communal village life; the psychological rewards of firmly belonging to one place, of cooperation with one's fellows, of frequent, whole-hearted celebrations, and of intimate ties to the land. In other ways, the sketch these numbers portray is not dark enough. It is hard for the average book reader to grasp the meaning of these numbers and their impact on every aspect of one's life. It is not even enough to spend months in a remote highland village to grasp this ghastly side. One must grow up there and then escape—from intellectual darkness, helplessness, continuous struggle for sheer survival, debilitating diseases, premature deaths, indignation suffered because of one's race, poverty, or backwardness—to know what it really means. The closest that one can come to understanding such misery from afar is through works of fiction.

But while the majority was living in abject poverty, a few thousand families—wealthy Guatemalans and foreign employees of American corporations—were living very well indeed. These individuals usually owned a few cars, one or more modern houses, or a large country estate. They maintained a retinue of servants. They often studied and traveled abroad. They thus made up a few scattered reefs of affluence and extravagance in an ocean of penury and depredations.[19b]

The American-owned and -operated United Fruit Company (UFCO) held a special place in this feudal society. UFCO began its Guatemalan operations at the turn of the century. At that time, an enterprising railroad baron developed and acquired control of the nation's transportation network, including Guatemala's only railroad and shipping port. This monopolistic position made it possible for the new company to railroad small banana-growing companies out of business and to gradually acquire a major share of Guatemala's banana business. As UFCO's economic power grew, it proceeded to make the political climate of its host country as congenial to profit maximization as possible. Given an income greater than that of any government in Central America, and given UFCO's willingness, while in Guatemala, to behave as the local politicos and power elite did, UFCO became a dominant force in Guatemalan politics. To many Guatemalans it was known as *El Pulpo*—an octopus holding sway over Guatemala's political and economic life.[22a]

By the 1940s, UFCO owned some 20 percent of Guatemala's arable land and was the country's largest employer. By then, UFCO's profits from its Latin American operations amounted to twice the revenues of the Guatemalan government. Its profits from Guatemala alone amounted to some 50 percent of total government revenues. Naturally, by the early 1940's UFCO was virtually exempt from paying taxes. The living conditions UFCO provided for its Guatemalan farm workers were far worse, for example, than those depicted in Steinbeck's *Grapes of Wrath* or *In Dubious Battle*, but they were better than those enjoyed by most Guatemalans under the employ of their own fellow countrymen.

UFCO was the largest and, probably, most hated, foreign company in Guatemala, but it was not the only one. About 80 percent of Guatemala's electric power was provided by a private, American-owned power company.[23a] In addition to foreign corporations, a few Guatemalan landowners, politicians, and industrialists were taking their fair share of the spoils too.

From 1931 to 1944 the country was under the rule of one Jorge Ubico, who came to power as the result of a "U.S.-engineered election."[22b] By today's standards Ubico was a benign, somewhat comical, dictator with Napoleonic aspirations and a great deal of admiration for Franco and Mussolini.[24] But to most of his subjects his long rule was no laughing matter. Executions, tortures, a salary some 1,300 times that of his average subject, election results 308,000 to 0 in his favor, being but a few of his misdeeds.

As elsewhere in the American continents, Native Americans suffered oppression, depredation, and exploitation. But in contrast to the U.S. and Canada, Native Americans constitute the majority of the population in Guatemala. Most of them lived, as mentioned, under conditions of unimaginable poverty. Under Ubico, discrimination against them was the law of the land; it being legal, for example, for wealthy landlords to shoot on sight any Native American found hunting wild game on their land.[25]

Like other Central American countries, Guatemala was a virtual protectorate, or semi-colony, of the United States.[26a] To avoid costly and unpopular direct interventions in this region, the U.S. created and trained professional armies. This led to the "militarization of political life and an institutionalising of armed terror as the basis of the stability of oligarchical rule."[26b] As a result, Central American governments in the early 1940s were "anti-democratic . . . a throwback to feudal despotism."[26c]

In 1944, a series of demonstrations, protests, and strikes ensued. In the face of widespread opposition to Ubico's rule, the army eventually refused his orders to crush the rebellion. Ubico resigned and went into retirement in New Orleans. There followed a few months of a new, equally repugnant dictatorship, which in turn was ousted from power through a second revolution in October, 1944.

Revolutions frequently bring about greater horrors than the horrors they set out to eliminate, e.g., Iran's Islamic Revolution. In contrast, Guatemala's October Revolution was an exceptionally successful affair. It was followed by fairly free elections, certainly the freest in Guatemala's turbulent history.[21b] The revolutionary party's presidential candidate was Juan Arevalo, a liberal writer and teacher who was in exile during the revolution. The old guard put forward a few candidates of its own. Arevalo won and became president in March of 1945.

Early during Arevalo's presidency a new democratic constitution was ratified. This constitution, which remained in force throughout the Guatemalan Spring (1945-1954), mandated checks and balances among the three branches of government, universal suffrage, freedom of speech, press, and assembly; as well as a few other items that Westerners take for granted but that were never before enjoyed by Guatemalans.

Arevalo's foreign policies were more independent of the U.S. than those of his predecessors. When the Korean War broke out, Guatemala expressed solidarity with the U.S. Unlike the U.S., Guatemala severed political relations with two repressive governments in its vicinity—Nicaragua and the Dominican Republic. Arevalo's government supported a movement of radical democrats, *the Caribbean Legion*, which was committed to the creation of democracies by any means, including revolutions (a movement which contributed, incidentally, to the rise of Costa Rican democracy[21c]). Arevalo felt that Central American countries ought to merge into a single nation, but failed to convince his dictatorial neighbors to do so. In short, Guatemala's foreign policies, like its internal policies, seem to have been democratically inspired.

Arevalo's administration enacted a Labor Code which laid down the foundations for a social security system and protected employees from arbitrary firings. This code marginally improved employees' rights and working conditions. However, true to Arevalo's gradualist philosophy, those conditions were still a far cry from those enjoyed then by American or Swedish workers.

Arevalo's government allocated more funds and resources to education, especially of the illiterate poor, than any previous Guatemalan administration. Official racial discrimination was ended, although under the best of circumstances it would have taken generations to close the social, economic, and cultural gap between the races.

A few hundred communists were politically active during Arevalo's tenure in office. Arevalo himself was decidedly anti-communist, but as in all other democracies today, communists were left unmolested. They were also permitted to hold a few low-level official posts. Though critical of Arevalo's slow, gradualist, approach, the communists supported his reforms. The Communist Party was small and had little access to the army, police, or cabinet. Given these weaknesses, along with Arevalo's popularity and anti-communism, the chances of a communist takeover were probably minuscule; slightly higher, perhaps, than they were in 1982's Spain.

The charge of communism is critically important to our saga, as it provided the sole official justification for subsequent American policies. Even today, most journalistic reviews and college textbooks take this charge for granted. Yet, the record itself unequivocally suggests that Americans have not been told the truth. To dispel doubts, let me quote two former State Department officials. First, a memo written in 1945 concerning suspicions that Arevalo had communist sympathies:

> Anyone even reasonably well informed about his teachings, writings and general activities would be inclined to pass over such

suspicions as being so utterly without foundation as to call for no response.[21d]

Second, a retrospective look (published in 1976) by another official:

> Arevalo held that communism, as a doctrine, was antidemocratic and that the international movement was an enemy of democracy and of the people of Latin America. Arevalo banned the Communist party and deported Communist leaders for illegal activities early in his administration. Yet he insisted that the civil rights of all citizens, including Communists who did not violate the law, be protected. As a result, Communist leaders did have an opportunity to air their beliefs and programs, and popular support for them grew under Arevalo. Communists from abroad were allowed to visit the country and local Communists held posts in his administration.[23b]

However, American policy makers were troubled by the 1944 revolution's democratic aftermath. The U.S. ambassador was implicated in several attempts to overthrow the young democracy, and in 1950 Arevalo formally requested his recall.[23c] The democracy badly needed financial aid; in nine years Guatemala received less than one million dollars. It needed arms to defend itself; since 1948 the U.S. turned down repeated requests to supply arms and applied strong and effective pressures on all its allies to do likewise. According to some Guatemalan writers, this embargo was so effective that by 1954 it left their country unable, not only to equip its army, but to provide game hunters with ammunition.

Notwithstanding Arevalo's entire record, Congress and leading American newspapers conducted an anti-Guatemalan campaign. "What is surprising," says one former State Department official, "is that there was virtually no expression of the Guatemalan side of the story in Congress" or in major American newspapers.

> For example, Guatemalan national resentment about how the United Fruit Company allegedly had gained its hold was not mentioned, nor was the fact that the company had almost exclusive control of Guatemala's major railroads, port, and of many of the ships which carried its foreign trade. . . . Perhaps the most notable omission was any reference to the many social and

economic reforms which had been introduced in Guatemala since Ubico's fall and the sharp contrast in the democratic practices of the Arevalo administration as compared with the dictatorial methods of many of his predecessors.[23d]

Arevalo left office in 1951, thoroughly disillusioned about American hostility to his efforts to establish capitalism with a human face. "In the ideological dialogue . . ." he said in his farewell address "the real winner was Hitler."[23d]

In short, while Americans were being killed by the thousands in Korea, defending a pro-American dictator against an anti-American totalitarian, and while the U.S. was paying hundreds of millions of dollars to prop up dictatorial regimes in Greece and Turkey, a Western-style democracy was emerging in Guatemala, just south of the Mexican border, from the ravages of feudalism. Amazingly, the U.S. was going out of its way to bring feudalism back.

The next elections were held in 1950. Though they involved some inexcusable government fraud, irregularities, violence, and intimidation of the opposition, they "marked the first time in Guatemalan history that executive power had freely passed from one civilian to another."[22c] The two chief contenders were Jacobo Arbenz, a man from Arevalo's party and a leader of the October Revolution, and an old order oligarch. After reportedly receiving more than 60 percent of the votes, Arbenz assumed the presidency.

Arbenz shared Arevalo's political philosophy. In his 1951 inaugural address, Arbenz set out to transform Guatemala "from a dependent nation with a semi-feudal economy to an economically independent country . . . from a backward nation . . . to a modern capitalist country . . . and . . . to accomplish this transformation in a manner that brings the greatest possible elevation of the living standards of the . . . people."[20b]

To accomplish these goals, Arbenz was willing to take greater risks than Arevalo. The centerpiece of his program was moderate land reforms. Under his plan, *idle* land in excess of 223 acres would be transferred from the 1059 largest landowners (including land owned by himself and by his foreign minister). The land was to be handed over to peasants, each receiving from 8 to 33 acres. Most of the recipients were to pay rent at the rate of 3-5 percent of the value of annual produce of the land. Previous landowners would receive partial compensation for their losses (based on the unrealistically low value they themselves assigned to it in their tax returns). By 1954, about 100,000 peasant families, or some 500,000 individuals (mostly Native Americans), were cultivating land that otherwise would have been idle and were often getting financial credits, technical aid, and training. As a result, food prices went down and living standards went up.

Arbenz's agrarian program could be criticized on various grounds. It was, for example, hastily conceived and implemented; it gave the government too much power and influence over the peasants; and, like inheritance tax in many American states, it marginally eroded the privileges of the upper class. But there is no doubt that the program served well the long-term interests of democracy, Guatemala, the U.S., and even the Guatemalan upper class itself. In the words of a former State Department official:

> To the land hungry peasant in Guatemala the agrarian reform probably looked like manna from heaven . . . policies of forced labor and debt peonage had been commonplace throughout most of Guatemala's history. Good farm land is scarce . . . where most of the population resides and most . . . landholdings are pitifully small. Suddenly, the agrarian law promised land for the landless, more land for those having too little to provide a living for their families, and an end to land monopoly and exploitation by wealthy landlords . . . Peasants and workers . . . were made to feel that the government had suddenly acquired a genuine interest in their welfare.[19c]

Needless to say, this program did not endear Arbenz to most of the 1,059 comfortable landowners, including UFCO, the largest of them all. UFCO also had to deal with a labor force demanding reforms, often with some government backing. UFCO also faced a threat to its monopoly of Guatemala's overland and overseas shipping. The threat in this case did not come from attempts to nationalize Guatemala's railroads (which in 1951 were charging the highest rates in the world) or its single port, as democratic governments elsewhere had done. The threat came from construction of a new railroad (parallel to UFCO's) and a new port on the Pacific Coast (besides UFCO's port on the Atlantic). Likewise, to break the monopoly of the American electric power utility, Guatemala refrained from regulating this utility's affairs—as Americans chose to do in their own country. Instead, it set about constructing additional power plants.

With Arbenz in power, Washington's McCarthyization of Guatemala escalated. Communists held some low-level positions in Arbenz's administration: for the President, Congress, and the media this sufficed to turn Guatemala into a "beachhead for Soviet Communism" in the Americas. The U.S. continued the arms embargo and twisted the arms of other Western democracies to do the same. At the same time, the U.S. supplied arms and money to the democracy's foes. In desperation, after years of vainly trying to purchase arms in the West, Arbenz decided to buy some arms from Czechoslovakia, thereby clinching the witch-hunters' case against the Guatemalan Spring.

The Eisenhower administration came to power in 1953. It wasted little time carrying Truman's Guatemalan policies to their logical conclusion. The final act, planned and bankrolled by the CIA, involved a 1954 invasion of Guatemala by a small band of mercenaries and disaffected oligarchs. Because they could not prevail over the Guatemalan army on their own, their invasion was boosted by bombing of the capital with planes flown by American pilots, a CIA-operated radio station, and bribes given to Guatemalan generals by the United States' ambassador. The invasion was preceded by the stationing of long-range U.S. bombers in Nicaragua; apparently, a nuclear warning to the Soviet Union to refrain from counteracting the invasion.[14]

Arbenz resigned. For a few days, the American ambassador played the role of a *de facto* Guatemalan president. Through a variety of tactics (including intimidation and bribes), he installed the man chosen by the CIA to lead the coup, Carlos Castillo Armas, as Guatemala's new ruler.

And so it was that, a short time before President Eisenhower was disserving the cause of peace, freedom, and American national security by turning down Soviet comprehensive disarmament proposals, he was disserving this cause by bringing Guatemala's one and only democratic experiment to an end. Likewise, shortly before President Eisenhower's speech writers were to perform their capable best to misinform the American people about the true nature of the Soviet proposals, they misled their countrymen about the true nature of the Guatemalan Spring:

> The people of Guatemala, in a magnificent effort, have liberated themselves from the shackles of international Communist direction and reclaimed their right for self-determination . . . I pay tribute to the historic demonstration of devotion to the cause of freedom given by the people of Guatemala and their leaders.[21e]

There is no reference here to the people of the CIA or UFCO. No mention of the "number of close connections" between the Eisenhower administration and UFCO, "beginning with Secretary of State Dulles, whose law firm . . . numbered UFCO among its clients."[22d] No acknowledgment of the dirty psychological warfare, complete with bribes, arms embargoes, and intimidations. No forecast of the likeliest outcome of this "liberation": decades of human rights abuses "as appalling as any in the hemisphere."[22e] No mention of nuclear brinkmanship. No mention of risking a rift on this issue with Britain and France.[21f,27] No mention of the fact that Guatemalans have never been as free as they had been during the few years of their mid-century Spring. No attempt to prove a Stalinist direction; on the contrary, the Soviets seemed to have regarded the October Revolution as a "petty bourgeois" democracy.[23e] Nor, when talking about regained freedom, could Mr. Eisenhower mean freedom to speak without fear, organize political parties, or read Dostoyevsky—which was brought to an end in 1954; but freedom to starve, be exploited, shot, and discriminated against—which was reinstated.

So much for intelligence and candor in high places. A truer assessment appeared elsewhere:

> Deep down everyone in Guatemala knows that Communism was not the issue. Feudalism was the issue, and those who profited from feudalism won.[21g]

In the 38 years which followed, Guatemala has shown greater respect for U.S. interests than it had shown during its brief democratic interlude. Shortly after assuming power, Castillo Armas dispossessed 100,000 families of their newly-acquired lands, returning these lands to UFCO and other rich landowners. (By 1970, UFCO changed its name to United Brands, Inc.[22f]) The oil and timber concessions which Arevalo and Arbenz denied American corporations were granted. In time, the number of thriving American corporations climbed into the dozens. The Guatemalan government was anxious to create an ideal business climate. For instance, American corporations in Guatemala were living in the executive's dreamland—a strike-free environment in which intransigent labor leaders were routinely incarcerated, tortured, and killed.

The price of this favorable business climate was onerous. Today, Central American societies and nations are even more polarized than they were in the mid-1950s, with the opposition even more anti-American than before. The Guatemalan Spring was largely a middle class affair; since then, many less educated peasants have joined the conflict. To one well-meaning American official, at least, the best hope is recurrence of the Guatemalan Spring. Surveying the spreading reprisals, massacres, and tortures, he commented in 1980: "What we'd give to have an Arbenz now."[28]

Though the price paid by ordinary Americans was burdensome enough, the heaviest toll was exacted from the Guatemalan people. Arevalo's constitution and the rule of law are gone; instead the country has been turned into a slaughterhouse, alternating from 1954 to 1991 between periods of bloodshed and relative calm. Since 1954, "state terrorism" has been institutionalized in Guatemala, the oligarchy and military waging "open warfare against all reformist elements."[26d] Intermittently throughout the last 38 years, government-backed organizations like *The Death Squadrons* and *An Eye for an Eye* were terrorizing the vast majority. Communists were assassinated without trial, as were outspoken liberals, clergymen, union leaders, intellectuals, other potentially subversive elements, and countless innocent bystanders.

By 1983, all this "spiral of progovernment and antigovernment violence" led "the country to the most extreme state of violence, to wit, the establishment of a reign of terror. This constituted a weapon of social repression used against unions, opposition groups, universities, political parties, cooperatives, leagues of peasants and the Church; in other words, against all the institutions and groups critical of the Government."[29a] In 1983, members of these groups were being murdered at an average rate of 35 per day. There were then about 240,000 political refugees and exiles abroad, and the number of people who had to leave their homes and re-settle else-where in Guatemala may have been as high as one million. These figures constituted, respectively, roughly 3 and 14 percent of all Guatemalans. There was "the daily appearance, throughout the country, of mutilated bodies with signs of having suffered brutal tortures before being machinegunned to death."[29b] The total death toll from political violence from 1954 to 1983 was estimated at over 40,000 lives, or one out of 200 Guatemalans. By early 1989, the country averaged five daily murders and kidnapings. By late 1990, the U.S. continued

> to finance the army despite its participation in suppressing and killing. . . . Until the army is drastically reformed and reduced, electoral politics will be a cruel game perpetrated on the people of Guatemala to assuage the consciences of those who supply arms and money to the army . . . . Despite the facade of Guate-malan democracy, teachers, students, workers and untold number of rural Indians continue to be kidnaped and murdered, their assassins never to be tried.[30]

Many victims were innocent civilians. The Army's fight against the guerrillas, according to the Organization of American States, in reality was often directed at the peasants. On June 6, 1982, for example, in one village "the Army rounded up all the families, tied them up and put them in a house which they then burned, killing all 200 people inside."[29c] By late 1990, "some 500 communities, their fields, and nearby forests have been burned and leveled to deprive left-wing insurgents of recruits, food, and shelter."[31]

Despite the relative calm and democratic facade of the late 1980s, U.S. foreign policy spelled the virtual end of social progress in Guatemala. UFCO and other landowners got back their idle lands, thereby restoring one-fifth of Guatemala's 1954 population to landlessness, economic dependence, and destitution. The literacy campaign and labor laws were written off. Full-time child labor, often beginning at eight years of age, was near universal in rural areas. Half the nation's children went on dying before reaching their fifth birthday.[20a] In 1989, farm workers were making the country's minimum wage—$1.75 a day—and were still employed in slave-like conditions.

It is interesting to compare Guatemala's stationary misery to social advances in Costa Rica. A few cold statistics would suffice. In 1960, 7 percent of all Costa Rican infants died before their first birthday; by 1981, this figure had declined to 1.9 percent. During the same period, infant mortality in Guatemala declined too, but at a slower pace (9.2 to 6.4 percent). From 1970 to 1980, maternal death rates in Costa Rica steeply declined; in Guatemala they rose. In 1981 Costa Rica, the principal causes of death were cancer and heart disease. In Guatemala they were the maladies of poverty and neglect: infectious, parasitic, and intestinal diseases, influenza, and pneumonia.[32] (Unfortunately, in the 1980s, a large foreign debt, pressures from Western business interests, and a shift towards plutodemocracy contributed to a rise in Costa Rican hunger, infant mortality, and other negative indicators of the quality of life.[33])

A more disturbing comparison involves totalitarian Cuba— conventionally viewed as a notable failure of American foreign policies, and feudal Guatemala—a success story. In some ways, even before drastic reductions in Soviet aid came into effect, Cubans under Castro were worse off than Guatemalans. They were, for example, subject to more thoroughgoing indoctrination and meddling in some of their private affairs. Their centralized, inefficient economy merely shifted its unwholesome dependence on one country (the USA) to another (the USSR). Also, the average Cuban was better off than the average Guatemalan even before Castro's rise to power. But these differences were more than off-set, in my opinion, by more significant advances in social conditions in postrevolutionary Cuba than in re-feudalized Guatemala.

By the early 1980s, Cuba had moved towards a more equitable distribution of income.[34a] Considerable progress had been made in life expectancy, social security, welfare, assistance to the aged and handicapped, the status of women, pervasive administrative corruption,[35] and nutritional levels. Medical and dental care were free. Education up to ninth grade was compulsory; secondary education was free. The 30 percent illiteracy rate was wiped out. Since 1970, infant mortality has been the lowest in Latin America. Many infectious diseases like malaria have been completely eradicated. In short, though Cuba in the 1980s was unfree, it "has shown itself to be notably efficient in meeting the basic needs of the population, especially of those sectors that were the most disadvantaged prior to the revolution"[34b] (that is, the vast majority).

In making this comparison, I certainly do not wish to imply that totalitarianism is better than democracy. I believe that democracy, had it been given a chance in Cuba, would have done better. Had the U.S. provided Arevalo and Arbenz with the kind of aid that the Soviet Union gave Cuba, or had the U.S. merely granted Guatemalan reformers the same freedom of action it gave their Mexican and Costa Rican counterparts, the average Guatemalan today would have been freer, in every sense of the word, than the average Cuban. The point I wish to make is this: in Guatemala our foreign policies triumphed, in Cuba they failed. As a result, though both Guatemalans and Cubans were unfree, the average Cuban—as long as his country was able to withstand American attempts of military, economic, and political strangulation—was better off.

This last point brings me to a dreadful question which I have never thought of before, and, which, just a few years ago, I would have been loath to consider. I have discussed in detail the cost of communism, e.g., dreariness, quiet desperation, and anti-individualism. One gruesome feature of communism's first few decades is avoidable deaths. In Stalin's USSR, for example, estimates range from 20 to 100 million, or roughly 20 percent of total population; in Tibet, one million, or 17 percent. What then have been the costs of American policies in Guatemala?

Again, let us ignore the refugees; the half-starved, illiterate, terrorized, and brutalized children and adults in their one-room, windowless shacks; the fear that engulfs everything and everyone; the burning of books. Let us focus instead only on the number of dead. As we have seen, the first, shallow layer of the communal grave comprised well over 40,000 political murders. But we must not stop here. With American aid, or at least without American intervention, there is every reason to believe that in Guatemala, as in early 1980s' Costa Rica and Cuba, death rates would have gradually gone down. Needless to say, Guatemalan children could have had more than an even chance of making it past their fifth birthday. An anti-malaria campaign, a bit more food, a vaccination campaign, sanitation, and a few such simple steps would have worked wonders. Because American policies in Guatemala killed most victims indirectly, through neglect and exploitation, it is impossible to assess their toll. Let us settle on the highly conservative estimate that American policies cost on average, from 1945 to 1991, 10,000 premature deaths a year. That is, 10,000 human beings who could have lived to old age but did not because of exploitation and neglect. For 47 years, that would amount to 470,000 avoidable deaths, or some 5 percent of the current population. Until freedom returns, this number will obviously continue to rise.

Guatemala, let me again assure the reader, is not the exception. One anti-communist explained the rise of communism in Vietnam in this fashion:

> During the 1930's . . . the primary interest of nationalists was to throw the French out and . . . become a sovereign state. . . . But the Vietnamese still were helpless . . . did not know . . . how to organize a revolution. They had no arms, no money, no system of attack. The French had a vast system of secret police and informers . . . the Western nations did not want to . . . assist a few unknown . . . Vietnamese radicals in planning the expulsion of the French. Quite the opposite . . . In consequence, it was natural for all revolutionaries . . . to gravitate toward Communism. Where else could they go for assistance and encouragement?[36]

Or take the Iranian tragedy:

> For more than a quarter century, strategic and selfish economic considerations prevailed over the U.S. concern for basic social and economic reforms in Iran. . . . Social and economic change was more a matter of rhetoric than actual consistent policy. . . . This kind of . . . "relationship" is a ready-made recipe for destructive revolutionary change. It is basically a bankrupt concept because it fails to allow for . . . socioeconomic change that would benefit a Third World society.[37]

One could go on, but my purpose here is not to prove the view that brinkmanship and imperialism have been America's beacons, only that the challenge this view poses to conventional or CIA-funded historical writings must be taken seriously. For this limited purpose, the foregoing suffices.

American Nuclear and Third World Policies: an Appraisal

Without hazarding a resolution of the deterrence/brinkmanship debate, we can reasonably surmise that American military and foreign policies conform to either interpretation, or, as appears more likely, to a combination of both. To conclude our discussion, it must be shown that, under any historical interpretation one chooses to adopt, one fundamental conclusion remains true: these policies have been foolish and immoral.

We have been forced to conclude that this was the case under the deterrence premise. Chapters 5-7 scrutinized American policies from this angle, strongly suggesting that they were unwise because the means chosen could not, by any stretch of the imagination, serve their end. Similarly, in view of the colossal harms these policies have caused, and in view of their total irrelevance to their stated chief goal of safeguarding civilization and freedom, they could only be judged as heartless. It is also probable that if our behavior—as seen through either deterrence or brinkmanship spectacles—is irrational and heartless, then so is any mix of the two: there is no reason to suppose that in this case the sum is somehow fundamentally different from its constituent parts.

To rest our case, we must move to the unappraised premise of brinkmanship and Third World imperialism. There is, to begin with, little to argue about immorality. To achieve the dubious objective of increasing the influence and riches of an already powerful and wealthy cabal, these policies sapped the economic, spiritual, and political resources of the majority of the world's people, they entailed countless avoidable individual tragedies, and they imperiled humanity's future.

Unfortunately, the question of wisdom can't be resolved in so clear a fashion. On the face of it, brinkmanship appears eminently rational. Under this interpretation, American policies acquire an impressive degree of coherence. Nuclear brinkmanship provided huge profits, weak trading partners, and inexpensive raw materials. In the absence of brinkmanship, American attempts to keep so many of the world's people in chains for so long might have boomeranged long ago. Moreover, avowal of thinly disguised militarism is popular with American voters and has appreciably contributed to the fortunes of many a politician: in this century, a sincere commitment to world peace has been tantamount to political suicide. Thus, the consistent practice of brinkmanship demonstrably enhances a politician's financial position, power, and prestige, while even a temporary lapse could grievously impair his or her worldly fortunes. By these standards, the practice, and the practitioners, of brinkmanship could lay strong claim to rationality.

To those choosing, however, to define wisdom not in terms of providing short-lived rewards to powerful groups and individuals within Western societies and within their Third World captive nations, but in terms of the vast majorities of both Western and Third World countries; to those choosing to define wisdom in terms of advancing the prospects of freedom, civilization, and survival; or to those choosing to define wisdom in terms of the long range interests of these powerful individuals themselves (e.g., the assured physical survival of their grandchildren and of the commercial and political organizations of which they are a part); brinkmanship appears unwise.

Upholders of this alternative view point to the inordinate costs of the arms race (Chapter 3), and, especially, to the consequences of a war from which no one will emerge victorious. They plead our obligations to all past and future generations, our contemporaries, and all other life forms. They believe that brinkmanship could have failed—what if one or another recipient of our ultimatums did not "flinch"? Granted, the Soviets had been rational, but how far could we push them before they too went over the brink? Is Czechoslovakian delivery of antiquated rifles to Guatemalan democrats worth taking this step into the unknown? And what if the Soviets' place is taken by a foe as committed to brinkmanship and bravado as we are? They question, besides, the efficacy of brinkmanship. Russian communism made its most rapid leaps forward *before* it reached nuclear parity with the West. Russia's nuclear arsenal dwarfs China's, but it is on Russian soil that communism has performed its astonishing swan song. There are good reasons to suppose, in passing, that communism would run its course in China too, but not that its demise would be caused by the nuclear policies of the United States of America.

Upholders of this alternative view go on to argue that, by the 1970s at the latest, the Soviets knew that the losses that they could inflict upon us in a second strike were "prohibitive to the *nth* degree."[38] Besides, the Soviets probably suspected that nature's revenge upon us in the event of nuclear war might have been as severe as the Kremlin's. They were indeed apprehensive, but not by objective military realities. Rather, they were frightened by the possibility that we were in fact mad enough to believe that our meaningless edge permitted us to dictate the outcome of diplomatic standoffs. It thus makes little sense to attribute our occasional diplomatic "victories" to such things as our more accurate warheads or our more powerful laser beams. A terrorist about to detonate a bomb in an airborne plane is taken seriously by the crew not because he is stronger than they are, but because he might be mad enough to bring about the mutual destruction of himself and everyone else.

Although I am unable to satisfactorily resolve this philosophical dispute on the nature of wisdom, I am decidedly on the side of those who feel that brinkmanship is not only heartless, but unwise. I cannot conceive of any way—short of moral appeals or Scroogian sojourns into the past, present, and future—to convince committed brinkmanship practitioners of their folly. For them, pre-nuclear notions of *realpolitik* and short-term rewards outweigh long-term costs to their fellow astronauts on Spaceship Earth, to their descendants, and perhaps even to their own future selves. For me, theirs is not only an immoral, but also an unwise, pact with the devil. Lacking proof, I must resort to a mathematician's sleight of hand: for the remainder of this book, I shall axiomatically and unreservedly assume that brinkmanship is as unwise as ordinary decency, common sense, and intuition suggest.

Summary

History shows that (1) the actual policies of a nation may sharply differ from its stated policies, and (2) the majority of citizens and politicians often mistake avowals for facts. Strategic thinking in the U.S., the military balance, and the history of the arms race are more congruent with the brinkmanship interpretation than with its deterrence counterpart. The brinkmanship hypothesis is further supported by: (1) Statements of some high ranking officials and mainstream analysts. (2) The atomic destruction of Nagasaki. (3) The repeated use of nuclear threats to further trivial political objectives. (4) Repeated allegations that the Soviet Union practiced brinkmanship. (5) The view of many influential U.S. officials "that the use of nuclear weapons must be regarded as absolutely normal, natural, and right." (6) Refusal of the United States, even by 1991, to disavow the first use of nuclear weapons. (7) America's half-century-long pursuit of nuclear overkill, nuclear "edge," and increased accuracy of nuclear warheads. (8) American reluctance to give Russian reformers such as Khrushchev and Gorbachev a helping hand in the economic, political, or disarmament spheres.

Policy makers and their media spokespeople justified consistent American support for repressive Third World regimes by arguing that they had no choice: had they abandoned their dictatorial friends, these friends would have been replaced by even more ruthless communists, who would then not only cause even greater suffering to their people, but also endanger the vital interests and freedoms of the American people. The entire historical record defies this self-serving interpretation. The U.S. preferred bloody but subservient Caligulas not only to communists, *but also* to democrats intent on bringing greater freedom, dignity, and independence to their people. Among the scores of examples which readily lend themselves, this chapter recounts the chilling chronicle of American intervention in Guatemala, the replacement of a civilized democracy by bloodthirsty American proxies, and the aftermath—38 infernal years for the vast majority; vast profits for a handful of American businesspeople and Guatemalan warlords. Because this tale is typical of American Third World policies as a whole, it lends support to the claim that American policies throughout the Cold War had pronounced brinkmanship and imperialistic tendencies.

Although brinkmanship and imperialism provided some short-term benefits to small Western minorities, they were immoral and heartless. They were also unwise because they risked the freedom, welfare, and survival of these minorities, the West, and the human race.

Chapter 9

ROOTS OF COLLECTIVE MISBEHAVIOR

By now, the corporations that dominate our media, like alcoholic fat cats, treat this situation as theirs by right . . . Their concept of a diversity of views is the full range of politics and social values from center to far right. The American audience, having been exposed to a narrowing range of ideas over the decades, often assumes that what they see and hear in the major media is all there is. It is no way to maintain a lively marketplace of ideas, which is to say it is no way to maintain a democracy.

Ben Bagdikian,[1] 1987

Both superpowers have succeeded in making a deep imprint on the beliefs and attitudes of people everywhere. Public debate and political thinking have become largely a product of manipulation. It is harder and harder for facts and knowledge to break through the false beliefs. The end result is a profound web of misconceptions . . . . At the heart of the arms race are a series of assumptions that are simply false. But in the superpowers, on the national media, those fundamentals are rarely questioned. Our hope lies in challenging them.

Alva Myrdal,[2] 1982

Among all the excuses which are alleged to Charon for not entering readily into his boat, he [David Hume] could not find one that fitted him; he had no house to finish, he had no daughter to provide for, he had no enemies upon whom he wished to revenge himself . . . "Upon further consideration" said he. . . . "I might still urge, Have a little patience, good Charon; I have been endeavoring to open the eyes of the Public. If I live a few years longer, I may have the satisfaction of seeing the downfall of some of the prevailing systems of superstition." But Charon would then lose all temper and decency. "You loitering rogue, that will not happen these many hundred years. Do you fancy I will grant you a lease for so long a term? Get into the boat this instant, you lazy, loitering rogue."

Adam Smith,[3a] 1776

Theories in the humanities and social sciences often trace complex realities to an all-inclusive single cause. Although such theories do occasionally make lasting contributions to knowledge, their ambitious reductionism—despite its intellectual appeal and momentary fame—invariably fails. B. F. Skinner was right in pointing to the operant character of some of our actions, wrong in thinking that it was by far the most important. Plato was right in thinking ideas are important, wrong in thinking that they are the only entities which really count. The same can be said about most grand theories in psychology, metaphysics, politics, and other disciplines. Reductionism has performed wonders in physics, but has no place in history. Only eclectic theories (which mirror to a certain extent the complex realities they seek to understand) come close to explaining these realities. Hence, this chapter will forego grand theorizing. Instead, it will highlight a few of the causes which may have shaped political decisions in Cold War America.

For an eclectic, the selection of topics is particularly difficult, for he sees some merit in just about any explanation he comes across. He must resign himself to presenting a highly simplified and fragmented picture. There is, for instance, no mention in this chapter of important cultural theories, the nature/nurture controversy, or inherent ills of representative democracy. Instead, two criteria determined the choice of material. First, besides throwing light on humanity's woes, this chapter includes explanations which lend additional support to this book's earlier indictment of Cold War America. Second, this chapter prepares the reader for the counterintuitive reform proposal of chapter 10. It does so by giving special prominence to psychological theories which—by sensitizing readers to their own failings—ease their transition from one way of viewing and doing politics to another. It does so, also, by highlighting those features of American politics which are most intimately connected to this proposal.

Collective irrationality and immorality can be explained in almost identical terms wherever they are found. The remainder of this book will therefore extend the discussion to many other social ills besides American disarmament and foreign policies. This comprehensive approach allows cross-fertilization; insights gained, for example, from environmental politics clarify our disarmament policies. Moreover, this more comprehensive approach has practical implications. Nowadays humanitarians conduct numerous battles on numerous fronts. They fight against American support for Third World dictatorships, environmental pollution, soil erosion, wholesale extinction of species, built-in obsolescence of consumer products, monopolies, corporate irresponsibility, corruption, erosion of civil liberties, unemployment, unsafe working conditions, homelessness, and starvation; and this list does not even come close to describing the multitude of humanitarian concerns. If this chapter succeeds in showing that all these social ills spring from the same roots, a different strategy would seem to be in order. Instead of wasting their meager resources in admirable but, in the long run, futile holding actions against so many surface manifestations of a single disease, humanitarians might consider a joint attack on the disease itself at its weakest point, thereby sapping both its roots and surface manifestations (Chapter 10).

Organizational Characteristics

Organizational Callousness

We may begin with a simple, and widely acknowledged, principle: when forced to choose between a course of action which benefits their short-term interests but harms society, and a course of action which benefits society but harms their short-term interests, and when free to make this choice on their own, organizations tend to choose actions that benefit them and harm society.

Organizations in democratic countries (where their harmful actions often come under attack) defend their right to pursue their socially harmful interests with various tactics. The most notable tactic is the *Phony Controversy*: the covering of straightforward issues in a thick fog of technical details and contentions. The following examples demonstrate the ubiquitousness of organizational callousness and of its phony controversy stock-in-trade.

In some ways, history is one long story of organizational callousness. The Athenian Empire fell in part because it sought its own short-term interests instead of the more general interests of democracy and the Greek World. The Roman Empire fell in part because its army pursued its narrow, private interests, instead of the public's. The Catholic Church broke up during the Reformation, in part because it was concerned with its organizational welfare instead of the public's. Great Britain lost most of its American colonies in part because some British organizations sought their own gains at the nation's expense.

In 1970s' Soviet Union, the simple steps needed to effect badly needed agricultural reforms were not being taken in part because such steps conflicted with the narrowly conceived interests of the Communist Party, of a few other powerful organizations, and of a few individuals. A former high-ranking Yugoslav official explained past collectivizations of peasant holdings in communist countries in similar terms:

> The fact that the seizure of property from other classes, especially from small owners, led to decreases in production and to chaos in the economy was of no consequence to the new class [communist party]. . . . The class profited from the new property it had acquired even though the nation lost thereby.[4]

Similarly, 1991 food shortages in the Soviet Union could be traced, in part, to actions of some still-powerful members of this class.

One could talk about the Charles Dickens' variety of child labor, and one can be reasonably certain, without studying the historical record, that this barbaric practice was vigorously defended by most organizations and individuals who derived short-term benefits from it. One could talk about worker exploitation, of the type depicted by Victor Hugo and John Steinbeck, and again be sure that it was brazenly championed by virtually all organizations, and by many individuals, whose short-term gains it served. One could fill endless volumes with quotations of such ignominious defenses, but in this context one will have to do. Here, then, is what a former employee of the East India Company (and a Christian Minister to boot) had to say about the sufferings of millions upon millions of David Copperfields, Tiny Tims, and Tom Joads:

> A man who is born into a world already possessed, if he cannot get subsistence from his parents on whom he has a just demand, and if the society do[es] not want his labour, has no claim of *right* to the smallest portion of food, and, in fact, has no business to be where he is. At nature's mighty feast there is no vacant cover for him. She tells him to be gone, and will quickly execute her own orders.[5]

In 1906, more than 10 percent of milk samples in New York City contained live tuberculosis-causing bacteria. Though it was well known by then that these bacteria could be killed by pasteurization (heating the milk), the dairy industry's spokesmen and scientists put up the usual fight. Among other things, they claimed that pasteurization would destroy the value of milk and price it off the market. Blessedly, they and the pathogens lost the fight.[6]

Organizational callousness and phony controversies are ubiquitous in environmental politics. No matter how conclusive the evidence against a substance (or practice) is, you can bet your life on one thing: any private or public organization, and many individuals, who derive short-term benefits from the production and sale of such a substance will fight tooth and nail to preserve it. Take, as just one example, the following 1981 summary of the smoking/cancer "controversy" by a British cancer researcher:

> Although there has been conclusive evidence for more than a quarter of a century of roughly the sort of scale of death that tobacco causes . . . spokesmen for the industry . . . still do not accept this. There can never be, really, clearer proof than we now have with tobacco. Yet the industry concerned will not accept in public that it is causing these deaths. I think that this will be true of many other industries which are found to cause deaths. . . . when an industry is found to cause substantial numbers of deaths, with a few exceptions . . . there will be deliberate attempts to mislead government and the public as to what the evidence is. Even if certain individuals in such industries want to be humane and want to work in some kind of way towards the general good, and they are effective at doing so, then

they will find themselves rendered impotent or fired, because it is not in the commercial interests of an industry to have its products advertised as causing this, that, and the other kind of disease.[7]

Most organizations involved in shaping and directing American disarmament policies are similarly callous.[8] Arms manufacturers and other commercial organizations prosper from the arms race; in a genuine peace conference, they might be negotiated out of existence. So, like the milk and cigarette merchants, organizational logic tells us, they will always adopt a hard (and profitable) line on the question of disarmament. I shall spare the reader documentation of this obvious, self-serving position.

The rival services of the American Armed Forces might be expected to subordinate their interests to the national well-being. Isn't this, after all, their calling? But, as the following quotations of highly regarded former insiders suggest, the different services obey the dictates of organizational logic with clockwork regularity.

A former high-ranking official and a co-author:

> Even in Vietnam . . . service interests were not subordinated to common concerns . . . the Pentagon practiced business as usual . . . the military departments did not give the war priority over the internal needs of the military organization.[9a]

In Vietnam, according to one Air Force Intelligence officer,

> The Air Force had to have the bombing of the North—it was the only real Air Force show in the Vietnam War. . . . Without the bombing the Air Force would hope for little publicity and glory—which would mean smaller appropriations . . . To criticize the bombing claims meant, therefore, to hurt your own organization and to benefit its rivals.[10]

A noted analyst:

> The M-16 rifle had been a brilliant technical success in its early models, but was perverted by bureaucratic pressures into a weapon that betrayed its users in Vietnam. . . . Between 1965 and 1969, more than one million American soldiers served in combat in Vietnam. . . . During those years, in which more than 40,000 American soldiers were killed by hostile fire and more than 250,000 wounded, American troops in Vietnam were

equipped with a rifle their superiors *knew* would fail when put to the test. . . . The original version of the M-16 . . . was the most reliable, and the most lethal, infantry rifle ever invented. But within months of its introduction in combat, it was known among soldiers as a weapon that might jam and misfire, and could pose as great a danger to them as to their enemy. These problems, which loomed so large on the battlefield, were entirely the results of modifications made to the rifle's original design by the Army's own ordnance bureaucracy. The Army's modifications had very little to do with observation of warfare, but quite a lot to do with settling organizational scores.[11]

A respected nuclear strategist:

An officer who is considered brilliant but somehow lacking in service loyalty . . . may as well pack up his things and go elsewhere. He will not rise very far. It . . . follows that some officers will reach very high rank . . . who would not be called brilliant by anyone . . . the officer who is really objective about his own service as compared with the sister services is not going to rise to high enough estate to make that objectivity of much service to the nation. That means that if the Navy is currently committed to aircraft carriers as its "capital ships," the naval officer destined to get on will automatically believe in carrier aviation. . . . An article in an Army journal may well stress the need for more helicopters . . . but it is far less likely to question whether new antitank devices have not made the tank obsolete. That would not look at all good if a congressional appropriations committee got hold of it.[12]

I have not yet encountered a single dissenting opinion on this subject. This "servicitis" (a term coined by the chairman of the House Armed Services Committee[13a]) is simply taken for granted, just as the fatal laughing disease was taken for granted by 1930s New Guinea cannibals. In 1985, this chairman's ultraconservative Senate counterpart openly stated:

If we have to fight tomorrow, these problems will cause Americans to die unnecessarily. Even more, they may cause us to lose. . . . I am saddened that the services are unable to put the national interest above parochial interest.[13a]

As we have seen (Chapter 6), the Defense Intelligence Agency prefers its own short-term interests to the national interest. Similarly, the major veterans' organizations, who "subsist on dues from individual and corporate members and from defense contractors who advertise in their publications . . . support the legislative interests of the services with which they are affiliated by employing large professional staffs."[9b]

The role of the gigantic Department of Defense is too obvious to be elaborated here, so let us look at the more obscure case of the Department of Energy (DOE), which has been in charge of development and production of nuclear weapons. In 1982, the nuclear weapons program accounted for roughly half of DOE's total budget. Predictably, DOE's views "on how many nuclear weapons we need, on how much nuclear material we should have in the pipeline and in the stockpile for future weapons tend to equal if not exceed the estimates of the Department of Defense itself."[9c]

Organizational Self-Destructiveness

When left to themselves, organizations not only tend to pursue their short-term interests at society's expense, but they often do so at the expense of their own long-term welfare and survival. A few examples should suffice to demonstrate this suicidal proclivity.

The chemical industry is often a showcase for this self-destructive aspect of organizational logic. There are often advance warnings, as in the case of the chemical PBB,[14] that a product might be dangerous, that it might eventually cost the company more money than it will bring in, and that it might even lead to bankruptcy. But such companies often ignore their own long-term welfare and vigorously defend their right to develop the chemical and maximize short-term profits. Appropriate disposal of chemicals in Love Canal would have cost $2 million (in 1979 dollars).[15] By 1987, the federal and state governments were suing the parent company for more than the $250 million they had already spent for partial cleanup and relocation.[16]

Similarly, the first alarms about the Earth's ozone layer were sounded in 1974. Seventeen years later, recurring 50 percent seasonal depletions over Antarctica and a 5 percent year-long depletion over the mid-Northern Hemisphere have been reported. Though the causes of these depletions remain uncertain, the chief suspect is CFCs (chlorofluorocarbons), a group of manmade chemicals. Moreover, these same CFCs also account for some 25 percent of the global warming trend (another major environmental peril). Notwithstanding the stakes (humankind's future), for the manufacturers and commercial users of CFCs the situation was clear enough. The observed depletions, they said, are "likely due to poorly understood natural causes."[17] As usual, the U.S. government lined up behind them. In a 1990 international conference, for instance, the United States of America cast "doubt on prospects for a global accord to protect the ozone layer"[18] (and to slow down the suspected trend of global warming) by declining to help developing countries cut the use of CFCs.

The 1970s whaling industry provides an even more tangible example of built-in suicidal tendencies. We need not concern ourselves here with questions of morality, aesthetics, justice, or ecological balance to see the whalers' folly in needlessly destroying forever the very resource upon which their industry is based.

Finally, consider the arms race. Now, in this case, if all the organizations which promoted this race kept winning, they and their decision makers, like everyone else, would have been wiped out in the most literal sense of the word: crushed, killed, evaporated, hurled, combusted, and irradiated. That they could pursue a policy which might have caused them such grave injuries borders on the incredible. However, the preceding examples strongly suggest that such a patently irrational course of action is eminently probable.

The challenge, then, is not only protecting the public from callous organizational and individual actions, but protecting the public interest, the long-term interests of these organizations, and the long-term interests of their members.[19] It follows that the correct approach to organizational callousness is not to think of, or rail against, such organizations' policy makers as public enemies, but to view them as the victims of blind forces. Despite their affluence and power, these victims deserve our sympathy and all the help we can give them to set themselves, and us, free.

In helping them, we must keep in mind those rare historical episodes where organizations moved from excessive preoccupation with the immediate future to long-term planning. These episodes suggest that benign proclivities are already embedded in organizational structure. Thus, the challenge for the reformer is not fighting unmitigated evil, but shifting the balance between the already existing forces of callousness and public-spiritedness.

Institutional Decay

Improperly regulated organizations obey a peculiar logic. With time, they become progressively less efficient, flexible, and responsive. Organizational inefficiencies in the U.S. military, in the British Colonial Office (Chapter 6), and in virtually every other large established organization on earth, illustrate various stages in this process of decay. Those still reluctant to accept the strange conclusion that organizations are far less rational than most of their individual members—that, for instance, the number of employees in the Arms Control and Disarmament Agency is unrelated to this organization's achievements or mission—might wish to recall Parkinson's tragicomic warning:

> To the very young, to schoolteachers, as also to those who compile textbooks about constitutional history, politics, and current affairs, the world is a more or less rational place. They visualize the election of representatives, freely chosen from among those the people trust. They picture the process by which the wisest and best of these become ministers of State. They imagine how captains of industry, freely elected by shareholders, choose for managerial responsibility those who have proved their ability in a humbler role. Books exist in which assumptions such as these are boldly stated or tacitly implied. To those, on the other hand, with any experience of affairs, these assumptions are merely ludicrous. Solemn conclaves of the wise and good are mere figments of the teacher's mind.[20]

Institutional Rigidity

History tells us that the future is often unpredictable. President Truman, who began our involvement in Vietnam by aiding French colonial rule, could not foresee that this decision would lead the U.S. to fight a full-scale losing war. He could not foresee the massive demonstrations against this war in the U.S. nor the decline in morale and performance of our troops. The history of science and technology is similarly replete with anecdotes showing that crystal gazing can be dangerous to one's professional reputation. A

Report on the Motor Car published in 1908 by a British Royal Commission concluded that the most serious future problem of this infant technology was going to be dust thrown up from dirt roads (not air pollution, traffic deaths, oligopolies, or resource depletion).[21a] A number of physicists of the very first rank believed, until they were proven wrong by the actual turn of events, that atomic bombs could not be made.

Given this disconcerting historical record, and given the information available at the time such predictions are made, the complexity of the situation, the fact that every action taken in such intricate settings has unintended consequences, and our limited understanding of people, institutions, and societies, it must be assumed that at times even the most rational and disinterested government will adopt faulty policies.

This inherent unpredictability suggests[22] that good statesmen should view such policies as the deployment of 450,000 American troops in the Arabian Peninsula, support of the South Vietnamese dictatorship, development of missiles with multiple warheads, use of nuclear reactors to boil water, and generation of massive quantities of CFCs, in the same way that accomplished scientists view hypotheses. At her best, a scientist chooses the most promising hypothesis and proceeds to test it. She may be brilliant, charismatic, energetic, and hardworking, but if she cannot learn from her mistakes, if she cannot draw the correct lessons from chance occurrences and new realities, if she cannot modify or discard her hypotheses, she is unlikely to go far.

The similarity between politics and science at their best, coupled with science's enviable record, strongly suggests that we should treat national policies as scientific hypotheses and view their implementation as a series of experiments which are designed, in part, to refute them. Whenever possible, we should commit an entire nation, or an entire industry, to the new policy only after it proves successful on a small scale. We should give preference to flexible and inexpensive policies which can be readily abandoned. We should, of course, hope that the original policy was correct, and we should not be too quick to abandon it. At the same time, early detection of, and adjustments to, failing policies should be institutionalized. We should be more inclined to forgive politicians their missteps and less inclined to forgive their inability, or unwillingness, to learn from them.

These theoretical considerations explain in part the advantage astronomy and medicine enjoy over astrology and shamanism. In the political arena, they cast light on democracy's superiority over totalitarianism (Chapter 1). However, everyday observations of the political scene tell us that we have not gone far enough in implementing these ideas in our society and institutions[22] (or in our daily lives—see below). The obvious tendency of our institutions for precisely the opposite—institutional rigidity—undoubtedly contributes to the collective irrationality of our policies.

Institutional Inertia

Two writers in a celebrated government report:

> Over the years, government has tended to wait until crises occur and then has reacted to them—rather than study and analyze issues beforehand."[23]

A former Deputy Administrator of the Environmental Protection Agency:

> Since government action depends on public demand, the government does not begin to attack a problem until that problem has become severe. The government always has to catch up, to find solutions for problems that long before have grown out of control. Although our government may be responsive, it is so only by delayed reaction. The lag time between need and response is measured in years . . . we are posed with a frightening question: Shall we always be able to afford that delay? . . . Left alone, our government will not always look after the public interest. In the environmental area there is a natural, built-in imbalance. Private industry, driven by its own profit incentives to exploit and pollute our natural resources, uses its inherent advantages to exert political pressure to resist environmental requirements. The machinations of industry explain at least in part why the abuses of pollution became so severe before steps were taken to establish controls. It was not until conditions approached a point of horror that the public woke up to the need for reform. . . . The most important lesson from our environmental experience is that government will not act to face hard national problems until the people demand that it do so. The government normally fails to

see these problems coming, since nearly all top officials are preoccupied with the crises that have already arrived. But the real difficulty is that solutions . . . will require wrenching changes in government policies . . . . This means that the key decisions on government policy will be subject to political pressure. . . . But any restriction . . . will surely encounter stiff opposition. Vested interests will send their lobbyists into action . . . hard policy decisions are unlikely to be made until the problems are so acute that they are obvious to the average citizen.[24]

Though government inertia is widespread, its presence is particularly frightening in relation to nuclear politics. If here too "decisions are unlikely to be made until the problems are so acute that they are obvious to the average citizen," the correct decisions would not be made on time to avert holocaust. We could perhaps afford this delay with sticks and stones, but we cannot afford it with nuclear bombs.

Money and Politics

The intimate links between money and organizational callousness are well-known: "To get elected these days, what matters most is not sound judgment or personal integrity or a passion for justice. What matters most is money. Lots of money."[25a] This commonsense insight is backed up by a considerable amount of research. For instance, in one study money emerged "as the first and most essential element in political party activity and effectiveness in the 1980s."[26a] The bidding price of Congressional seats keeps rising. By 1986, campaign expenditures for incumbents were $.3 million in the house and $3.3 million in the Senate.[13b] Apart from "the exceptionally wealthy," says chief Washington correspondent of a major daily, "raising political money has become a throbbing headache that drains vital time and energy from the job of governing. This chore leaves many members part-time legislators and full-time fund-raisers."[13c] Naturally, organizations which benefit from the arms race enrich the campaign coffers of politicians who are sympathetic to the arms race, or who are willing to promote it in order to get elected and re-elected. One member of Congress quipped once that "business already owns one party and now it has a lease, with option to buy, on the other."[27a]

Though there must be some incorruptible politicians around, this joke contains a kernel of truth. At the very least, a typical politician will consider favorably the views of arms manufacturers on whose support his career depends, knowing that civic courage would most likely go unnoticed by most of his constituents, that it would grate a small and articulate minority, and that it would lead his financial backers to abandon him and sustain his opponents.

Common sense suggests that political donations are worthwhile investments. Indeed, studies show a "disturbing correlation between . . . campaign contributions and how members of Congress . . . vote on bills important to special interest groups."[25b] Similarly, a review of the 1980 and 1982 congressional elections suggests that "campaign spending has a significant effect on the outcomes of congressional elections."[26b]

Take, for example, the late Henry Jackson, who for many years was "the most powerful man in the U.S. Senate in military affairs and matters of national security."[28] On such matters, according to one observer, Jackson rarely lost a debate. Jackson's goals "fitted in well with those of the huge Boeing industries" which were headquartered in his home state of Washington, and this earned him the epithet "the Senator from Boeing." Now all this does not necessarily cast a shadow on Jackson's integrity; he might have genuinely believed in the convergence of Boeing's and the nation's interests. The question is rather: Why was a man as misinformed as Jackson elected and re-elected to the U.S. Senate? The money that Jackson received from organizations like Boeing provides a partial answer to this question.

The public is used by now to occasional outbursts on this issue, not only from reformers but from frustrated or about-to-be-retired members of the power elite. Two "old-line conservatives" who, by 1986, "have been senators a combined total of 68 years:" "It is not 'we the people' but political-action committees and moneyed interests who are setting the nation's political agenda and are influencing the position of candidates on the important issues of the day," said one senator. "We are gradually moving elections away from the people," said the other, "as certainly as night follows day."[29]

A syndicated columnist surveying the 1990 Washington scene:

This is a town of clinical depression, mainly because members of Congress have been reduced to beggars, spending all their time raising campaign money to scare away potential opponents. . . . The inmates have taken over, trapped in an asylum of their own making. . . . The overriding new truth of national politics is that both sides, both Democrats and Republicans, are getting their money from the same PACs [political action committees] and people—that is why there seems to be such new consensus in Washington debate.[30]

According to an official of the Federal Election Commission, money opens American elections to foreign influences. Federal election laws prohibit in theory direct foreign contributions, but not in practice. For instance, before the 1982 elections, "44 political action committees with ties to foreign corporations and investors contributed just over $1 million to 1,764 candidates for Congress."[31]

Though the following FBI undercover operation discloses an extreme case, it still highlights the norm. Agents posing as employees of wealthy foreigners requested interviews with congressmen and other public officials. During the interviews, the agents handed them cash in exchange for promises of special favors. Dozens of officials, six representatives, and one Senator were filmed accepting bribes. After exhausting all appeal channels, at least four legislators spent some time in federal prisons.

According to one account, "with predictable media focus on the easily understood issue of corruption, an even more chilling thesis of the . . . case went unnoticed: the fact that supposed agents of a foreign nation could so easily bribe some of the most powerful members of the United States Congress."[32] There is at least one other disturbing aspect of this case, for it suggests that the practice of political bribery, albeit the tacit and legal variety, is almost universal.

The Defense Department and the Armed Services cannot give outright gifts or campaign contributions, but they control vast amounts of money. Naturally, some of this wealth, courtesy of the American people, has been used to advance causes which were inimical to the national interest. Until it was disbanded in 1965, the "famous 999th Air Force Reserve Squadron commanded by

Major General (Senator) Barry M. Goldwater, USAF . . . permitted eighty-three congressmen and senators to spend short periods of active duty in such prime military observation posts as London and Paris. But the 999th was only a surface manifestation of a more deep-seated and persistent phenomenon."[9a]

A mainstream analyst commented on a recent scandal, a scandal which led to an open hearing in the U.S. Senate. In this hearing,

> The slimy underbelly of American politics slithered into full view, [exposing] how U.S. senators grub for campaign funds from moneyed interests seeking to buy influence. . . . It was the best lesson the nation has yet had on the costs and the consequences of a campaign-finance system that has corroded government at the highest levels. Even if all five senators are cleared in the end, this trial-like procedure is likely to evoke a public verdict that the system itself is guilty of murder, with integrity the casualty. . . . [This scandal] is not different in kind from the defense industry interests that lavish money on members of the armed services committees, the union political action groups that funnel cash to the labor committee lawmaker, or the Wall Street interest that fuel the campaigns of incumbents who oversee securities-industry lawmaking. They are all threads in the dark tapestry that now smothers our political system, like a smelly blanket under which lawmakers lie in bed with those who would procure their favors for cash. There is a name for those who solicit such attention, and it is not "senator."[33]

My dictionary defines *bribe* as "a price, reward, gift or favor bestowed or promised with a view to pervert the judgment or corrupt the conduct especially of a person in a position of trust (as a public official)," and *corruption* as "impairment of integrity, virtue, or moral principle" or as "inducement (as of political official) by means of improper considerations (as bribery) to commit a violation of duty." We only have to add the premise that the duty of a politician is to look after the public interest to conclude that these definitions fittingly apply to American politics.

A former counsel for President Carter concurs with this seemingly harsh judgment: "It's one step away from bribery. PACs contribute because they count on you to vote with them."[13d]

Let me conclude this section with the sober reflections of two political scientists:

[The] political finance system . . . undermines the ideals and hampers the performance of American democracy. . . . Officials . . . are . . . captives of the present system. Their integrity and judgment are menaced—and too often compromised—by the need to raise money and the means now available for doing it. . . . The pattern of giving distorts American elections: candidates win access to the electorate only if they can mobilize money from the upper classes, established interest groups, big givers, or ideological zealots. Other alternatives have difficulty getting heard. And the voters' choice is thereby limited. The pattern of giving also threatens the governmental process: the contributions of big givers and interest groups award them access to officeholders, so they can better plead their causes. . . . The private financing system . . . distort[s] both elections and decision making. The equality of citizens on election day is diluted by their inequality in campaign financing. The electorate shares its control of officials with the financial constituency.[34]

Revolving Doors

A subtler way of influencing government decisions depends on social contacts. For instance, promoters and politicians might hobnob at the same dives or parties. Needless to say, in such settings a promoter's virtually inexhaustible money supply is highly serviceable.

The cozy relations among the various organizations whose internal logic dictates promotion of the arms race are cemented by another strong tie: the continuous and massive flow of personnel among them. This applies, in particular, to senior-level officials who spend at least part of their time in Washington, D.C.[27b] For example, the 1987 U.S. Secretaries of Defense and State had been, prior to assuming government posts, vice-president and president of the corporation that was awarded a lucrative government contract for the development of the MX missile.[35] To students of organizational logic, this arrangement appears strictly equivalent to the following: awarding a bid for guarding the communal coop to the most notorious pair of chicken-eating foxes.

Thus, many organizations which derived short-term benefits from the arms race were hard at work puffing it. They did this through public relations, propaganda, and mind-manipulation directed at their members and the public at large, and through cultivating special relations with government (relations which included campaign contributions, socializing, favors of all kinds, and a flow of personnel from government ranks to the private sector and vice versa). All this seems to justify the conclusion that the defense industry has been a "*de facto* participant in the policy-making process,"[27c] and that national defense policies have been determined by an "iron triangle" made up of the following entities:

I. The Department of Defense and other relevant government organizations, such as NASA and the nuclear weapons branch of the Department of Energy.

II. Congress, especially influential members from districts and states whose economy depends heavily on war-related economic activities.

III. War-related corporations, public and private research institutions, trade associations, media corporations, educational institutions, and labor unions.

It goes without saying that similar triangles (or polygons) slanted decisions in every part of the political arena. It is not only America's foreign and military policies which are "triangulated," but government decisions in every field and at every level; from Sacramento to Albany, from encroachment on California's redwoods to pollution of the Gulf Stream Waters.

Elections and Officials

I have already discussed the unwholesome influence of money. In a rational world, a candidate's campaign chest would have little bearing on his electibility. This chest's decisive influence strongly suggests that our electoral process is a caricature of rationality. Aldous Huxley put it well:

> Human beings act in a great variety of irrational ways, but all of them seem to be capable, if given a fair chance, of making a reasonable choice in the light of available evidence. Democratic institutions can be made to work only if all concerned do their best to impart knowledge and to encourage rationality. But today, in the world's most powerful democracy, the politicians and their propagandists prefer to make nonsense of democratic procedures by appealing almost exclusively to the ignorance and irrationality of the electors. "Both parties," we were told in 1956 by the editor of a leading business journal, "will merchandize their candidates and issues by the same methods that business has

developed to sell goods. These include scientific selection of appeals and planned repetition. . . . Radio spot announcements and ads will repeat phrases with a planned intensity. Billboards will push slogans of proven power. . . . Candidates need, in addition to rich voices and good diction, to be able to look 'sincerely' at the TV camera."

The political merchandisers appeal only to the weaknesses of voters, never to their potential strength. They make no attempt to educate the masses into becoming fit for self-government; they are content merely to manipulate and exploit them. For this purpose all the resources of psychology and the social sciences are mobilized and set to work. Carefully selected samples of the electorate are given "interviews in depth." These interviews in depth reveal the unconscious fears and wishes most prevalent in a given society at the time of an election. Phrases and images aimed at allaying or, if necessary, enhancing these fears, at satisfying these wishes, at least symbolically, are then chosen by the experts, tried out on readers and audiences, changed or improved in the light of the information thus obtained. After which the political campaign is ready for the mass communicators. All that is now needed is money and a candidate who can be coached to look "sincere." Under the new dispensation, political principles and plans for specific action have come to lose most of their importance. The personality of the candidate and the way he is projected by the advertising experts are the things that really matter.

In one way or another, as vigorous he-man or kindly father, the candidate must be glamorous. He must also be an entertainer who never bores his audience. Inured to television and radio, that audience is accustomed to being distracted and does not like to be asked to concentrate or make a prolonged intellectual effort. All speeches by the entertainer-candidate must therefore be short and snappy. The great issues of the day must be dealt with in five minutes at the most—and preferably (since the audience will be eager to pass on to something a little livelier than inflation or the H-bomb) in sixty seconds flat. The nature of oratory is such that there has always been a tendency among politicians and clergymen to over-simplify complex issues. From a pulpit or a platform even the most conscientious of speakers finds it very difficult to tell the whole truth. The methods now being used to merchandise the political candidate as though he were a deodorant positively guarantee the electorate against ever hearing the truth about anything.[36a]

Aldous Huxley's indictment, which appeared in a 1958 book

chiefly concerned with the preservation of freedom, still stands. The "peculiar rules of engagement" in the 1988 presidential campaigns, according to *Newsweek*, included:

> Boil the "message of the day" down to snappy one-line "sound bites" that look good on the news and are reinforced by color visuals; avoid saying something that may drown out the rehearsed message; when forced to play defense, either change the subject or use one-liners to turn your opponent's words back on himself—political jujitsu."[37]

A skeptical attitude towards elected officials is embedded in American folklore. "I'd rather meet [Satan] and shake him by the tail," said Mark Twain, "than any other statesman on the planet." "All of our so-called successful men are sick men, with bad stomachs, and bad souls" said John Steinbeck.[38] Or take this parody:

> I've got a letter, parson, from my son away out West,
> An' my ol' heart's as heavy as an anvil in my breast,
> To think the boy whose futur' I had once so proudly planned
> Should wander from the path o' right an' come to such an end!
> . . . .
> He writes from out in Denver, an' the story's mighty short;
> I just can't tell his mother; it'd crush her poor ol' heart!
> An' so I reckoned, parson, you might break the news to her—
> Bill's in the Legislatur', but he doesn't say what fur.[39]

To be sure, these literary pieces simplify reality, overlook exceptions, and come uncomfortably close to stereotypic thinking. Still, it is probably fair to say that the average politician is less adept than his fellow citizens at resisting the temptations of power.

We have seen a similar situation in the Armed Forces, where, according to a mainstream American analyst, "an officer who is really objective about his own service as compared with the sister services is not going to rise to high enough estate to make that objectivity of much service to the nation."[12] Similar generalizations hold for many wielders of power in our society. Organizational recruitment and promotion hinge on loyalty to the organization, not to higher values. More often than not, those who make it through the ranks are the subservient, compromising team players; the intriguing backstabbers; the workaholics consumed by the love of money and power; the compartmentalized thinkers. They are the survivors of an evolutionary process—*against* critical thinking, intellectual integrity, fair play, and principled individualism. It is these pathetic survivors who carry the burden of organizational callousness and self-destructiveness on their shoulders.

Nor can we draw much solace from the professional backgrounds of our "successful" men. In the nature of the case, the judicial branch of government is comprised of lawyers. But in the 1980s, roughly 42 percent of Congress, compared to only some 0.5 percent of the American labor force, have been similarly trained.[40] In addition, 33 percent of Congress identified themselves as businessmen or bankers. Similar statistics probably apply to senior officials in the Executive Branch.

Information

In his famous funeral oration, Pericles reportedly told his fellow Athenians that "although only a few may originate a policy, we are all able to judge it."[41] Pericles' views have been satirized and laughed at ever since, and not without good reasons. Indeed, the working—and remarkably successful—philosophy of sophists, tyrants, and demagogues in both the ancient and modern worlds was more nearly based on the opposite premise—that while just about any George, Dick, and Harry can originate national policies, only few politicians and voters can adequately judge them. Free elections do not by themselves vouchsafe rationality:

> Democracy, taken in its narrower, purely political, sense, suffers from the fact that those in economic and political power possess the means for molding public opinion to serve their own class interests. The democratic form of government in itself does not automatically solve problems; it offers, however, a useful framework for their solution. Everything depends ultimately on the political and moral qualities of the citizenry."[42]

Among other things, these qualities—citizens' ability to decide which policies are consistent with their interests and convictions—

depend on a few characteristics of the issues and on the way organizations control the thoughts and actions of their members and of the public at large.

Most critical issues of our age require much study and reflection to be properly evaluated. Recall, for example, the many arguments raised for the arms race and against peaceful coexistence (Chapter 7). The unequivocal picture which emerges from a disinterested review of these arguments is that the case for peaceful coexistence, provided the Russians and Chinese were willing to go along, was unquestionably better. But the point I wish to stress here is the almost hopeless complexity of this issue and the impossibility of adequately dealing with it in public speeches and in the contemporary news media. Even on such comparatively straightforward cases as slavery, contaminated milk, and child exploitation, anti-humanitarians managed to dazzle a large portion of the public. Is it any wonder that they have been more successful on far more technical, complex, and seemingly two-sided issues such as disarmament, foreign policy, or environmental pollution?

Moreover, every voter, politician, and organization man must judge numerous complex issues, not just one. Experts who spend lifetimes studying any of these issues are engaged in endless "controversies." How then can a voter or organization man who must work, sleep, and, if we are to believe current surveys, watch television an average of six hours or more every day of his life, decide which policies would best serve his interests and convictions?

An individual's predicament is further complicated by the absence of clear alternatives. To be sure, we are given a choice, but usually only among staunch defenders of the status quo. "Do you suppose," Khrushchev once asked the tycoon Averell Harriman, "we consider it a free election when the voters of New York State have a choice only between a Harriman and a Rockefeller?"[43] Is it a meaningful election, do you suppose, when, in 1984, the voters of the United States had a choice between a man who would, if elected President, increase military expenditures by 13 percent, and a man who would "only" increase it by 3 percent? Or when, in 1988, they had a choice between men who said precious little, and who were probably insufficiently familiar with, such burning challenges as hazardous wastes, energy conservation, thousands of preventable infant deaths, or hundreds of thousands of avoidable teenage pregnancies?

The complexity of issues and absence of meaningful choice are further exacerbated by the close ties between organizations and their members. Take, for example, the membership of war-related entities. In 1990 (before mobilization for the Persian Gulf started), their ranks included over two million Americans in uniform, one million civilians employed by the Defense Department, and millions employed in military industries. The ranks of these millions were, in turn, swelled up by relatives and friends who wished them well or depended on them for financial support. Obviously, not all these good people were hardliners. But being human, and knowing that the arms race served their short-term interests, it is only to be expected that they would be favorably disposed towards any argument in its favor.

Additional factors serve to secure members' compliance with organizational goals and policies. Some principled individuals never try to join faceless institutions. Of those who try, only potential team players who are either misinformed or uninformed about the social implications of the organization's activities are likely to be hired. Once people join, their job security, promotion, and social standing hinge on their ability to conform or identify their organization's interest with the public's.

"If a nation expects to be ignorant and free," Thomas Jefferson said, "it expects what never was and never will be . . . the people cannot be safe without information."[36b] Citizens can judge a policy, provided they know what it is; they can judge a politician, provided they know what he or she stands for. In the remainder of this section I shall trace humankind's peril to one of its roots—the unreliability of the majority's chief sources of information.

Corporate Media

This book's reconstruction of the Cold War bears little resemblance to orthodox historical writings. This divergence places me in an uncomfortable position. Both this book and conventional sources of information presume to describe and interpret the same events. Hence, either I am hallucinating or the majority's main sources of information are scandalously inadequate. Before checking into the nearest asylum, I decided to examine the situation in non-military fields. To my relief, I found out that iconoclastic disarmament historians are not alone; the views of some independent specialists in just about any political domain are strikingly at odds with traditional views. Some information specialists (those studying our sources of information directly) note similar discrepancies in surveys of mass media and education as a whole. If these dissenters are right, then the first steps towards political literacy involve overthrow of long-held beliefs, not merely their amplification and refinement; uncovering misrepresentation and humbug, not merely pointing to shallowness and insufficiency. There is no royal road to political literacy and no substitute for open-mindedness. Here I can only try to bolster my case by presenting conclusions reached in two fields—foreign affairs and tobacco-related deaths.

The corporate media's coverage of the Iranian revolution:

> By and large the American news media . . . have characterized the [1979] Iranian conflict as the work of turbaned religious zealots in league with opportunistic Marxists, rather than—as they might have—the reaction of people outraged by a repressive regime. By doing so the press has helped to misinform American public opinion and narrow the range of debate.[44]

A vehement anti-communist commenting on American involvement in Vietnam:

> By 1957 the politicians and the press of the United States considered Ngo Dinh Diem the Miracle Man of Vietnam . . . America was being deluged with propaganda praising Ngo Dinh Diem—when in reality he was reigning as a tyrant and sowing the seeds for a National Liberation Front victory, driving South Vietnam into civil war and defeat.[45]

Media suppression of evidence that tobacco kills:

> On February 24, 1936, Dr. Pearl delivered a paper to the New York Academy of Medicine. His paper concluded that tobacco shortens the life of all users, a piece of genuinely spectacular news affecting millions of readers and listeners. The

session was covered by the press, but they either remained silent about the news or buried it. . . . In 1954, the American Cancer Society released results of a study of 187,000 men. Cigarette smokers had a death rate from all diseases 75 percent higher than nonsmokers. . . . It was increasingly clear that tobacco-linked disease is the biggest single killer in the United States, accounting for more than 300,000 deaths a year, the cause of one in every seven deaths in the country, killing six times more people annually than automobile accidents. But though the statistics are conclusive to medical authorities, [by 1986 they were still] treated as controversial or non-existent by the news media. . . . The print and broadcast media might make page 1 drama of a junior researcher's paper about a rare disease. But if it involved the 300,000 annual deaths from tobacco-related disease, the media either do not report it or they report it as a controversial item subject to rebuttal by the tobacco industry. . . . *Newsweek*, for example, had a cover story January 26, 1978, entitled "What Causes Cancer?" The article was six pages long. On the third page it whispered about the leading cause—in a phrase it said that tobacco is the least disputed "carcinogen of all." The article said no more about the statistics or the medical findings of the tobacco-cancer link, except in a table, which listed the ten most suspected carcinogens—alphabetically, putting tobacco in next-to-last place. A week later, *Time* . . . ran a two-column article on the causes of cancer. The only reference it made to tobacco was that "smoking and drinking alcohol have been linked to cancer."

If there was ever any question that . . . in the media . . . advertising influences news and other information given to the public, tobacco makes it unmistakably clear. The tobacco industry since 1954 has spent more than $9 billion on advertising, most of it in newspapers, magazines, radio, and television. Newspapers, magazines, radio, and television have effectively censored news and entertainment to obscure the link between tobacco and death. During that period more than eight million Americans have died from tobacco-linked disease.[46a]

For the most part, then, the American mass media are doing a poor job of informing people about policies and policy makers and of educating them about the issues. To be sure, the flaw is not outright lies, but the quality of presentation, the range of opinions, extensive coverage of one side in a controversy—business, government, the comfortable establishment—and little coverage of all others. The media define political reality and proceed to present the range of permissible opinions. Given the slow evolution of our political world view, the implications are disheartening:

> Our picture of reality does not burst upon us in one splendid revelation. It accumulates day by day and year by year in mostly unspectacular fragments from the world scene, produced mainly by the mass media. Our view of the real world is dynamic, cumulative, and self-correcting as long as there is a pattern of evenhandedness in deciding which fragments are important. But when one important category of the fragments is filtered out, or included only vaguely, our view of the social-political world is deficient.[46b]

In more general terms, the media foster the self-serving illusion that history unfolds on an hourly, daily, or weekly basis. The sensationalism, trivia, and flashy headlines deflect us from the path of unprofitable questions like "why" or "what for." With history's slow and indecipherable ways under cover, consumers are unlikely to break their comforting addiction to intellectual mud baths.

Another deficiency is irrelevance, as Aldous Huxley explains:

> In regard to propaganda the early advocates of universal literacy and a free press envisaged only two possibilities: the propaganda might be true, or it might be false. They did not foresee what in fact has happened, above all in our Western capitalistic democracies—the development of a vast mass communications industry, concerned in the main neither with the true nor the false but with the unreal, the more or less totally irrelevant. In a word, they failed to take into account man's almost infinite appetite for distractions. . . .
>
> Only the vigilant can maintain their liberties, and only those who are constantly and intelligently on the spot can hope to govern themselves effectively by democratic procedures. A society, most of whose members spend a great part of their time, not on the spot, not here and now and in the calculable future, but somewhere else, in the irrelevant other worlds of sport and soap opera, of mythology and metaphysical fantasy, will find it hard to resist the encroachments of those who would manipulate and control it.
>
> In their propaganda today's dictators rely for the most part on repetition, suppression and rationalization—the repetition of catchwords which they wish to be accepted as true, the suppression of facts which they wish to be ignored, the arousal and ra-

tionalization of passions which may be used in the interests of the Party or the State. As the art and science of manipulation come to be better understood, the dictators of the future will doubtless learn to combine these techniques with the non-stop distractions which, in the West, are now threatening to drown in a sea of irrelevance the rational propaganda essential to the maintenance of individual liberty and the survival of democratic institutions.[36c]

In part, the print and broadcast media's failings can be traced to organizational callousness. Their chief goal—making money—is not necessarily served by disinterested reporting. Moreover, the controls that full commercial competition would have provided are often absent. By the mid-1980s, despite 25,000 media outlets in the United States, 29 corporations controlled "most of the business in daily newspapers, magazines, television, books, and motion pictures."[46c] The non-cabled television industry suffered from an advanced and obvious case of oligopolism. The great majority of daily newspapers were regional monopolies. Of some 1,700 daily newspapers in the U.S., 98 percent were local monopolies with most of their combined circulation controlled by fewer than 15 corporations. In fact, by 1985, according to the American Newspaper Publishers Association, only 32 cities had separately owned and operated dailies. Similarly, fewer than 12 corporations controlled most American book publishing.[1]

Senior officials of media corporations and other members of the power elite move in overlapping social circles, enjoy similar lifestyles and incomes, share similar professional backgrounds, interests, and world views, and often move from one type of organization to another (the infamous revolving door). Moreover, media corporations depend on government and business for news scraps and advertising, and literally cannot afford to be their watchdog. Given these conditions, it would take exceptional circumstances such as the Vietnam War in the early 1970s, growing signs of global environmental decline in the early 1990s, or a clash with their own short-term organizational objectives, for the media to begin doing their job.

As in the case of all other organizations, conformity in media corporations is assured through a meticulous process of hiring, promotion, and firing. The crowning achievement of this process is not reporters who daily compromise their principles, but sadly misinformed reporters who mistakenly see themselves as purveyors of truth and justice.

Thus, it is only a meager residue of non-conformity, vision, and originality that must run the gauntlet of censorship (self-righteously described by its Western practitioners as an "editorial process")—a time-honored bit which not only reins in junior journalists, broadcasters, book writers, and artists, but their senior colleagues as well. It goes without saying that the situation has gone from bad to worse since Mark Twain wrote the following words:

> The editor of a newspaper cannot be independent, but must work with one hand tied behind him by party and patrons, and be content to utter only half or two-thirds of his mind . . . writers of all kinds are manacled servants of the public. We write frankly and fearlessly, but then we "modify" before we print.[47]

It takes much more than an occasional airing of the truth to break away from the resultant climate of opinion, for we have by now grown accustomed to a daily diet of irrelevancies and half-truths. By switching channels, subscribing to a different tabloid, and shunning people who are openly critical of conventional beliefs, we too unknowingly discourage efforts to drag us out of the cave of political illiteracy.[48]

Government

In some ways, the U.S. Government is doing a remarkable job of informing the people. Assessments of the military balance, for example, have so far depended on official U.S. sources, not on Russian, Chinese, or South African sources. However, the institutional constraints which compel our government to disseminate information are not strong enough to curtail its mind manipulation activities. Among other things, it tries to shape our conceptions of reality through public relations campaigns, censorship, timely news releases, official leaks, mock-up incidents like the Tonkin Gulf episode, or spineless presidential commissions. We have seen earlier a few examples of our government's attitude towards the truth, so here we need only recount a few additional aspects.

The Defense Department and other organizational promoters of the arms race employ various tactics to shape public opinion. The ongoing and massive Defense Department's public relations campaigns, which have been planned and executed much better than our recent wars and military missions, had been detailed long ago (1970) in Senator Fulbright's *The Pentagon Propaganda Machine*. One quotation will suffice:

> Of considerable importance to the Defense Department in selling the military point of view is the stream of American citizens who pass through terms of military service. We have become a nation of veterans—now [1970] more than 28 million. This means that more than one-fifth of our adult population has been subjected to some degree of indoctrination in military values and attitudes. And all have been, whether they liked it or not, that dream of the public relations man—a captive audience.[49a]

Thus, even before organizational promoters of the arms race turn their attention to the public at large, they enjoy the support of a "large and sympathetic audience."[49b]

As another time-honored public relations tactic, consider Royal and Presidential commissions. All the experts selected to serve on such commissions have the needed credentials and reputations. They may all, in their final report, tell the public the truth—as they see it. However, seasoned observers can readily prognosticate, with only a small margin of error, the commission's recommendations, because only proven conformists, careerists, or upholders of the status quo—and hardly ever those likely to question fundamental assumptions—are asked to serve.

Finally, reflections of a former Secretary of Defense:

> U.S. national security officials (myself included) have faced a dilemma about how to speak of . . . [the military balance]. When the balance has been moving adversely, it is important to redress it. That makes it necessary to express some concern in official statements. Yet if the concern is mistranslated as a judgment about the present balance . . . it could lead to unwarranted conclusions about the weakness of U.S. capabilities and thus damage the U.S. political position.[50]

Whatever else one might think of this revealing passage, it makes one thing perfectly clear: this self-proclaimed democrat takes it for granted that his task is not to tell the public the truth, but to protect the national interest (as he sees it) by shaping public opinion.

Years after the event, the truth might come out, as it did, for example, with the 1979 publication of a book on a CIA-sponsored coup which took place in Iran a quarter of a century earlier. Similarly, by May 1990 Americans learned that in 1962 their country betrayed the anti-apartheid activist Nelson Mandela. Though this belated emergence of the truth is of great value to scholars, it is of limited value to the public. After all, the public in a functional democracy must judge contemporary issues, not history.

Experts

Experts are hired, promoted, and fired, in part, on the basis of conformity to organizational discipline and goals. The consequences are predictable:

> The traditional view of expert opinion is . . . radically mistaken. An expert is traditionally seen as neutral, disinterested, unbiased. . . . On the view proposed here . . . an expert is best seen as a committed advocate. . . . It is notorious that the opinion of an expert . . . can often be predicted from knowledge of which group has his affiliation.[21b]

A 19th century philosopher:

> Party interests are vehemently agitating the pens of so many pure lovers of wisdom. . . . Truth is certainly the last thing they have in mind. . . . Philosophy is misused, from the side of the state as a tool, from the other side as a means of gain. . . . Who can really believe that truth also will thereby come to light, just as a by-product? . . . Governments make of philosophy a means of serving their state interests, and scholars make of it a trade.[22a]

President Eisenhower:

> In . . . the free university, historically the fountainhead of free ideas . . . a government contract becomes virtually a substitute for intellectual curiosity. . . . The prospect of domination of the nation's scholars by Federal employment, project allocations, and

the power of money is ever present—and is gravely to be regarded.[52]

Military experts deserve a special mention in this book. According to one irate historian:

> President Kennedy was carried to power by an alarmed electorate who had been informed (by him) of a "missile gap" in the Soviet Union's favour—a gap which was wholly fictional. President Reagan has . . . been swept to power upon a similar tide. . . . An academic discipline which has failed to challenge, frontally, these major exercises in public deception—which has covered up for them, or even provided the trumpeters and drummers for the whole mendacious exercise—a discipline which has left it to a handful of honourable dissenters, outsiders, and amateurs to contest, with small resources, the well-funded lies of State— such a discipline must stand self-condemned.[51]

Another observer puts it this way:

> The defense intellectuals are clever. They have been employed under defense contracts and in government not to find ways of preventing war but of preserving it. Those who speak of limited nuclear war can easily envision an area of common interests which might enable the U.S. and Soviet nuclear giants to achieve an agreement to terminate hostilities short of total destruction, even after a nuclear exchange has begun. It is strange, then, that they can dismiss as unrealistic the idea that similar common interests could lead to an agreement to end all war and all war preparations.[53]

A retired American arms manufacturer, explaining his objection to the early 1980s' proposal of mobile MX missiles:

> Can the Soviets steal the schedule and reprogram their guidance systems . . . to negate the whole idea? It is not very likely, but in the weird world of nuclear strategy, anything that is at all possible has to be considered. I have been around nuclear strategists for many years and I know how they think. I am certain that if the MX missiles are deployed in a mobile configuration, someone will write a paper suggesting that the Soviets could break the scheduling code. Someone else would write a paper suggesting

that since we don't know whether the Soviets could break the code or not, we should, for maximum security, assume that they could. This would open a new window of vulnerability, and off we would go to a new level of escalation.[54]

Here is a typical episode:

> When Lawrence Korb moved into private industry after five years as an assistant secretary of Defense, and then, in 1986, as a private citizen, endorsed a group statement opposing further Pentagon budget increases, two of [John] Lehman's [Reagan's Secretary of the Navy] close lieutenants protested to Korb's new employers, the Raytheon Company. Those pressure calls [which jeopardized Raytheon's ability to get contracts] cost Korb his high-salaried job as Raytheon's vice president for corporate operations. . . . "I think [Korb said] people who use methods like that should not be entrusted with public positions . . . I was outraged, because my feeling was that people ought to be free to express their opinions. I couldn't imagine a great company like Raytheon caving in to that kind of pressure.[13e]

By 1990, our war intellectuals were getting desperate. A formal study by the RAND Corporation—a paragon of establishment respectability—was fretting about an alleged Soviet plot for starting World War III. A columnist in the mainstream press commented:

> What is it that provokes this insane flight of fancy in otherwise normal men? It is the prospect of peace, and with it the impending reduction of the $300-billion U.S. defense budget. Included in that sum is an estimated $2 billion a year paid to defense consultants . . . who concoct the scenarios to justify new weapons . . . For so many years they have lived off these kinds of articles and speculation, and now they are going to lose their bread and butter.[55]

All this runs counter to textbook lore, in which scholars are often portrayed as bowing to nothing but the truth. To be sure, some experts still live up to this ideal, but these courageous individuals operate outside, or on the fringes, of the political system. Most scholars yield to the practical needs of professional survival in an imperfect world.

Take, for instance, the case of a respected cardiologist who was contracted by a certain pharmaceutical outfit to test the safety of a new drug. Despite his comparative affluence and professional independence, despite the potential risks to thousands of heart patients, he doctored the experimental data to conform to the outfit's commercial interests. At the time, 50 other researchers were similarly disqualified by the Food and Drug Administration, suggesting that, even in this limited area of drug testing, cold-blooded fraud is more prevalent than one would like to think.[56]

Admittedly, this is the fringe. Most pundits are too decent or prudent to engage in outright lucrative fraud, and they are rarely asked to do so. They are only expected to defend the highly improbable, but not inconceivable, views which happen to suit organizational interests. When they don't, they suffer much and accomplish little. When they do, they retain their jobs and promotional opportunities, receive the approbation of their colleagues, supervisors, and society at large, and do not even lose caste in the academic community. In short, they have nothing to gain and much to lose from rocking the boat. Under such conditions, the record shows, indistinct shades of morality are usually put aside.

Education

Throughout the Cold War, the typical, virtually standardized, educational curriculum presented a grossly inaccurate picture of American society, history, and politics. Besides these institutionalized distortions of the past and present, the curriculum gave short shrift to subjects essential to comprehending contemporary politics, e.g., logic, the scientific method, radical ecology, or Russian literature. It made little effort to foster individualism, a love for justice, compassion for the underdog, critical thinking, and openmindedness. It showed little interest in the quality of interaction among students. It highlighted trivia and bypassed critical issues. For instance, it seems more important for our children to know that millions of Americans live in abject poverty and helplessness and be aware of the arguments that could be raised for and against this state of things, than to know the name of the 34th American President or the correct spelling of "quibble."

Our educational system aims at meaningless test scores, conformity, and information storage. It attempts to shape students' behavior and beliefs, not to give them the tools they need to form their own opinions. A 1982 proclamation of the Texas State Board of Education reveals the usually unstated goals of America's prevailing educational theories and practices: "Textbook content shall promote citizenship and the understanding of the free-enterprise system, emphasize patriotism and respect for recognized authority . . . Textbook content shall not encourage life-styles deviating from generally accepted standards of society."[57]

To give democracy a chance, students must know something more than comforting fairy tales about their country's history and politics. They must understand how their government is supposed to work, *and* how it really works. They must be acutely aware of their country's strengths *and* failings. They must be familiar with the characters and philosophies of key historical figures, not with contrived caricatures. They must not be shielded from the truth—any truth—regardless of how uncomfortable this truth might be. They must be able to spurn the financial and emotional rewards of conformity and obedience to authority. At least under extreme circumstances, they must be willing to place the public good above their narrow self-interest. A truly democratic educational system, in other words, would try to combine individualism and compassion, rationality and public-spiritedness. It would never compromise the truth. It would replace hymns to successful knaves and make-believe heroes with dispassionate efforts to recapture the past and present, complete with their fools, scoundrels, and idealists.

For the sake of analysis, I have treated each of the foregoing information sources independently of the others. In the real world, they all form a single web:

> Indoctrination is to democracy what coercion is to dictatorship . . . In a totalitarian society, the mechanisms of indoctrination are . . . transparent. . . . Under capitalist democracy, the situation is considerably more complex. The press and the intellectuals are held to be fiercely independent, hypercritical, antagonistic to the "establishment," in an adversary relation to the state. . . . True, there is criticism, but a careful look will show that it remains within narrow bounds. The basic principles of the state propaganda system are assumed by the critics. . . . An independent mind must seek to separate itself from official doc-

trine, and from the criticism advanced by its alleged opponents; not just from the assertions of the propaganda system, but from its tacit presuppositions as well, as expressed by critic and defender. This is a far more difficult task. Any expert in indoctrination will confirm, no doubt, that it is far more effective to constrain all possible thought within a framework of tacit assumption than to try to impose a particular explicit belief with a bludgeon. It may be that some of the spectacular achievements of the American propaganda system, where all of this has been elevated to a high art, are attributable to the method of feigned dissent practiced by the responsible intelligentsia.[58]

Human Characteristics

Individual Callousness

Since 1953, Russian leaders were intermittently pursuing peaceful coexistence. From 1985 through 1991, especially, and at a great personal risk to themselves, they were preaching and practicing the philosophy of global interdependence. At the same time, and at a great risk to humanity, American leaders were deftly playing the time-honored game of Machiavellian politics. Armed with the belief that the enemy was nuclear war, environmental decline, poverty, and economic chaos, Russia was making unprecedented concessions in an effort to convince American voters and politicians that it was sincere and reasonable. The United States expressed delight with these developments, but utterly failed to extend a helping hand to Russian humanitarians or make a single *meaningful* concession of its own.

A similar situation prevails in most nations—between those who practice civil disobedience and those who run them over; between principled political aspirants who speak about the issues and the opportunists who obfuscate the issues—between the Gandhis and Churchills, the Berrigans and Reagans, the McGoverns and Nixons.

Callousness played a key role in history's stage long before the Persian Wars of the ancients and will surely continue to do so long after our own Persian War. Take, for instance, the city-state of Athens. Following the conclusion of the Persian Wars, the still present Persian threat prompted some Greek states to enter into a voluntary alliance with Athens. Shortly thereafter, the Athenian confederacy was turned into a benign but much resented empire. Secessions were suppressed by force, strategic decisions were made in Athens alone, and money collected from member states for the common cause was used for strictly Athenian purposes. A historian of this period, writing in 1900, attempts to explain this failure of Athenian democracy (a failure which contributed to Athens' downfall):

> Most Athenian citizens were naturally allured by a policy of expansion which made their city great and powerful without exacting heavy sacrifices from themselves. . . . The empire furthered the extension of their trade, and increased their prosperity. The average Athenian . . . was not hindered by his own full measure of freedom from being willing to press, with as little scruple as any tyrant, the yoke of his city upon the necks of other communities."[59]

Or take 1914 Europe. The prospects of World War I, Bertrand Russell says,

> filled me with horror, but what filled me with even more horror was the fact that the anticipation of carnage was delightful to something like ninety percent of the population. I had to revise my views of human nature.[60]

One laboratory study[61] examined the practical effectiveness of humanitarian strategies. In this artificial setting, American college students can make money by delivering messages through a computer. They are led to believe that monetary gain depends on the cooperation of a similarly placed fellow "student" (in reality, a computer program). However, if neither side cooperates with the other, a mutually paralyzing deadlock results and both suffer monetary losses. The other "student" employs a pacifist strategy. He always concedes the first round to the subject. He does so even though this concession puts him at a serious disadvantage—if the subject wins the first round the subject can, by administering painful shocks to the pacifist, win all other rounds. In subsequent rounds, the pacifist insists on fair play, thereby forcing the subject to either concede equality or use painful shocks to retain an unfair advantage and make a few shekels. When the pacifist is shocked as a result of his principled stand, he steadfastly eschews retaliation (he can shock the subject too). So we have here a situation in which a cooperative person always concedes an advantage in order to demonstrate his good will and avoid a mutually detrimental deadlock. He then presses for equality. If he fails to attain equality, he receives painful electric shocks. Although he can retaliate, he never does. In this setup, all subjects believe themselves to be under pressure from two teammates (in reality, a computer program) urging a callous strategy.[62] Also, all subjects are led to believe that the pacifist is a Quaker who is morally committed to nonviolence.

In the first four rounds, 87 percent of the subjects behaved callously. In later rounds, and especially after direct appeals from the pacifist, this fraction declines to 59 percent. That is, under social and monetary pressures, close to two-thirds consistently dominate and hurt a cooperative and nonviolent person.

The results for these . . . experimental manipulations suggest that when the pacifist fails it is not primarily because he fails to project a clear image of his intentions. Naively we had assumed that the various manipulations would only serve to strengthen the pacifist's case—the personal profile information, the availability of communication, the opportunity to forgo harmful actions—all of these would ostensibly contribute to the effectiveness of the pacifist's bargaining strategy. Behind this lay the assumption that the pacifist would more than likely benefit from anything that served to bring his character, his claims, and his commitments into sharper focus. Our results suggest that this assumption needs to be questioned or at least seriously qualified. While the pacifist appeal can persuade some adversaries away from their initial positions, and it does influence a small proportion to do so, particularly under the condition of personal communications, it also fails to influence many [subjects] who plan to dominate. But beyond these obvious alternatives it may have another effect; it may encourage exploitation among [subjects] who otherwise do not entertain such plans prior to interacting with the pacifist. . . . Reassured by their knowledge of the pacifist that they could dominate with impunity, they did not soften their demands but planned for continued exploitation. The pacifist's tactics apparently invite exploitation and aggression even among those who do not begin with such intentions.[61]

Indoctrinability

"There is no nonsense so arrant," says Bertrand Russell, "that it cannot be made the creed of the vast majority by adequate governmental action."[63] The evidence for our susceptibility to suggestion, propaganda, and indoctrination comes from various sources.

It is a matter of common experience. Most Russians used to believe in the curious brand of Marxism they imbibed from their social environment. Hitler came to power, in part, by appealing to his listeners' emotions. Closer to home, propaganda is a key element in our elections, government pronouncements, news broadcasting, various cults, and education. Similarly, "our" religion is almost always a function of just one variable: the indoctrination we received in early childhood. A character in a Steinbeck's novel puts it thus: "Let's say that when I was a little baby, and all my bones soft and malleable, I was put in a small Episcopal cruciform box and so took my shape. Then, when I broke out of the box, the way a baby chick escapes an egg, is it strange that I had the shape of a cross? Have you ever noticed that chickens are roughly egg-shaped?"[64]

Experimental evidence similarly confirms our susceptibility to manipulation, suggestion, propaganda, and indoctrination. Our behavior can, for instance, be influenced by subliminal perceptions. For example, messages played too fast on a tape recorder to be assimilated on the conscious level can reportedly reduce the incidence of shoplifting.

Some genuinely ill individuals can be cured, and some healthy individuals made ill, through the power of suggestion. In Australia's Northern Territory, I have been told, a spell cast by a reputed medicine man is potent enough to ail, wither away, or even kill tradition-bound Natives.

Hypnosis seems to give one person impressive powers over another. Yet, about 15 percent of the adult population can become deeply hypnotized.[65] An even more striking example is provided by post-hypnotic suggestion. In one demonstration to which I was a witness, the subject was instructed to open the nearest window as soon as the hypnotist lights a cigarette. Following his release from the hypnotic state, the subject took an active part in the ordinary conversation which followed. When the hypnotist lit a cigarette, the man was visibly distressed. He apparently wished to open the window, but this wish placed him in an awkward position. It was too cold outside to open a window and just then he was engaged in a conversation which could not be politely interrupted. Yet, he excused himself and opened the window.

Conceptual Conservatism

As we have seen, our susceptibility to indoctrination is exploited by the power elite. As much as we hate to do so, we must concur with Aldous Huxley's views:

> It is perfectly possible for a man to be out of prison and yet not free—to be under no physical constraint and yet to be a psychological captive, compelled to think, feel and act as the representatives of the national State, or of some private interest within the nation, want him to think, feel, and act. . . . The victim of mind-manipulation does not know that he is a victim. To him, the walls of his prison are invisible, and he believes himself to be free.[36d]

As far as politics is concerned, and regardless of educational background, class, or party, most of us are sadly misinformed. We often have strong feelings about politics. We are convinced that we understand what is going on, that our political actions are in line with our convictions and interests. But in all this we are often mistaken. To perceive political realities, we must do much more than acquire new information. We must, rather, open-mindedly weigh the evidence and, if need be, discard old beliefs and adopt new ones. In the world as it is constituted now, political liberation presupposes a series of conceptual shifts. As we shall see, both psychology and history show that human beings are not very good at letting go of strongly held but unreasonable beliefs.

Let us examine failed prophecies first. As a rule, a prophet takes care to make his prophecies vague enough, or to project them far enough into the future, so that they cannot be proven wrong in the prophet's lifetime. Sometimes, however, prophets throw professional caution to the wind and make testable predictions. And here is an interesting question: What happens when prophecy fails?

Among the many historical incidents throwing light on this question there is the story of Mohammed and Mount Safa. The mountain, you will recall, disobeyed the Prophet's orders to come over to where he and his followers were passing the time of day. Although Mohammed was quick to attribute the mountain's stead-fastness to Allah's mercy (had the mountain moved, they would have all been crushed), this was a clear professional failure. Yet, to my knowledge, no one is on record as having abandoned Islam on account of this washed out claim to divinity.

A group of psychologists[66] observed members of a small occult sect who were convinced that the world was soon coming to an end. After that fateful day came and went, most believers still clung to their faith. As in the case of Mohammed's followers, these occultists managed to rationalize the knockout blow to their creed. All this suggests that one common response to a disconfir-mation of belief is not its abandonment, but "increased fervor among the true believers."[66]

These historical and psychological observations cast perhaps some light on the hardliners' conduct. For instance, the conversion of the Acheson-Lilienthal Report into the Baruch Plan was based in part on the expectation that our atomic monopoly would last 20 years. In September 1949 this prediction was laid to rest by the first Soviet atomic test. Surely, now that prophecy failed, was the time to talk to the Soviets? Not for the true believers; five months later, the U.S. chose to develop the H-bomb without trying to negotiate with the Soviets. And sure enough, by 1955 (at the latest)[67] both sides conducted their first successful H-bomb test. The repeated disconfirmation of the hardliners' beliefs and policies in the one-third of a century which followed did not lead to their abandonment, but to "increased fervor among the true believers."

Even Gorbachev's quiet revolution failed to meet their exacting standards:

> Just what might it take to get such "hard line conservatives" to believe otherwise? Notwithstanding a stream of astonishing and courageous initiatives and concessions by the Soviet leader, the critics' complaints and warnings about "the perfidious Russians" are unabated. A length, one might begin to wonder if the conser-vatives' suspicions of Mr. Gorbachev are susceptible to *any*

imaginable refutation. This is a significant question, albeit a question that is rarely posed.[68]

One can only hope that one day, reason and kindness alone, and not the simultaneous explosions of thousands of "superbombs," will suffice to shake their faith.

Experimental work on chicken behavior provides a powerful metaphor for the hardliners' misconduct. Baby chicks can be fitted with distorting goggles which make an object appear one-sixth of an inch off its actual position. Unable to learn that their eyes can deceive them, that the food they see is not in the spot it appears but a minuscule distance away, such chicks, if left alone, starve to death in the midst of plenty. Our leaders' distorting goggles similarly induced them to forget the grave risks of accidental war, nuclear proliferation, environmental decline, and the existence of other potential adversaries besides the Soviets, prompting them to peck unswervingly in the direction of Moscow. And, like those emaciated chicks, if left alone, they (and the rest of us) might have perished because they could not adjust to new realities.

It is difficult to demonstrate the critical importance of conceptual conservatism in politics. Most historians invoke such explanations as greed, blind ambition, or saving face instead of invoking the difficulty of abandoning discredited beliefs. This psychological difficulty has, however, been noticed by some perceptive power brokers.

Before the destruction of Hiroshima and Nagasaki, according to a former special assistant to the President for national security affairs, no one seriously considered a warning to Japan's rulers that they could no longer put off the bitter pill of surrender. Sustained consideration of such a warning

> would have required a reversal of the most deeply ingrained of all the behavior patterns of the Manhattan Project, the commitment to secrecy. . . . The secrecy that had begun with a proper concern not to arouse Hitler's interest had become a state of mind with a life and meaning of its own, so deeply ingrained that anyone who had asked . . . just *why* it was a secret now . . . might have had to wait for the answer. It was a secret now because it had been a secret throughout the war . . . But would it really be better or worse, now, if he [the enemy] *did* know? That question went so

deeply against the grain, even for the most farsighted men in the undertaking, that they never examined it thoroughly. It is no accident that the two men to raise the question of warning directly with Truman . . . did not begin with any ingrained assumption that continued secrecy was somehow vital to success.[69]

A former under secretary of state:

It will not be easy for America to conform its foreign policy to the recognition that the Cold War is effectively ended, since, among other reasons, many political leaders . . . formed their view of the Cold War in the vicious days of Iosif Stalin and have never since altered that frozen impression . . . The rhetoric emanating from Washington still often reminds me of . . . the [late 1970s] report of a lonely Japanese soldier discovered hiding in a cave on one of the more remote Pacific Islands. He was still cowering in fear of discovery for no one had ever come by to tell him that World War II had long been over. . . . Even our most flexible-minded political leaders may . . . be appalled at the prospect of breaking their well-entrenched habit of regarding the Cold War as the fundamental framework in which policy must be formulated.[70]

Former Soviet President Mikhail Gorbachev:

Revolutions always begin in the mind. The way to save civilization and life itself does not lie in thinking up new technologies for ever more accurate and lethal weapon systems, but rather in liberating the mind from prejudices—political and social, national and racial—from arrogance, self-conceit and the cult of force and violence.[71]

Though conceptual conservatism permeates every aspect of our lives, it is particularly noticeable in science. Unlike ordinary voters and policy makers, scientists are trained to be objective and flexible, to detach their egos from their theories, to think it possible that they are mistaken. Yet, in some ways, the history of science is comprised of endless tales of the innovative individual's struggle against his own, and then against his colleagues', conservatism.[72]

Take, for instance, the history of childbed fever, a disease which once claimed countless lives in maternity wards. After many false starts, Ignaz Semmelweis discovered a simple preventive measure. "If you do not wish to kill your patients," he told his fellow gynecologists, "you must disinfect your hands before handling a patient. You cannot, in particular, dissect a cadaver or examine a sick patient and then proceed to deliver a baby with soiled hands." Now, one could scarcely imagine a more conclusive proof than the one proffered by Semmelweis, a greater urgency, a smaller sacrifice or inconvenience, or a better educated public than the one to which his pleas were directed. Yet, Semmelweis and his plea had been ignored for years and years and young women kept dying at childbirth.[73]

If stories like this have been repeated hundreds of times, if this conceptual malady afflicts science (which is often regarded as humankind at its intellectual best), then it goes without saying that the same forces play an important role in politics too. There is a more pronounced ideological component in politics than in science. Political decisions are enmeshed in practical considerations. They are not made by professional truth-seekers but by professional power-seekers. They are not judged by experts but by depressingly misinformed and insufficiently educated lay people. It stands to reason, therefore, that conceptual conservatism plays a critical role in the irrationality of our political decisions.

Perhaps the strongest experimental evidence for conceptual conservatism comes from recent studies.[74,75] In one such study, scientists from two major research universities were given a false formula which led them to believe that balls are 50 percent larger than they really are. They were then asked to transfer water from two actual balls to a box. Their own measurements dramatically discredited the formula in both instances. While they were getting, say, four quarts using the water transfer method, the formula was wrongly leading them to expect six.

Under such circumstances, not one of these highly qualified participants flatly rejected the formula. In response to questions about the volumes of balls, including balls identical in size to the ones they have been working with a short time before, over 90 percent based their replies on the false formula, not on the evidence of their senses.

These results are counterintuitive. When asked to predict theirs or others' behavior, most psychologists and lay people grossly underestimated the tendency to cling to the discredited formula. In addition to confirming the near universality of conceptual conservatism, these findings suggest that human irrationality is often attributable to the psychological difficulty of replacing one belief with another:

> The . . . outcome—all subjects clung in practice to an observationally absurd formula and none rejected it outright even on the verbal level—is surprising. Even when we deal with ideologically neutral conceptions of reality, when these conceptions have been recently acquired, when they came to us from unfamiliar sources, when they were assimilated for spurious reasons, when their abandonment entails little tangible risks or costs, and when they are sharply contradicted by subsequent events, we are, at least for a time, disinclined to doubt such conceptions on the verbal level and unlikely to let go of them in practice.[75]

Conformity

Imagine that you have volunteered to take part in a study of visual discrimination. When you show up, eight other subjects are already in their seats. You sit down in the only empty chair and the session gets under way.

The session consists of eighteen rounds of tests. At each round, all nine of you are shown a single line along with a group of three lines of varying lengths. Each of you is then asked, in turn, which of the three lines is equal in length to the single line. The seating arrangement is such that you usually hear the answers of all but one of your fellow subjects before your turn to answer arrives. To your surprise, they often give answers which your senses tell you are wrong, and which, if you were alone, you would have rarely given.

This was a study in conformity, not visual discrimination. You were the only subject; the other eight were accomplices who were instructed beforehand to give wrong answers. About one-fourth of all subjects successfully withstands this form of social pressure; one-twentieth completely succumbs; the remainder ranges in between (conforms to the majority's manifestly incorrect opinion only in some experimental rounds). This study confirms everyday intuitions: although all people are susceptible to social pressure, a few can overcome it successfully, a few cannot, and most can overcome it only in part.[76] Also, while in Rome we do as the Romans do, not merely as a matter of conscious policy, but partly because of a strong, subconscious tendency to go along: "The optimistic assumptions that underlay the [Bay of Pigs] invasion were not seriously challenged . . . partly because . . . all the members of the advisory group surrounding the President . . . felt it better to . . . conform to the dominant optimism."[77]

Obedience to Authority

Imagine yourself taking part, along with another subject, in a study of memory and learning. The session begins with explanations of the study's goals and your tasks. Your respective roles— teacher and learner—are determined by drawing lots. You land the teaching position. During the experiment, the learner is strapped into an "electric chair" from which he cannot escape, with electrodes attached to his wrist. His task is memorizing word associations. Your task involves teaching him these associations and giving him electric shocks of increasing severity when he fails to remember them. Throughout the experiment you are seated in front of an impressive shock generator, with 30 switches which go up in intensity from 15 to 450 volts. The shock level these switches produce is marked in words on the shock generator, beginning with "slight shock," going through "moderate," "strong," "intense," "extremely intense," all the way to a point beyond the reading, "danger: severe shock."

As the session unfolds, the learner keeps making irritating mistakes. If you ask, the experimenter demands that you go on raising the shock level, up to the very highest. At 150 volts (the tenth switch), the learner demands to be released. The experimenter, if you ask, tells you that the session must go on. If you continue beyond this level, the learner's protests grow increasingly vehement and emotional. At 285 volts the protests "can only be described as an agonized scream." At 300 volts, the learner tells you that he will no longer take part in the session, nor provide answers to the memory test. The experimenter tells you to continue and to regard silence as the wrong answer. If you go on, the learner keeps screaming violently up to 330 volts. Beyond that point he is completely silent. For all you know, he might be dead. Nevertheless, the experimenter urges you to go on.

This, more or less, is the protocol of Stanley Milgram's celebrated study of obedience to authority. The teacher is the subject, while the learner is a skilled actor who actually receives no shock. Two out of every three subjects went all the way to 450 volts. They did so even though they were under the impression that they missed being in the other person's shoes merely by chance. They went to the very end despite the warning signs on the shock generator and despite the pleas and anguish of a fellow human being.

> With numbing regularity good people were seen to knuckle under to the demands of authority and perform actions that were callous and severe. Men who are in everyday life responsible and decent were seduced by the trappings of authority . . . into performing harsh acts.[78]

Most subjects did not relish the suffering they inflicted on fellow humans. They gave the learner the weakest shock possible when the choice was left to them. They showed no signs of malice or spite. They were transparently ill at ease during the experiment; often trembling or sweating excessively. They protested and continued only after the experimenter demanded that they go on. Their conduct is traceable to obedience, conceptual conservatism, and conformity, not to sadism.[79]

In one variation, both the teacher and learner were the experimenter's accomplices. The subject was in charge of recording experimental "results." Here the subject's dilemma was not between defying authority or actively inflicting pain, but between defying authority or helping one person inflict pain on another. In this case, over 90 percent cooperated to the very end. The similarity between these experimental situations and the predicament of organization men is self-evident. Just like the passive recorder in this experimental variation, these men play a minor, and often passive, part in organizational misdeeds. The similarity between this situation and the predicament of all of us who indirectly contribute to organizational misdeeds by paying taxes, buying certain products, or declining to become informed about the issues, is equally self-evident.

One incomplete analogy to the arms race is provided by Nazi Germany. The victims of Nazi atrocities often cooperated with the authorities. At any given point, cooperation seemed rational. At every point the victims could rebel, but rebellion seemed to involve greater risks than going along. According to one thoughtful observer, the most frightening idea about the Nazi holocaust is not that something like this could be done to us, but that *we* could do it to others. Also, the holocaust suggests the ability of modern power to induce actions "jarringly at odds with the vital interests of the actors."[80] Like the guards and prisoners of Treblinka, "we collaborate day by day in maintaining the institutions of the warfare state which seems . . . plausibly set to destroy us."[81]

This chilling analogy is instructive, but only if we bear its incompleteness in mind. Though arguments in favor of the arms race were as unscientific as were the intellectual foundations of Nazi concentration camps, they were not as morally repulsive. The horrors of Treblinka were daily experienced by its occupants, but the horrors of the arms race and nuclear war required considerable mental efforts to visualize or grasp. It is precisely such differences that made it possible for the modern warfare state to gain the support of good people who would have been among the first to fight the obvious evils of the Third Reich.

The Stalinist holocaust provides another incomplete analogy to the arms race. In both Stalinist Russia and Cold War America, deception was accomplished through extensive control of the media and the educational system. In both, such forces as conceptual conservatism and obedience to authority led decent people astray. In both, a seemingly humanitarian ideology played a key role. "To do evil," says one Gulag veteran, "a human being must first of all believe that what he is doing is good, or else that it's a well-considered act in conformity with natural law. . . . The imagination and spiritual strength of Shakespeare's evildoers stopped short at a dozen corpses because they had no *ideology*. Ideology . . . gives the evildoer the necessary steadfastness and determination."[82a]

Other Human Failings

The foregoing account of individual failings is obviously incomplete. Nothing has been said, for instance, about selfishness, hero worship, greed, and compartmentalized thinking. Little has been said, in particular, about weakmindedness and lack of familiarity with logic, the scientific method, and empirical rules of evidence; about our inability or unwillingness to consistently apply the little we are familiar with to either politics or our daily lives. "It is not their character so much that I have a contempt for, though that contempt is thoroughgoing," said Woodrow Wilson of the hardliners who torpedoed America's membership in the League of Nations (thereby helping to write the scripts for World War II and Cold War I), "but their minds."[83]

Yet, something seems to be lacking in this chapter's long indictment of human behavior, for it contradicts our everyday experience. Most of us are capable of kindness, courage, and compassion. We come up at times with extraordinary insights into ordinary problems. Almost everyone has some admirable qualities and can do certain things better than many of his or her fellows. Can all the bad things psychologists tell us about human behavior be reconciled with such common observations?

Maybe they can; in the final analysis, our misbehavior might be largely attributable to ignorance. Our educational system and cultural influences could be designed to strengthen the rational component of our nature and "vaccinate" us against unkindness, irrationality, conceptual conservatism, unwarranted obedience, and conformity. Moreover, such steps are sorely needed to improve the democratic process, make us freer and happier, and make the future of both democracy and civilization more secure. But, as everyday experience and opinion surveys suggest, most of us might already be human enough to achieve these goals. We may act as we do because we lack one thing: the truth about the things that really matter. Once we wrest this truth from its self-appointed guardians, our obvious failings notwithstanding, it is conceivable that we shall begin voting for our interests and principles, not against them; for statesmen free to serve us, not for politicos forced to serve somebody else.

Long ago, Alexander Solzhenitsyn asked: "What . . . will happen in our country [USSR] when whole waterfalls of Truth burst forth?" He then went on to say: "And they will burst forth. It has to happen."[82b] "How could he make such a rash forecast?" I asked myself upon reading these lines in the mid-1970s. Soviet totalitarianism and lies, I thought then, were good for a few centuries. And yet, if only for a few years, truth did triumph on Russian soil. So, before the scientist in me begins hedging, let me quickly conclude this chapter by saying: Waterfalls of Truth will one day burst forth in our country too. It has to happen.

Summary

This chapter highlights a few of the institutional and individual characteristics which underlie the collective irrationality and heartlessness of American politics. On the institutional level, it notes the tendency of improperly regulated organizations to promote their short-term interests at society's expense. Such organizations are inclined towards self-destructiveness, gross inefficiencies, inflexibility, and inertia. They outlive their usefulness, accumulate power, and promote anti-humanitarian actions by stirring phony controversies, contributing money to political campaigns, providing jobs for former and would-be government officials, and turning elections into circuses and politicians into puppets and clowns. Above all, they do this by skillfully manipulating the worldview, opinions, and beliefs of the public. Under the best of circumstances, voters would be faced with a formidable task in trying to (1) make sense of the great diversity and complexity of contemporary issues, (2) realize the absence of meaningful alternatives, and (3) disregard their economic and other ties to callous organizations. Given the decisive influence of America's mass media, government, hired experts, and cradle-to-grave educational system on our political worldview, given the proclivity of these information sources to promote the status quo by inventing reality, the climb from the cave of political illiteracy takes exceptional qualities. Moreover, many individual failings contribute to our tendency to vote and act against our convictions and interests. Under social pressure and when given a chance, the majority would take advantage of a principled and well-meaning fellow human being. All people are susceptible to propaganda and indoctrination. We often cling to discredited beliefs. We tend to think and act as others do. We tend to obey immoral commands as long as these commands are handed down by respected authority.

Overall, we are not as informed, rational, resistant to social pressure, and charitable as we would like to think.

Chapter 10

A SURGICAL REFORM STRATEGY

Ideas that have great results are always simple ones. My whole idea is that if vicious people are united and constitute a power, then honest folk must do the same. Now that's simple enough.

Lev Tolstoy,[1] 1869

Perhaps the most touching and profound characteristic of childhood is an unquestioning belief in the rule of common sense. The child believes that the world is rational and hence regards everything irrational as some sort of obstacle to be pushed aside. . . . The best people, I think, are those who over the years have managed to retain this childhood faith in the world's rationality. For it is this faith which provides man with passion and zeal in his struggle against the twin follies of cruelty and stupidity.

Fazil Iskander,[2] 1970

Do not go gentle into that good night.
Rage, rage against the dying of the light.

Dylan Thomas,[3] 1951

Has Humanity a Future?

A Kurt Vonnegut's fictional character once wrote a book titled "What Can a Thoughtful Man Hope for Mankind on Earth, Given the Experience of the Past Million Years?" The book itself is rather short, consisting of one word and a period: "Nothing."[4] Given indeed this experience, given the ever-growing number of technological threats and potential breaking points, given the overwhelming complexity of our social ills; given, moreover, the seemingly inexorable march of history (a march which seems to bring us ever closer to the maelstrom); Vonnegut's black humor appears realistic enough: it seems that, no matter what we do, the earth will sink and drown.

Depending perhaps on one's temper, one might look at the same record and wonder at the heights to which we have climbed in such a comparatively short time. Our ancestors routinely practiced fertility rites, human sacrifice, and self-flagellation; they ate human flesh, used the skulls of their enemies as drinking cups, and enslaved their fellows and spouses. Held in the clutches of shamans, taboos, and irrational fears, they were not, on the average, as free, as decent, and as rational as we are now, even if we manage, at the end, to suffocate in our own waste, blow ourselves apart, or lose our freedom. Further back in time, our forebears were ape-like creatures; still farther, they were snakes. An irreversible environmental decline, a nuclear holocaust, or a Brave New World will merely show what we have known all along—that we are capable of the worst follies, crimes, and fears. But they will not deny what everyday experience shows even more forcefully—that we possess a fair measure of wisdom, courage, and kindness. The historical record, and we, its perpetrators, form a crazy quilt of vice and virtue, folly and wisdom, fear and courage. This, combined with the novel element which science and technology introduce into contemporary history, render a return to the wasteland of the dark ages distinctly possible. But they do not guarantee this return, nor do they utterly negate a brighter prospect. There is, in particular, the remote but nevertheless well-founded hope that, if we just manage to keep the biosphere, democracy, and civilization going a few more centuries, we may become fully human.

Be it as it may, I can't concede that the end is nearby. Moreover, there is something to be said for the view that we must struggle against "all forces which are opposed to peace, to cooperation, to life and love. . . . giving up is not worthy of a human being."[5] So, without pretending to have resolved this legitimate debate on the future of humanity, I shall arbitrarily take it for granted that the struggle for a better world is not, in principle, devoid of hope.

Successful Reform Presupposes an Informed Public

"I am convinced," says a typical observer of the nuclear arms race, "that political leaders, left to themselves, will not be able to prevent a nuclear holocaust."[6] "Left alone," a former Deputy Administrator of the Environmental Protection Agency tells us, "our government will not always look after the public interest."[7] Both commentators, and many others,[8] agree that the key to curing our social ills is an informed public: "The main, perhaps the only, hope for the future is that the public will learn the facts in time and that an aroused public opinion will force reluctant politicians to stop the nuclear arms race and reduce armaments."[6] "The most important lesson from our environmental experience is that government will not act to face hard national problems until the people demand that it do so."[7]

Borne out as they are by the entire historical record, these views appear plausible. The powers that be are unlikely to be swayed by appeals to rationality, decency, fair play, or even their own long-term interests. At the present stage of human development, they can be moved only by irresistible forces. In a democracy, the only irresistible force may well be an informed people. So the question of strategy may boil down to this: How can this sleeping giant—the people—be awakened?

Forlorn Strategies

Democratic reformers have traditionally resorted to a number of strategies. One time-honored strategy involves starting an altogether new party with a broad reform platform. Another involves gaining control of an already existing major party.

Both strategies have been tried repeatedly in the past, and both, in the majority of cases, have failed. A new party, or a radically new platform of an established party, can succeed when the severity of the problems becomes obvious to the voters. Yet, submerged as they are in a sludge of irrelevance and misinformation, voters are unlikely to reach this enlightened state on time. A broad reform platform will antagonize many well-meaning voters, either because it takes the wrong stand on some issues, or because no voter is well-informed on all the issues. We are a conservative people, and not without good reasons. Unlike Marx's workers, we have a lot more to lose than our chains, and we know from the sad experience of others that revolutionary changes often bring disaster. Even if a new party, or an old party with a radically new platform, gains control over one or two branches of government, it might not be able to accomplish much because its program will be strongly resisted in so many centers of power within our republic.

For these, and for many other reasons that need not be elaborated here, this strategy of reform—starting a new party or attempting a takeover of an existing party—seems fruitless.

Another traditional strategy focuses on specific reforms. The specific reformer takes one issue, such as space militarization, the proposed construction of a nuclear power plant someplace, inadequate health care for the poor, or American support for dictatorial Turkey, and joins or organizes a political crusade against it. Sometimes his scope is broader, say, nuclear disarmament, nuclear power, poverty, or American policies in the Third World, but he goes no farther.

Until the mid-1940s, specific reformers had their fair share of victories. Since then, science and technology have proven too fast for them. On the whole, despite some notable successes, specific reformers have been losing ground. If they continue on the same course, they are likely to win a few sporadic battles, but—in a world in which everything is connected to everything else—lose the war.

Take, for instance, a specific reformer struggling to ban a carcinogenic pesticide. After years of hard work and sacrifices, she might win or lose. But even if she wins, is it a victory when, as a result of her actions, the manufacturer increases the volume of exports of this particular chemical so that total dispersal into the global environment remains the same? Is it a victory when the sum total of all hazardous chemicals in the biosphere rises? When the same manufacturer comes up with a similarly obnoxious substitute? When thousands of people must stand in the unemployment line as a result of her action? When, at any given moment throughout her struggle, most cities in the northern hemisphere can be reduced to radioactive rubble? When, on any given day, three or more species that have always shared this green and round planet with us have been irreversibly lost? Yet, these are precisely the kind of victories reformers have had since 1945.

All this is not meant to disparage specific reformers. Some of their accomplishments, e.g., greater equality for racial minorities and women, or the 1980 Alaska Wilderness Bill, are impressive. Similarly, specific reformers play a critically important role in raising public consciousness, in establishing a tradition of dissent, civic-mindedness, and pluralism, and in providing the groundwork and foundations for future progress. But, despite its near universal appeal, despite its accomplishments, despite the idealism, courage and sacrifices of its unsung practitioners, the strategy of specific reforms is unlikely to get us out of the present quagmire. On this question, the historical record is unambiguous.[9] Specific reformers are trying to push back the minute hand on humankind's time bomb, but they only succeed in slowing its steady advance.

Another image these struggles bring to mind is that of a lonely canoeist in a fast-flowing river. Despite strenuous efforts to paddle upriver and escape a dangerous waterfall whose roar she can already hear in the distance, she is steadily approaching death. Riverside observers of this drama may not know whether she can escape the waterfall at all, but they can be reasonably sure that the old way of feebly paddling upriver is not going to save her. Likewise, people observing the drama of contemporary history from the recesses of an academic library may not know whether humankind will escape from the logic of events, but they can be reasonably sure that the old strategy of specific reforms will come to grief.

Hard work, dedication, and good will must be combined with a viable strategy. But a strategy that produced so few victories in the past 46 years, a strategy that has been applied for so long on so many fronts and saw a net decline in the human prospect, a strategy that consistently attacks numerous surface manifestations of a social disease instead of its causes, a strategy that weakens the humanitarian camp by dividing it into disconnected branches, a strategy that institutionalizes the ills it sets out to correct, a strategy that inadvertently bestows upon the system the facade of democracy it so badly needs—such a strategy cannot possibly embody the correct approach to safeguarding freedom and civilization.

"It is not only my task to look after the victims of madmen who drive a motorcar in a crowded street," said Dietrich Bonhoeffer about some of his fellow Germans, "but to do all in my power to stop their driving at all."[10] To avert totalitarianism, war, environmental decline, injustice, economic and spiritual stagnation, we ought to start thinking about the eradication of mad driving, instead of merely looking after the ever-growing number of victims.

A Surgical Reform Strategy

In a democracy, the main hope for curbing the arms race and other social ills is an informed public. Only an informed public can be mobilized in the right direction, and only an informed public can vote intelligently and constructively. Broad platform reformers try to inform and mobilize the public on a variety of issues; a given specific reformer focuses on one; but they all operate in a system which takes unfairness for granted. In our system, politicians are openly and legally bribed by anyone who can afford to do so, the public is daily inundated by a tidal wave of irrelevance and misinformation, elections are unfair and irrational. Is it any wonder, then, that all reform attempts end up, at best, in a compromise on any given issue between public and private interests?

My whole idea is simple. For the time being, specific and broad reform strategies must give way to a surgical approach. Before trying to cure one or another social ill, democratic reformers must see to it that their appeals to reason and justice reach the public, unfiltered and undistorted. If they want peace, freedom, enlightened foreign policy, environmental responsibility, social justice, devolution of political and economic power, or civil rights, they must go through the heartrending exercise of leaving these social ills alone for a while, forging a united front, and directing their attention on those defects in the political process that make these ills possible. Before trying to change the majority's way of thinking, they must change their own. They need to struggle exclusively and uncompromisingly for *fairness in politics*: comprehensive legislation that would ban private money from the political arena, make elections more rational and fair, and re-establish an open marketplace of ideas. They ought to do so not because venality, irrationality, and falsehood in Western politics are the most pressing social ills of our day—they are certainly not—but because their abatement gives the greatest promise of enhancing the human prospect. They need to take this indirect road because it may well be the best way of solving the one or another specific problem which is of greatest concern to them: in politics—unlike Euclidean geometry—the shortest distance from one point to another is not a straight line. They ought to do this because political reality is a three-dimensional interdependent web, not a two-dimensional collection of parallel lines.

This chapter will only draw a rough sketch of the needed Fairness in Politics Legislation and offer a few tentative reflections on this legislation's nature and rationale.

An exclusive struggle for fairness in politics enjoys distinct advantages. It amplifies the faint glimmers of reform by focusing them into a single point. It presupposes only an elementary commitment to fair play and democracy. By campaigning on one issue, reformers can draw into their camp people of good will from all shades of the political spectrum. A single-issue platform is easy to understand and hard to obfuscate. The struggle for fairness in politics will not have to start from scratch, for many reformers are already involved in one or another aspect of this struggle. Moreover, this struggle enjoys a measure of sympathy in Congress, other power centers, and the humanitarian camp as a whole.

We only need to remind ourselves of amateur sport competitions to see that the surgical reformer's indirect route is not as irrelevant as it appears on first sight. Suppose you belong to a basketball team which is eager to play against a slightly weaker team. Suppose you invited them to a match which they accepted, but only on the condition that your team fields three players (to their five) throughout the game. You might decide to accept this condition; if you are extremely lucky, you might even win. But cold logic suggests that your best path to victory is obtaining fair rules first and playing basketball second. Likewise, cold logic suggests that political duels stand the best chance of being won by changing first the dueling protocol.

Though political contests are played for greater stakes than athletic contests, they do not adhere to the same standards of fair play. Contenders for public office, for instance, are not allotted equal sums of money to spend on their campaigns, which means that they are not given equal access to the voters. As we have seen, such rules corrode the political process and throw much light on existing democracies' social ills. The "terrible pressures" a politician faces in our system, said a John F. Kennedy's ghostwriter, "discourage acts of political courage" and often drive him to "abandon or subdue his conscience."[11] Searching for campaign money," said a former U.S. Vice President, "is a disgusting, degrading, demeaning experience. It is about time we cleaned it up."[12]

The proposed legislation would altogether eliminate money and monetary pressures from our body politic. It would forbid politicians to accept money or its equivalents from any source other than the public treasury while running for office, while in office, and a few years after leaving office. All serious contenders for the same elected position would be provided with equal amounts of campaign funds.

As we have seen, elections are presently conducted like horse races. Politicians are sold in the same way Las Vegas sells its gambling and entertainment wares. Political candidates appeal to the voters' fears and prejudices, not to their reason and humanity. Flooded in a sea of irrelevant, trivial, and distracting information, voters are often oblivious to the real issues.

In addition to enfeebling moneyed interests, fairness in politics calls for rational elections. For instance, the needed legislation may provide voters with standardized pamphlets containing descriptions of candidates' policies and records. It may ban political advertisements which reduce candidates to spineless clowns (in the same way that commercials for cigarettes were expunged from our TV screens, and for similar reasons).

To judge policies and politicians, voters must be provided with objective information about them. To do their job well, politicians must confront the world as it is. In the U.S., neither voters nor politicians are confronted with the truths they need. As a result, Americans often elect to public office the wrong people who then pursue misguided policies. The causes of this information problem are clear enough. We do not expect a suspected embezzler to incriminate himself, and we do not chiefly depend upon what he says to convict or exonerate him. Why, then, should we expect any but the most outstanding statesmen to tell us or themselves the truth? Why should we depend upon what they choose to tell us to convict or exonerate them and their policies? Why should we depend on the mainstream media, hired experts, and educators to tell us all we need to know, if their access to information is limited, if they have been victims of lifelong indoctrination, and if truthfulness and objectivity do not coincide with their interests?

"The people cannot be safe without information," yet it is too much to expect the government, educational establishment, media, other organizations, and hired experts to tell us and themselves the truth. We must find other means of protecting impartiality and the democratic process. One solution to this problem may rely on the traditional democratic approach of checks, balances, and the separation of powers: those who are charged with the task of telling the truth should have no stake in it. The proposed legislation may, for instance, severely limit the freedom of the three traditional branches of government to collect and disseminate information. Instead, it may mandate the creation of an *independent* agency whose members are elected by the public and whose only task is to collect information and disseminate it to the public and government. Safeguards can be put in place so that this agency is judged on the basis of how well it uncovers and presents information to the public and the politicians, not on the basis of what information it uncovers.

The introduction of additional checks and balances is consistent with our political traditions. The semi-autonomous Federal Reserve System, for example, was established in 1913 to protect the dollar from politically motivated shenanigans. The time has arrived, I think, to safeguard democracy and survival by creating an even more autonomous information agency.

Another vital link in ensuring fairness in politics concerns the media. For instance, the proposed legislation might involve large-scale divestiture of media outlets. It might require the print and broadcast media to give considerable space to independent writers, announcers, agencies, public interest groups, and private citizens, and it would give the media no say about what goes into this space. The worrisome power of advertisers can be reduced through the creation of a central clearing house: advertisers would still be free to reach as many people as they can afford to, but the choice of the medium itself will be made by this public agency on a strictly random basis. Government news releases might be followed by highly critical analyses which would, among other things, question basic premises. The critics themselves might be chosen at random from an international pool of knowledgeable or concerned people, and not on the basis of conformity and subservience.

Under the best of circumstances, years will pass before political fairness changes our way of dealing with such issues as militarism, environmental decline, and needless poverty. Moreover, given the enormous complexity of human societies, a concerted struggle for fairness might fail or even backfire. Yet the burning question "Can humankind afford such ominous delays and risks?" is irrelevant. The only relevant question is: "Which strategy is likeliest to remove this multitude of perils in the shortest possible time?" There are no sure roads into a more secure future; the cataclysm may come no matter what we do. We can do no more than select the most promising road and travel it as fast as we can.

The pathetic masquerade going under the name of politics now, and which, if allowed to continue on its present course, might bring politics to an end, can be replaced by a more fair, rational, unbiased, democratic, and lasting political process. If the people who are aware and who care could somehow break away from village green politics; if they could come to see the interconnectedness of their problem to all others; if they could subordinate personal and organizational welfare to the common good; if, by some miracle, they could abandon their intuitive conception of political action; if they could single-mindedly and cooperatively pursue political fairness; and if our species' luck does not run out in the meantime; humanity might make a significant step forward.

Summary

Besides political activism, successful reform presupposes an optimal strategy. Parties espousing radically new programs are unlikely to achieve their goals. Taken as a whole, the strategy of fighting directly for the things one cares most about—despite its intuitive appeal and millions of well-meaning and dedicated practitioners—is counterproductive. Even if successful, the fights against the stealth bomber, America's lifeline to Guatemala's dictators, or the Diablo Canyon nuclear power plant, do not in the long run serve the cause of peace, freedom, and justice. In a political system that institutionalizes bribes, half-truths, and merchandizing, the struggles of broad-platform and specific reformers resemble wrestling matches in which one fighter must tie both hands behind his back.

Democracy may be capable of rational actions, but only if given a chance. Humanitarians should give it that chance by concentrating their scarce energies and resources on those defects in our way of doing politics which make otherwise sane human beings vote against their interests and convictions. The struggle against deep-seated structural flaws in our political system must precede the struggles against their terribly important surface manifestations. For the time being, such actions as civil disobedience, militancy, demonstrations, teach-ins, marches, or door-to-door campaigning should be directed only at eliminating money from politics, rationalizing elections, and providing institutional safeguards for the truth. Humanitarian organizations and individuals need to temporarily set aside their specific concerns and cooperatively and uncompromisingly struggle for fairness in politics. Despite their grave urgency, despite their apparent directness, simplicity, and relevance, most other actions divert precious resources from this crucial campaign for fairness.

NOTES AND REFERENCES

For informative, partially integrative, surveys of the Cold War, see: Cohen, Avner and Lee, Steven (eds). *Nuclear Weapons and the Future of Humanity* (1986). Kurtz, Lester R. *The Nuclear Cage* (1988). Malcolmson, Robert W. *Nuclear Fallacies* (1985). Parenti, Michael. *The Sword and the Dollar* (1989). Schwartz, William A. et al. *The Nuclear Seduction* (1990).

For the sake of brevity and convenience, in this book the term "Cold War" refers to the period 1945-1991. This should not be taken to imply that the Cold War started in 1945, that it ceased by 1992, or that something like it—against Russia or some other country(s)—will not continue long into the future.

Chapter 1: TOTALITARIANISM

1. *Khrushchev Remembers* (translated by Strobe Talbott, published by Little, Brown and Company; Boston, 1970).

a) p. 521.

b) pp. 367-368. Years later, Khrushchev remarked on Stalin's consent to the invasion: "I would have made the same decision myself if I had been in his place."

c) This gamble was taken, according to its author, despite the full understanding of the Soviet leadership "of what the consequences of putting the missiles on Cuba might be—namely, war with the United States" (p. 499). Even with the benefit of hindsight, Khrushchev still regarded his gamble as a "spectacular success" and a "triumph of Soviet foreign policy," which, by "bringing the world to the brink of atomic war," enabled the Soviets to win "a Socialist Cuba" (p. 504).

d) p. 152.

2. *East of Eden* (1963 edition), chap. 13, I.

3. One runs at times across statements like: "The reconciliation of man with the environment is a qualified success story" (Ashby, Eric. *Reconciling Man with the Environment*, 1978, p. 86). But, in either 1978 or 1992, such statements betray, at best, wishful thinking.

4. Jaspers, Karl. *The Future of Mankind* (translated from the 1956 German edition by E. B. Ashton), p. 4.

5. Because physical health and psychological well-being are more closely related to fate and personal circumstances than to politics, they are not included in the text as formal components of freedom. Obviously though, people who feel compelled to eat sand or who are dying from a painful lung cancer are not as free as their healthier counterparts.

6. Suetonius, Gaius. *The Lives of the Twelve Caesars* (2nd century, A.D.), bk. IV.

7. Al-Khalil, Samir. *Republic of Fear* (1990).

a) p. 275. b) p. 110.

8. Miller, Judith, and Mylroie, Laurie. *Saddam Hussein and the Crisis in the Gulf* (1990), pp. 37-38.

9. *The Practice and Theory of Bolshevism*, 1964 reprinting, p. 11. Russell goes on to say: "If a more just economic system were only attainable by closing men's minds against free inquiry, and plunging them back into the intellectual prison of the Middle Ages, I should consider the price too high."

In the text I occasionally follow Russell's characterization of Marxism as a religion, and for the same reasons (see his Chapter VIII, p. 70).

10. *The Christian Science Monitor*, November 15, 1983, p. 20.

11. Stockholm International Peace Research Institute. *World Armaments and Disarmament: SIPRI Yearbook 1983*, p. 117.

12. *The Bulletin of the Atomic Scientists*, November 1982, pp. 62-63.

13. Solzhenitsyn, Alexander I. *The Gulag Archipelago* (1974), vol. I, p. 69.

14. *Vanity Fair*, February 1990, p. 124.

15. Taubman, William, and Taubman, Jane. *Moscow Spring* (1989).
a) p. 185. b) p. 119.

16. Melville, Andrei and Lapidus, Gail W. (eds). *The Glasnost Papers* (1990), p. 161

17. Democritus, who flourished in the fifth century, B.C., puts it this way: "Poverty in a democracy is as much to be preferred to what is called prosperity under despots as freedom is to slavery." Quoted in: Russell, Bertrand. *A History of Western Philosophy* (1945), pt. I, chap. IX, p. 72.

18. Cited in: Kennedy, Robert and Weinstein, John M. (eds). *The Defense of the West* (1984), p. 43.

19. Parenti, Michael. *Inventing Reality* (1986), p. 142.

20. Smith, Hedrick. *The Russians* (1976).
a) p. 495. b) Stalin, quoted on p. 25.

21. CIA 1982 statistics, cited in: Dibb, Paul. *The Soviet Union* (1986), p. 2.

22. *The Current Digest of the Soviet Press* (selections from the Soviet press, translated into English).
a) Vol. 35, no. 25, (1983), p. 19.
b) Vol. 35, no. 33, (1983), pp. 26-27.
c) Vol. 35, no. 33, (1983), pp. 19-20. A *Rude Bravo* article condensed and paraphrased in *Pravda*, August 20, 1983.

23. For a more vivid example of the havoc such a system can create in some people's souls, see Yuri Trifonov's sensitive short story, *The Exchange*. In: Proffer, Carl and Proffer, Ellendea (eds). *The Ardis Anthology of Recent Russian Literature* (1976).

24. *Statistical Abstracts of the United States* (1988; 108th edition).
a) p. 808. b) p. 809.
c) Calculated from data in sections 13, 23. This comparison does not imply an endorsement of anti-ecological and anti-humanitarian agricultural practices in the USA. But these practices could also be found in the USSR, and the governments of both agreed that agricultural excellence could be best measured in terms of labor productivity and total output. Given these shared practices and assumptions, a comparison of the two systems tells us much about their relative efficiencies.

25. *The Detroit News*, December 23, 1990, pp. 3A, 7A.

26. Arthur Young, quoted in: Mill, J. S. *Principles of Political Economy* (1871 edition), bk. II, chap. VI, section 7.

27. May, Brian. *Russia, America, the Bomb and the Fall of Western Europe* (1984).

a) On pp. 69-70 May argues that while Soviet agriculture still suffers from "chronic Russian inefficiency, it is vastly more productive than the old system." For instance, farm workers made up 75 percent of the labor force before the revolution, but only 25 percent in the early 1980s, and grain production has, roughly, doubled. But he altogether misses the point when he concludes from this that "Soviet agriculture has been misrepresented." His comparison ignores the leaps made in agricultural technology since the October Revolution. The correct question is why were the improvements in Russia comparatively slight, not whether some improvements took place. Also, the meaningful comparison is not to the pre-revolutionary archaic system, but to contemporaneous agricultural systems. For instance, why was Israeli agriculture, which had its beginning roughly in the same period as Soviet agriculture, more efficient?

b) John Kenneth Galbraith in a 1981 article, cited on p. 136.

28. Miller, Wright. *Who are the Russians?* (1973), p. 159.

29. Developments in China lend additional support to this assertion. Privatization of Chinese agriculture contributed to steady and dramatic increases in total agricultural output. For example, in 1980 total output was 2.6 larger than in 1978. Bialer, Seweryn. *The Soviet Paradox* (1986), p. 252.

30. My sources, Hedrick Smith (above), and Andrei D. Sakharov (*My Country and the World*, 1976, p. 47), give a few conflicting details. According to Sakharov, for instance, Khudenko was sentenced for eight years. Note also that when writing about these and other specific events I don't try to adhere to scientific standards of admissible evidence. At least until 1985, deliberate lies and large-scale cover-ups often left no choice but to rely on hearsay. So any individual story could be incorrect in many details, and, for all I know, might have never taken place. But despite the inaccuracies and uncertainties, there is little doubt that the rough sketch I am portraying reflects historical realities.

31. Miller, William Green (ed). *Toward a More Civil Society?* (1989).

a) p. 5. b) p. 86. c) p. 201. d) p. 279. e) p. 157.

32. *Survival*, March 1990, pp. 108-109.

33. Quoted in: Aristotle. *Nicomachean Ethics*, book VI.

34. Morris, Charles R. *Iron Destinies, Lost Opportunities* (1988), p. 84.

35. Orwell, George. *Homage to Catalonia* (1938).

36. Medvedev, Zhores. *Soviet Science* (1978).

a) pp. 146-147.

b) Medvedev's view of the quality of Soviet science is far more favorable than the view presented in the text. His book also provides detailed descriptions of the thoroughgoing politicization of Soviet science.

37. Rubin, Barry. *Paved with Good Intentions* (1980), pp. 30-33. For a more favorable view of Soviet conduct during this episode, see Abrahamian, Ervand. *Iran Between Two Revolutions* (1982), pp. 210, 228.

38. *Khrushchev Remembers: The Glasnost Tapes* (1990), p. 55.

39. My account of the Winter War and of Finnish history is based on: Wuorinen, John H. *A History of Finland* (1965); Kirby, D. G. *Finland in*

the Twentieth Century (1979); Upton, Anthony F. *Finland in Crisis, 1940-41* (1964).

40. *Detroit Free Press*.
   a) October 26, 1989, p. 6A. b) October 27, 1989, p. 14A.
41. Bialer, Seweryn. *The Soviet Paradox* (1986), pp. 270-1. See also: Luttwak, Edward. *The Grand Strategy of the Soviet Union* (1983).
42. Dibb, Paul. *The Soviet Union* (1986).
   a) pp. 33, 39.
   b) p. 238. Another calculation arrives at an even higher estimate of Soviet subsidies—$100 billion between 1972 and 1981. Cited in: Luttwak, Edward N. *The Grand Strategy of the Soviet Union* (1983), p. 161.
43. A more recent calculation suggests that 1974 was a turning point from an economic asset to liability; that after peaking in 1980, the costs of empire declined; and that the importance of these costs has been exaggerated. See the Spechlers' article in: Menon, Rajan and Nelson, Daniel N. (eds). *Limits to Soviet Power* (1989).
44. *Parade Magazine*, March 4, 1984, pp. 10-11.
45. *Earth Island Journal*, Fall 1990, p. 10.
46. Asia Watch Committee. Quoted in: Szulc, Tad. *Then and Now* (1990), p. 466.
47. Thucydides. *The Peloponnesian War* (Benjamin Jowett's translation), bk I, 19.
48. Mikhail Gorbachev. Cited in: Lifton, Robert Jay and Markusen, Eric. *The Genocidal Mentality* (1990), p. 267.
49. Motyl, Alexander J. *Sovietology, Rationality, Nationality* (1990), p. 187.
50. Heisbourg, Francois (ed). *The Strategic Implications of Change in the Soviet Union* (1990), p. 21.
51. The causal link between democracy and social justice was already evident at the dawn of Athenian democracy. For example, Solon's reforms prohibited the enslavement of Athenian citizens who were unable to pay their debts. Later, legislative reforms provided for regular welfare payments to the poor.
52. Walt Whitman might have had something like this in mind when he wrote about "the democratic wisdom underneath, like solid ground for all" (see his poem, "The Commonplace").
53. As far as I am aware, the first clear repudiation of the myth of authoritarian efficiency, and the most powerful theoretical explanation of democracy's greater observable efficiency, can be found in Karl R. Popper's *The Open Society and its Enemies*. My discussion of this myth has been strongly influenced by Popper's work.

Chapter 2: CONSEQUENCES OF NUCLEAR WAR

1. From his poem: "A New World."
2. Barnaby, Frank and Thomas, Geoffrey (eds). *The Nuclear Arms Race—Control or Catastrophe?* (1982).
   a) pp. 7-16. b) p. 15. c) p. 170.
3. Stockholm International Peace Research Institute. *Nuclear Radiation in Warfare* (1981).

a) pp. 4-11. b) p. 14. c) p. 12. d) p. 88.

4. United States Department of Defense and Department of Energy (Glasstone, Samuel and Dolan, Philip J., eds). *The Effects of Nuclear Weapons* (1977; 3rd edition).

5. Congress of the United States, Office of Technology Assessment. *The Effects of Nuclear War* (1979).
a) p. 21. b) p. 35.

6. United Nations Report A/35/392. *Comprehensive Study on Nuclear Weapons* (1981).
a) parag. 152. b) parag. 153. c) parag. 163. d) parag. 260.

7. Goodwin, Peter. *Nuclear War, the Facts on Our Survival* (1981), p. 31.

8. A more pessimistic assessment of the wartime medical effects of ionizing radiation can be found in: Institute of Medicine, National Institute of Health. *The Medical Implications of Nuclear War* (1986).

9. Kazutoshi Hando in: The Pacific War Research Society. *The Day Man Lost: Hiroshima, 6 August 1945* (1972), p. 14.

10. The Committee for the Compilation of Materials on Damage Caused by the Atomic Bombs in Hiroshima and Nagasaki. *Hiroshima and Nagasaki: The Physical, Medical, and Social Effects of the Atomic Bombings* (1981).
a) p. 14. b) pp. 7-11.

11. Peterson, Jeannie (ed). *The Aftermath* (1983).
a) p. 16. b) p. 19.

12. Hachiya, Michihiko. *Hiroshima Diary* (1955).
a) p. 4. b) p. 8.

13. Lifton, Robert J. *Death in Life* (1967).
a) p. 27. b) p. 29.

14. McNamara, Robert. *Blundering into Disaster* (1986), p. 5.

15. O'Keefe, Bernard J. *Nuclear Hostages* (1983).
a) p. 197. b) p. 231.

16. Clarke, Magnus. *The Nuclear Destruction of Britain* (1982).

17. United States Council on Environmental Quality and the Department of State. *The Global 2000 Report to the President of the U.S.* (1980), vol. II.
a) p. 356. b) p. 248.

18. Medvedev, Zhores. A. *Soviet Science* (1978), p. 95.

19. Medvedev, Zhores. A. *The Legacy of Chernobyl* (1990), p. 280.

20. Komarov, B. *The Destruction of Nature in the Soviet Union* (1980), p. 103.

21. Miller, G. Tyler, Jr. *Living in the Environment* (1987; 5th edition), p. 371.

22. Suvorov, Viktor. *Inside the Soviet Army* (1982), p. 59.

23. H. J. Muller, quoted in: Moody, Paul, A. *Genetics of Man* (1975; second edition), p. 427.

24. *New York Times*, January 23, 1990, p. B5.

25. National Research Council. *The Effects on the Atmosphere of a Major Nuclear Exchange* (1985).

26. London, Julius and White, Gilbert F. (eds). *American Association for the Advancement of Science Selected Symposium: The Environmental Effects of Nuclear War* (1984).
a) p. 125. b) p. 91 c) p. 123. d) p. 128.

27. *Environment*, June 1988, p. 13.

28. American Chemical Society. *Cleaning our Environment: A Chemical Perspective* (1978; 2nd edition), p. 131.

29. *Scientific American*, January 1988, pp. 30-36.

30. *Earth Island Journal*, Fall 1990, p. 8.

31. United States Surgeon General. *Healthy People* (1979).

32. *Historical Statistics of the United States, Colonial Times to 1970*, Part 1, p. 55.

33. Levi, Werner. *The Coming End of War* (1981), p. 8.

34. Schwartz, William A. et al. *The Nuclear Seduction* (1990).

   a) p. 127.

   b) p. 4. The number of cities depends on the number of missiles (24 in the new submarines, 16 in the older ones) and the area which can be covered by warheads launched from a single missile. Hence, the number of missiles (with 7 warheads for new missile submarines, 10 for the old) must be taken into account when calculating the number of targeted cities. Schwartz et al.'s calculation of 168 is probably too high.

   c) pp. 210-211. d) pp. 128-129.

   e) pp. 212-213. All quotes are Raymond Garthoff's.

35. Pringle, Peter and Arkin, William. *SIOP, the Secret U.S. Plan for Nuclear War* (1983), p. 239.

36. Polmar, Norman. *The American Submarine* (1983; second edition), p. 131.

37. Catudal, Honore M. *Nuclear Deterrence—Does it Deter?* (1985), pp. 480-481.

38. See Nikita S. Khrushchev's fascinating account in: *Khrushchev Remembers: The Glasnost Tapes* (1990). Some analysts believe that practical nuclear parity existed in 1962 (e.g., Schwartz, William A. et al. *The Nuclear Seduction*, 1990, pp. 52-53).

39. Former U.S. Senator J. W. Fulbright, quoted in: *The Sunday Oregonian*, November 20, 1983, p. F3.

40. Kennedy, Robert. *Thirteen Days* (1969).

   a) p. 111. b) pp. 111-112. o) p. 48. d) quoted on p. 210.

41. Dillon, G. M. (ed). *Defence Policy Making* (1988), p. 76.

42. John Steinbruner persuasively argues that such incidents "cannot be explained away simply as unusual mistakes . . . They reflect rather the sort of thing that must be expected to happen when high crisis strikes the very complicated, inevitably decentralized, very large organizations that constitute modern strategic forces." In: Griffiths, Franklyn and Polanyi, John C. (eds). *The Dangers of Nuclear War* (1979), p. 39.

43. Bundy, McGeorge. *Danger and Survival* (1988).

   a) p. 446. b) p. 444.

44. Chomsky, Noam. *Necessary Illusions* (1989), p. 274.

45. A similar series of coincidental events took place during the 1956 Suez crisis. See: Bracken, Paul. *The Command and Control of Nuclear Forces* (1983), pp. 65-68.

46. Gregory, Shaun. *The Hidden Cost of Deterrence* (1990).

   a) p. 196.

47. Cox, John. *Overkill* (1977).

   a) p. 118. b) p. 115.

48. *Parade Magazine*, August 14, 1983.

49. *Common Cause Magazine*, 1984, vol. 10, no. 1, p. 15.

50. Miller, William Green (ed). *Toward a More Civil Society?* (1989), pp. xvi-xix.

51. A few other variations of accidental war are described in: Wilson, Andrew. *The Disarmer's Handbook* (1983), Chapter 15. For an attempt at a theoretical study of conditions which might lead to unintentional nuclear war, see: Frei, Daniel, with Catrina, Christian (United Nations Institute for Disarmament Research). *Risks of Unintentional Nuclear War* (1982).

52. In: Egner, Robert E. and Denonn, Lester E. *The Basic Writings of Bertrand Russell* (1961), p. 732. See also Pierre Elliott Trudeau's comments in *The Bulletin of the Atomic Scientists*, February 1985, p. 13.

Chapter 3: COSTS OF THE ARMS RACE

1. From the *Brothers Karamazov*, Book V, Chapter IV. Alyosha Karamazov's answer to this question is: "No, I wouldn't consent."

2. *Newsweek*, July 11, 1988, pp. 42-44.

3. Schwartz, William A. et al. *The Nuclear Seduction* (1990), p. 177.

4. Gregory, Shaun. *The Hidden Cost of Deterrence* (1990), p. 60.

5. Stockholm International Peace Research Institute. *World Armaments and Disarmament: SIPRI Yearbook.*
   a) 1982; pp. 363-389. b) 1984; p. 69. c) 1989; p. 10.

6. *Natural History*, November 1990, p. 35.

7. The International Institute for Strategic Studies. *The Military Balance* 1987/88, p. 238.

8. *Statistical Abstracts of the United States* (1988, 108th edition).
   a) pp. 43, 314. b) p. 323.

9. Vidal, Gore. *At Home* (1988), pp. 127-128.

10. Brown, Harold. *Thinking About National Security* (1983), pp. 216-217.

11. Jacobsen, Carl G. *The Nuclear Era* (1982), p. 112.

12. Ruth Sivard, cited in: *Corvallis Gazette-Times*, March 29, 1984.

13. Miller, G. Tyler, Jr. *Living in the Environment* (1990; 6th edition).
   a) estimated from data on pp. 267, 270.
   b) p. 268. c) p. 466. d) pp. 270-271.

14. Some economists agree with my more cautious conclusions. For instance,

There is a strong temptation to link the poor performance of both Western and socialist economies in recent years with the size of their military budgets. There is always an attraction in simple, single explanations for a miscellany of troubles. . . . However, except when there are major changes in trend in military expenditure, it is a mistake to consider that the military sector is responsible for such macro-economic developments as upswings in prices or in unemployment. In particular, the worsening economic performance in the industrial economies during the last decade cannot properly be attributed to changes in military spending. . . . The main economic point to make about military expenditure is a very simple one: it uses up resources which might alternatively be employed to provide consumer satisfactions.

Frank Blackaby in: Ball, Nicole and Leitenberg, Milton (eds). *The Structure of the Defense Industry* (1983), pp. 7, 19, 20.

15. Medvedev, Zhores A. *Nuclear Disaster in the Urals* (1979). For an update, see: Medvedev, Zhores A. *The Legacy of Chernobyl* (1990), pp. 279-286.

16. *Detroit Free Press*, December 7, 1988, p. 9A.

17. Worldwatch Institute. *State of the World 1991*.
   a) p. 139. b) p. 143.

18. *Earth Island Journal*, Fall 1990, p. 8

19. Pringle, Peter and Arkin, William. *SIOP, the Secret U.S. Plan for Nuclear War* (1983), p. 231.

20. General Maxwell D. Taylor, quoted in: Brodie, Bernard. *War and Politics* (1973), p. 193.

21. Yarmolinsky, Adam and Foster, Gregory D. *Paradoxes of Power* (1983).
   a) p. 68. b) p. 94.

22. At times the diminution in academic freedom is blatant. Can we really expect the truth to emerge from the pen of scholars who accepted the Defense Intelligence Agency's invitation "to bid on contracts for third-world research"? (*The Chronicle of Higher Education*, May 8, 1985, p. 1).

23. Fulbright, J. W. *The Pentagon Propaganda Machine* (1970).
   a) p. 11. b) pp. 157, 141, 142.

Chapter 4: WEAPONS OF THE COLD WAR

1. From the Foreword to the 1969 Perennial Classic edition (Harper & Row) of *Brave New World*, p. xi.

2. United Nations Report A/35/392. *Comprehensive Study on Nuclear Weapons* (1981).
   a) parag. 11. b) parag. 74.

3. Schwartz, William A. et al. *The Nuclear Seduction* (1990), p. 183.

4. The U.S. military was exploring the use of recombinant DNA technology in biological warfare as early as 1982. *Nature* (1982), vol. 297, pp. 527; 615-616. See also: Piller, Charles and Yamamoto, Keith R. *Gene Wars* (1988).

5. U.S. Department of Defense. *Annual Report. Fiscal Year 1982*, p. 37.

6. Tsipis, Kosta. *Arsenal* (1983), p. 122.

7. Bracken, Paul. *The Command and Control of Nuclear Forces* (1983).

8. Jasani, Bhupendra (ed). *Outer Space—A New Dimension of the Arms Race* (1982).
   a) p. 239. b) p. 119. c) pp. 41-63.

Chapter 5: STRATEGIC THINKING IN THE UNITED STATES

1. Mill, J. S. *Principles of Political Economy* (1871, 2nd edition); from the section: *Preliminary Remarks*.

2. Frankel, C. The Specter of Eugenics. In: Ostheimer, N. C. and Ostheimer, J. M. (eds). *Life or Death—Who Controls?* (1976), pp. 23-24.

3. Popper, Karl R. *The Open Society and its Enemies* (1966; 5th edition), vol. 1, chap. 10, section v, p. 189.

4. Bottome, Edgar. *The Balance of Terror* (second edition; 1986), p. xiv.

5. *Detroit Free Press*, June 9, 1990, p. 1A.

6. *San Francisco Chronicle*, May 30, 1990, p. 1A.

7. Chomsky, Noam. *Necessary Illusions* (1989).

8. Rumble, Greville. *The Politics of Nuclear Defence* (1985), p. 123.

9. Luttwak, Edward. *Strategy* (1987), p. 206.

10. Holdren, John P. in: Cohen, Avner and Lee, Steven. *Nuclear Weapons and the Future of Humanity* (1986), p. 46.

11. Gray, Colin S. and Payne, Keith. *Foreign Policy*, vol. 39 (summer 1980), p. 14.

12. Ronald Reagan, quoted in: *The Oregonian*, November 27, 1983, p. A2.

13. Quoted in: Bundy, McGeorge. *Danger and Survival* (1988), p. 573.

14. *The Chronicle of Higher Education*, May 4, 1988, p. A8.

15. *USA Today*, September 27, 1989.

16. If they managed to develop them at all—by the late 1980s, for instance, the good Soviets were just overcoming the challenge of solid fuels.

17. United States Department of Defense. *Annual Report, Fiscal Year 1982*, p. 44.

18. Such as the cruise missiles he seemed to be so fond of, again ignoring nuclear overkill and the likeliest outcome: more cruise missiles and less security for both sides.

19. A more detailed exposition of Harold Brown's doctrine of appearances can be found in his *Thinking About National Security* (1983), pp. 83-84, 265. Brown's views are shared by many others. For example, a former head of the Arms Control and Disarmament Agency testified in a 1983 Senate hearing: "The nuclear weapon is primarily a political, not a military force . . . the risk of nuclear war is far less today than the risk that the unity of the West will be destroyed . . . by psychological and political pressures emanating from the nuclear balance." But despite its many well-paid adherents, this concern is plainly illogical: "If . . . there was indeed a political wound from the alleged Soviet superiority . . . it was a self-inflicted wound. Instead of constantly referring to a non-existent . . . vulnerability, US spokesmen could simply have pointed out that . . . superiority, if it existed, had no military value . . . The political effect, such as it is, was created by the same people who then proceeded to stress its importance." See: Stockholm International Peace Research Institute. *World Armaments and Disarmament: SIPRI Yearbook 1984*, p. 42.

20. Question: How many bombs would have hit Moscow in a retaliatory strike after the Soviets have destroyed in a disarming first strike all the American nuclear bombs and delivery vehicles they possibly could? Answer: 60. See McGeorge Bundy, in: Bertram, Christoph (ed). *Strategic Deterrence in a Changing Environment* (1981), p. 112.

21. General Brent Scowcroft, Chairman. *Report of the President's Commission on Strategic Forces* (1983).

22. Stockholm International Peace Research Institute. *World Armaments and Disarmament; SIPRI Yearbook* (1984).

a) p. 383.

b) pp. 417, 418. Raymond L. Garthoff (in: Neidle, Alan F. *Nuclear Negotiations*, 1982, p. 24), former U.S. disarmament negotiator and ambassador to Bulgaria, is equally blunt on this point.

[The] theoretical possibility that about 90 percent of American ICBMs could be destroyed by a Soviet first strike . . . would by no means eliminate a very substantial American capability to strike the Soviet Union in retaliation . . . [and] is less damaging to our strategic position than would be the reverse for the Soviet Union.

23. Hachiya, Michihiko. *Hiroshima Diary* (1955), p. 48.

24. *Time*, January 1, 1990, pp. 67-68.

25. Garthoff, Raymond L. *Deterrence and the Revolution in Soviet Military Doctrine* (1990), pp. 199-200.

26. Catudal, Honore M. *Soviet Nuclear Strategy from Stalin to Gorbachev* (1988), pp. 165-173.

27. A brief review of American strategic thinking by the late Bernard Brodie—the most highly regarded American strategist—can be found in his: The development of nuclear strategy. In: Brodie, Bernard, et al. (eds). *National Security and International Stability* (1983), pp. 5-22. Until fairly recently, this book has been one of a handful in which Soviet officials were invited to air their views. Like religion and love, democracy is easy to preach but exceedingly hard to practice.

28. *Detroit Free Press*, March 2, 1990, p. 9A.

Chapter 6: THE MILITARY BALANCE

1. Quoted in: *The Bulletin of the Atomic Scientists*, March 1983, p. 2.

2. Cox, Arthur M. *Russian Roulette* (1982).

a) quoted on p. 101.

b) Excerpted from Arbatov's commentary, pp. 179-180.

3. Quoted in: O'Keefe, Bernard J. *Nuclear Hostages* (1983), p. 161.

4. Quoted in: *Issues in Science and Technology*, Spring 1988, p. 26.

5. *The Bulletin of the Atomic Scientists*.

a) October 1983, p. 29. b) October 1983, pp. 28-32. c) April 1983, pp. 45-46. d) June 1988, p. 56. e) July/August 1988, p. 56. f) December 1982, p. 48. g) October 1983, p. 30.

6. According to President Carter, "Just one of our relatively invulnerable . . . [missile] submarines—less than two percent of our total nuclear force of submarines, aircraft, and landbased missiles—carries enough warheads to destroy every large and medium-sized city in the Soviet Union. Our deterrent is overwhelming." Quoted in: Capra, Fritjof. *The Turning Point* (1982), p. 240.

7. Pringle, Peter and Arkin, William. *SIOP, the Secret U.S. Plan for Nuclear War* (1983), p. 163.

8. Suvorov, Viktor. *Inside the Soviet Army* (1982).
  a) pp. 232-233. b) p. 245. c) p. 239. d) pp. 239-245.

9. According to the Association of American Universities, "the Reagan Administration's efforts to restrict public access to various types of information have hindered scientific progress, damaged the nation's economy and security, and eroded academic freedom." Report summary in: *The Chronicle of Higher Education*, March 30, 1988.

10. Holloway, David. *The Soviet Union and the Arms Race* (1983).
  a) see for example, pp. 84-86. b) pp. 134-140. c) quoted on p. 14.

11. Jacobsen, Carl G. *The Nuclear Era* (1982), pp. 25-26.

12. According to former President Carter, if the President's goal "is to rapidly escalate the American defense budgets, then those are the kind of estimates he will get." (*New York Times*, March 2, 1986, p. 32.) A few other examples of institutional distortions are given in Chapter 7. Additional instructive examples can be found in: Daniel, Donald C. (ed.) *International Perceptions of the Superpower Military Balance* (1978), pp. 21-28.

13. Collins, John M. and Cordesman, Anthony H. *Imbalance of Power* (1978).
  a) All quotations are from Cordesman's analysis, pp. xv-xxviii.
  b) cited on pp. 108-109. c) pp. 23-24. d) p. 172.

14. Garthoff, Raymond, L. *Perspectives on the Strategic Balance* (1983).
  a) p. 7. b) pp. 17, 18, 21.
  c) pp. 27-28. All this is not meant to dismiss static indicators, but merely to place in them in a proper perspective. After all, they did decide the outcome of the Winter War and they undoubtedly contributed to Soviet victory in World War II.

15. The International Institute for Strategic Studies. *The Military Balance*.
  a) 1982/83. b) 1987/88, p. 230.

16. Peterson, Jeannie. *The Aftermath* (1983).

17. United Nations Report A/35/392. *Comprehensive Study on Nuclear Weapons* (1981).

18. Barnaby, Frank and Thomas, Geoffrey (eds). *The Nuclear Arms Race—Control or Catastrophe?* (1982).

19. Stockholm International Peace Research Institute. *Nuclear Radiation in Warfare* (1981).

20. Gervasi, Tom. *The Myth of Soviet Military Supremacy* (1986).
  a) p. 338. In late 1985, according to Gervasi, the Soviet Union had some 7,865 deliverable strategic warheads and the U.S. had 13,761; giving the U.S. a 75 percent advantage.
  b) p. 397. Assuming a complete surprise attack by either side and neither side firing its missiles before the first wave of incoming missiles reaches its targets, Congressional Budget Office statistics suggest that the survivability ratio in 1982 was one to nine (601/5316) in favor of the U.S.

21. Garthoff, Raymond L. *Deterrence and the Revolution in Soviet Military Doctrine* (1990), p. 131.

22. Brodie, Bernard et al. (eds). *National Security and International Stability* (1983), p. 14.

23. Bundy, McGeorge. *Danger and Survival* (1988), pp. 353-354.

24. Snow, Donald M. *The Nuclear Future* (1983), pp. 49-50.

25. Menon, Rajan and Nelson, Daniel N. (eds). *Limits to Soviet Power* (1989).

   a) pp. 11-12. b) p. 212. c) p. 171. d) p. 11.

26. Polmar, Norman. *The American Submarine* (1983; second edition), p. 131.

27. *Scientific American*, November 1982, p. 57.

28. In fact, one could argue that the Soviets' strategic "triad" consisted of only one whole leg (land-based intercontinental ballistic missiles, one half leg (submarines), and one quarter leg (bombers), yielding a total of less than two legs. Conversely, one could argue that the West's "triad" was in reality a seven-legged monster: the three traditional legs; cruise missiles; bombers stationed at sea, Western Europe and Korea; the French nuclear arsenal; and the British arsenal.

29. Israel reportedly developed "a ballistic missile able to reach the Soviet Union." Schwartz, William A. et al. *The Nuclear Seduction* (1990), p. 175.

30. National Academy of Sciences. *Nuclear Arms Control* (1985), p. 137. See also: Tsipis, Kosta. *Arsenal* (1983), pp. 164-166.

31. United States Department of Defense. *Annual Report, Fiscal Year 1982.*

   a) p. 47. b) p. 29. c) p. 89.

32. Luttwak, Edward. *Strategy* (1987).

   a) p. 206.

33. *Time*, January 1, 1990, p. 67.

34. See Michael T. Klare's article in: Menon, Rajan and Nelson, Daniel N. (eds). *Limits to Soviet Power* (1989).

35. "Static peacetime inputs alone are very poor indicators of dynamic wartime . . . performance." Epstein, Joshua M. *Measuring Military Power* (1984), p. 131.

36. Steven L. Canby in: Harkavy, Robert and Kolodziej, Edward A. (eds). *American Security Policy and Policy-Making* (1980), p. 98.

37. Commander of the U.S. Army in Europe was disappointed "to hear people talk about the overwhelming Soviet conventional military strength. We can defend the borders of Western Europe with what we have. I've never asked for a larger force." Quoted in: Knelman, F. H. *Reagan, God, and the Bomb* (1985), p. 197. For more detailed discussions of the myth of Soviet conventional superiority see: Cockburn, Andrew. *The Threat* (1983). Dibb, Paul. *The Soviet Union* (1986), pp. 156-167. Catudal, Honore M. *Nuclear Deterrence—Does it Deter?* (1985), pp. 224-233. The International Institute for Strategic Studies. *The Military Balance 1987/88*, pp. 226-232. Morris, Charles R. *Iron Destinies, Lost Opportunities* (1988), pp. 418-434.

38. Stockholm International Peace Research Institute. *World Armaments and Disarmament: SIPRI Yearbook* (1983).

   a) pp. 154-157. b) p. 265.

39. Stanley Sienkiewicz, in: Brown, James and Snyder, William P. (eds). *The Regionalization of Warfare* (1985), pp. 85-86. In Sienkiewicz' view, the following factors contributed to this outcome: the superior training, professionalism, and motivation of Israeli pilots and soldiers, superiority of

U.S.-manufactured weapons, better surveillance and warning systems, and the element of surprise.

Another analyst goes farther. The chief cause of the "continued overwhelming success of the Israelis against enormous numerical odds" is not, he suggests, "Arab incompetence," but the "enormous fighting edge" Israel's Western weapons had over Syria's Soviet weapons (Morris, Charles R. *Iron Destinies, Lost Opportunities*, 1988, p. 390). The West's decisive superiority in the Persian Gulf War lends further support to this view.

40. Bertram, Christoph (ed). *America's Security in the 1980s* (1982).

a) p. 41

b) p. 42. Similarly, in 1981 the Navy Secretary stated that the U.S. Navy was "far superior in both numbers and quality." Quoted in: Knelman, F. H. *Reagan, God, and the Bomb* (1985), p. 197.

41. The Boston Study Group. *The Price of Defense* (1979), p. 24.

42. Jacobsen, Carl G. *Soviet Strategic Initiatives* (1979), p. 135.

43. Bialer, Seweryn. *The Soviet Paradox* (1986).

a) p. 69. b) p. 63. c) p. 263.

44. Herodotus. *The Persian Wars* (George Rawlinson's translation), bk. v, parag. 78.

45. Alone, the British, French, or Chinese nuclear forces "would be capable of inflicting tremendous damage against urban targets." National Academy of Sciences. *Nuclear Arms Control* (1985), p. 16.

46. "It is fair to regard the Warsaw Pact as more a symbol of Soviet weakness than of Soviet strength. . . . there is little about which Moscow or East European rulers can be fully assured in the Warsaw Pact." Daniel N. Nelson in: Nelson, Daniel N. (ed). *Soviet Allies* (1984), pp. 266-267.

47. Solzhenitsyn, Alexander I. *The Gulag Archipelago* (1974), vol. 1.

a) pp. 261-262. This could be a conservative estimate. Another writer believes that, by war's end, *one million* Russian soldiers and officers were fighting against the Soviet Army (Suvorov, Viktor. *Inside the Soviet Army*, 1982, p. 239).

b) We may note, in passing, history's strange ways. According to Solzhenitsyn (p. 159), Khrushchev's oldest son died in a penal battalion, a personal tragedy which probably contributed to Khrushchev's de-Stalinization campaign.

48. Luttwak, Edward N. *The Pentagon and the Art of War* (1986).

a) p. 191.

b) Quotations are from pages 21, 18, 188, 191, 192, 19, 20. For two actual examples of the American military's state of decay, see Luttwak's description of the 1983 Grenada invasion (pp. 51-58) and his analysis of the Air Force Systems Command (pp. 166-180). It is too early to tell whether the swift victory in the Persian Gulf War was achieved *despite* this decay.

49. McPherson, Karen A. in: Edmonds, Martin. (ed). *Central Organizations of Defense*, pp. 213, 218, 219.

50. Dillon, G. M. *Defence Policy Making* (1988), p. 67.

51. Parkinson, C. Northcote. *Parkinson's Law* (1957).

52. Cockburn, Andrew. *The Threat* (1983). All quotations are from pp. 184, 44, 86, 236.

53. Medvedev, Zhores A. *Soviet Science* (1978), pp. 146-147.

54. *Khrushchev Remembers* (translated by Strobe Talbott, published by Little, Brown and Company; Boston, 1970), p. 343.

55. Such misinformation is occasionally found in surprising quarters. See, for example, Bottome, Edgar. *The Balance of Terror* (1986 revised edition); Medvedev, Zhores A. *Soviet Science* (1978).

56. *Armed Forces Journal International*, August 1983, p. 68.

Chapter 7: HISTORY OF THE COLD WAR

1. Wallace, Henry A. *Toward World Peace* (1948), pp. 4, 46.

2. Quoted in: Nathan, Otto and Norden, Heinz (eds). *Einstein on Peace* (1960), pp. 538-539.

3. Berlin, Isaiah. *Historical Inevitability* (1954), p. 53.

4. Solzhenitsyn, Alexander. *Warning to the West* (1976), p. 74.

5. Reported by Jerome B. Wiesner in: Tsipis, Kosta et al. (eds). *Arms Control Verification* (1986), p. xiv.

6. Krass, Allan S. *Verification: How Much Is Enough?* (1985), p. 253.

7. Zuckerman, Solly. *Nuclear Illusion and Reality* (1982).
   a) pp. 122-125. b) p. 118.

8. *The Bulletin of the Atomic Scientists*, March 1985, p. 9.

9. Seaborg, Glenn T. *Kennedy, Khrushchev, and the Test Ban* (1981).
   a) Averell W. Harriman, quoted on p. 242. b) p. 4. c) p. 9.

10. Leontief, Wassily W. The distribution of work and income. *Scientific American*, September 1982, pp. 188-204.

11. Friedman, Milton. *Capitalism and Freedom* (1962).

12. Heilbroner, Robert L. *The Limits of American Capitalism* (1966).

13. Ball, Nicole, and Leitenberg, Milton. (eds). *The Structure of the Defense Industry* (1983), p. 47.
   a) Judith Reppy on p. 47. b) David Holloway on p. 75.

14. Quoted in: Collins, John M. *U.S.-Soviet Military Balance 1980-1985* (1985), p. 9.

15. *Time*, January 1, 1990.
   a) p. 69. b) p. 72. c) p. 68. d) p. 70.

16. Garthoff, Raymond L. *Deterrence and the Revolution in Soviet Military Doctrine* (1990).
   a) for a brief review, see pp. 186-189. b) pp. 199-200.

17. Brown, Harold. *Thinking about National Security* (1983), p. 187.

18. Strobe Talbott, diplomatic correspondent for *Time Magazine*, summarized the record (see: Nye, Joseph S., Jr. *The Making of America's Soviet Policy*, 1984, p. 205):

> Only . . . when they have felt less threatened by their external enemies have the Soviet leaders decided that they could be more lenient toward . . . their own people . . . Only in such moments have they been able to tolerate cultural innovations, economic experimentation, and some very rudimentary political pluralism. The possibility that the United States can contribute to the amelioration of the Soviet system by the reduction of Soviet-American tensions is one of the few positive

lessons for the future that emerges from the otherwise erratic, perplexing, and rather dismal history of the relationship.

Sovietologist Seweryn Bialer (*The Soviet Paradox*, 1986, p. 120) concurs: "In the Soviet Union, hard international times almost always produce hard domestic lines."

It is thus possible to argue that the mellowing of Soviet domestic and foreign policies in the mid 1950s and 1980s took place *despite* the harsh international climate the Eisenhower and Reagan years created. Still other analysts believe that Soviet immigration policies are shaped for the most part by domestic, rather than international, factors. See Laurie P. Salitan's article in: Bialer, Seweryn (ed). *Politics, Society, and Nationality Inside Gorbachev's Russia* (1989).

19. Smith, Hedrick. *The Russians* (1976), chap. 20, p. 500.

20. Holloway, David. *The Soviet Union and the Arms Race* (1983).

   a) p. 15. b) Margaret Gowing, 1977, quoted on p. 20. c) pp. 26-27.

21. Bundy, McGeorge. *Danger and Survival* (1988), p. 117.

Despite the pleas on his behalf by some of Churchill's closest associates and advisors, Bohr waited more than a month before being granted an interview with the British Prime Minister. The rude ending was characteristic of the meeting as a whole. Churchill's reply to Bohr's request for permission to send him a memorandum on the subject was: "It will be an honour for me to receive a letter from you, but not about politics." (Cited in: Lieberman, Joseph I. *The Scorpion and the Tarantula*, 1970, p. 35). If nothing else, Churchill's conduct, and this reply, should give pause to those of us who have been taught to uphold Churchill as an exemplary champion of freedom.

This episode is characteristic of the tragic schism between politicians and their scientists-servants. In a book written before the outbreak of World War I, H. G. Wells presciently wrote:

> Destruction was becoming so facile that any little body of malcontents could use it; it was revolutionising the problems of police and internal rule. Before the last war began it was a matter of common knowledge that a man could carry about in a handbag an amount of latent energy sufficient to wreck half a city. These facts were before the minds of everybody; the children in the streets knew them. And yet the world still . . . "fooled around" with the paraphernalia and pretensions of war. It is only by realising this profound, this fantastic divorce between the scientific and intellectual movement on the one hand and the world of the lawyer-politician on the other that the men of a later time can hope to understand this preposterous state of affairs. (Wells, H. G. *The World Set Free*, 1914, Chapter 2, Section, 5).

Bertrand Russell:

> It is the custom among those who are called "practical" men to condemn any man capable of a wide survey as a visionary: no man is thought worthy of a voice in politics unless he ignores or does not know nine tenths of the most important relevant facts. (In: Nathan, Otto and Norden Heinz, eds. *Einstein on Peace*, 1960, p. xv.)

Martin J. Sherwin believes that Bohr's proposals "reveal more than the insights and oversights of an individual scientist; they represent the transfer of the scientific ideal into the realm of international politics." In: Graebner, Norman A. (ed). *The National Security* (1986), p. 111.

Albert Szent-Gyorgyi (in: *Annual Review of Biochemistry*, 1963, vol. 32, p. 13) goes farther:

> I have touched upon two facets of science, its ways of thinking and the tools it creates. The danger of our days is that politics has run away with the tools, leaving the way of thinking behind. The forces created by science can be handled only by the mentality which created them.

22. O'Keefe, Bernard J. *Nuclear Hostages* (1983).
   a) p. 122. b) Harry Truman, quoted on p. 130. c) p. 218.
23. Lieberman, Joseph I. *The Scorpion and the Tarantula* (1970).
   a) pp. 194-195. b) p. 273.
24. Hamilton, Michael P. (ed). *To Avoid Catastrophe* (1977).
   a) p. 27. b) p. 36. c) p. 40.
25. Bundy, McGeorge. *Danger and Survival* (1988).
   a) p. 177. b) p. 203.
26. Herken, Gregg. *The Winning Weapon* (1980), p. 171.
27. Myrdal, Alva. *The Game of Disarmament* (1976).
   a) p. 75. b) pp. 76-77.
28. Brodie, Bernard et al. (eds). *National Security and International Stability* (1983).
   a) pp. 327-356. b) paraphrased on p. 336.
29. Stein, Jonathan B. *From H-bomb to Star Wars* (1984).
30. Noel-Baker, Philip. *The Arms Race* (1958).
   a) The title of this section is taken from Chapter 2 of Noel-Baker's book.
   b) quoted on pp. 21-22. c) p. 234.
31. Paterson, Thomas G. et al. *American Foreign Policy* (1977).
   a) p. 489. Khrushchev's explanation for reaching this accord can be found in: *Khrushchev Remembers: The Glasnost Tapes* (1990), pp. 72-80.
   b) quoted on p. 490.
32. Quoted in: Cox, John. *Overkill* (1977), p. 177.
33. A case by case refutation of mainstream historians' inventions of reality will take a few lifetimes, thousands of pages, and voluminous yearly updates. One typical concoction can be found in: Stoessinger, John G. *The Might of Nations* (1979; *sixth* edition), pp. 395-396.
34. Frankland, Mark. *Khrushchev* (1967).
   a) p. 166. b) p. 169.
35. Graebner, Norman A. (ed). *The National Security* (1986), p. 71.
36. *Memories*, April/May 1990, pp. 64, 66.
37. Neal, Fred W. (ed). *Detente or Debacle* (1979).
   a) George Kistiakowsky, p. 63. b) p. 100.
38. Suvorov, Viktor. *Inside the Soviet Army* (1982).
39. National Academy of Sciences. *Nuclear Arms Control* (1985).
   a) p. 193. Including the number of unmanned seismic stations, pro-

cedures for their installation and operations, and practical rules governing on-site inspections.

b) p. 203. c) p. 86.

40. Alan F. Neidle (in: Neidle, Alan F., ed. *Nuclear Negotiations*, 1982, p. 77), a former ACDA official, believes that the Soviets made "some very extraordinary concessions." Those involved in these negotiations, he adds, "including myself, believe that the Soviets were genuinely serious."

41. Sykes, Lynn R. and Evernden, Jack F. The verification of a comprehensive test ban. *Scientific American*, October 1982.

42. Stockholm International Peace Research Institute. *World Armaments and Disarmament: SIPRI Yearbook.*

a) 1983; p. 568. b) 1983; p. 569. c) 1990; p. 51. d) 1983; pp. 533-534.

43. *Sane World*, September/October, 1985.

44. Kaufmann, William W. and Korb, Lawrence, J. *The 1990 Defense Budget* (1989), p. 3.

45. Piller, Charles and Yamamoto, Keith R. *Gene Wars* (1988).

a) p. 25. b) p. 43.

46. Cited in: *Chronicle of Higher Education*, May 4, 1988, p. A8.

47. U.S. Department of Defense. *Annual Report, Fiscal Year 1982*, pp. 60-61.

48. Garthoff, Raymond L. *Perspectives on the Strategic Balance* (1983), p. 9.

49. Miller, William Green (ed). *Toward a More Civil Society?* (1989).

a) p. xviii. b) p. 182.

50. Smith, Hedrick. *The Power Game* (1988).

a) p. 576. b) p. 640. c) p. 639. d) p. 640-641.

51. Yarmolinsky, Adam and Foster, Gregory D. *Paradoxes of Power* (1983), p. 137.

52. Campbell, Christopher. *Nuclear Weapons Fact Book* (1984), p. 53.

53. Quoted in: *The Sunday Oregonian*, 1983, November 20, p. F3. Other insiders put it this way: This new plan was totally nonnegotiable since it "required basic restructuring of Soviet strategic forces while meshing perfectly with Reagan's modernization plans." See: Destler, I. M. et al. *Our Own Worst Enemy* (1984), p. 234.

54. *Scientific American*, November 1982, p. 61.

55. Morris, Charles R. *Iron Destinies, Lost Opportunities* (1988).

a) p. 405. b) pp. 120-126.

56. Schwartz, William A. et al. *The Nuclear Seduction* (1990), p. 190.

57. *Detroit Free Press*, June 20, 1990, p. 6A.

58. Bosworth, Barry P. et al. (eds). *Critical Choices* (1989), p. 82.

59. *Detroit Free Press*, June 5, 1990, p. 9A.

60. *Detroit Free Press*, March 2, 1990, p. 1A.

61. Cited in: Dillon, G. M. *Defence Policy Making* (1988), p. 113.

62. Gorbachev, Mikhail S. *Toward a Better World* (1987), pp. 12-13.

63. James B. Conant, cited in: Lilienthal, David E. *The Journals of David E. Lilienthal. Vol. II. The Atomic Energy Years* (1964), p. 581.

64. Richard Ned Lebow in: Hanrieder, Wolfram F. (ed). *Technology, Strategy, and Arms control* (1986), p. 66.

65. For instance: "The composition and policy of the Reagan administra-

tion constitute a radical discontinuity in American political history." Knelman, F. H. *Reagan, God, and the Bomb* (1985), p. 14.

66. Mandelbaum, Michael (ed). *The Other Side of the Table* (1990), p. 189

67. Brodie, Bernard. *War and Politics* (1973), p. 216.

68. Gelb, Leslie H. with Betts, Richard K. *The Irony of Vietnam: The System Worked* (1979), pp. 100-104.

69. For a more detailed documentation and analysis of Hardline Supremacy, see: Barnet, Richard J. *Roots of War* (1972), pp. 109-115.

70. For a recent review, see Judith Ann Thornton's article in: Menon, Rajan and Nelson, Daniel N. (eds). *Limits to Soviet Power* (1989).

71. Luttwak, Edward N. *The Pentagon and the Art of War* (1984), p. 286.

72. Commoner, Barry. *The Closing Circle* (1974; Bantam edition).

73. John P. Holdren. In: Cohen, Avner and Lee, Steven (eds). *Nuclear Weapons and the Future of Humanity* (1986), p. 76. Edward N. Luttwak agrees (*Strategy: The Logic of War and Peace*, 1987, p. 186): "Arms control . . . does not restrain the competitive impulse but merely diverts it."

74. Both candidates possibly believed that the gaps they were talking about actually existed, but this is not the point. The point is: of the millions of competent Americans who might have been willing to serve a stint in the White House, how did we come to select men with such dangerous and incorrect opinions?

According to Daniel Elsberg (in: Thompson, E. P. and Smith, Dan, eds. *Protest and Survive*, 1981, pp. vii, viii): "In mid-1961, the year of the projected 'missile gap' favoring the Russians, the United States had within range of Russia about 1000 tactical bombers and 2000 intercontinental bombers, 40 ICBMS, 48 Polaris missiles, and another 100 intermediate range missiles based in Europe. The Soviets had at that time some 190 intercontinental bombers and exactly *four* ICBMs: four 'soft,' nonalert, liquid-fueled ICBMs at one site at Plesetsk that was vulnerable to a small attack with conventional weapons." In Elsberg's view, this represented American nuclear superiority "so overwhelming as to amount to monopoly."

75. See Michael T. Klare's article in: Menon, Rajan and Nelson, Daniel N. (eds). *Limits to Soviet Power* (1989).

76. A more recent illustration of this and other tactics can be found in: Rosefielde, Steven. *False Science* (1987).

77. Cox, Arthur M. *Russian Roulette* (1982), pp. 104-105.

78. Taubman, William, and Taubman, Jane. *Moscow Spring* (1989), p. 57.

Chapter 8: BRINKMANSHIP AND IMPERIALISM?

1. Cited in: Haldeman, Harry R. (Bob) *The Ends of Power* (1978), p. 83.

2. Quoted in: Wittner, Lawrence S. *Rebels Against War* (1969), pp. 180-181.

3. Capek, Karel. *War with the Newts* (first published in 1936; the text gives a slightly modified version of M. & R. Weatherall's translation), p. 340.

4. Malcolmson, Robert W. *Nuclear Fallacies* (1985).
a) Bernard Brodie, quoted on p. 13. b) Bernard Brodie, quoted on p. 44. c) John Foster Dulles, quoted on p. 44. d) General Curtis LeMay, quoted on p. 53. e) Colin S. Gray, quoted on p. 15. f) p. 16.

5. Quoted in: Bottome, Edgar. *The Balance of Terror* (1986; 2nd edition), p. 34.

6. Pericles in a 430 B.C. speech to his fellow Athenians. Paraphrased in: Thucydides. *The Peloponnesian War* (Benjamin Jowett's translation), bk. II, 63.

7. Henry Kissinger, cited on p. 117 of: Rumble, Greville. *The Politics of Nuclear Defence* (1985).

8. Laird, Robbin F. *The Soviet Union, the West and the Nuclear Arms Race*, (1986), p. 53.

9. Luttwak, Edward N. *The Pentagon and the Art of War* (1986).
a) p. 231. b) pp. 122-123.

10. John P. Holdren in: Cohen, Avner and Lee, Steven (eds). *Nuclear Weapons and the Future of Humanity* (1986), pp. 41-83.
a) p. 46. b) p. 48.

11. Bundy, McGeorge. *Danger and Survival* (1988).
a) p. 94. b) pp. 239; 278-80.

12. Leitenberg, Milton. In: Eide, Asbjorn and Thee, Marek. *Problems of Contemporary Militarism* (1980).
a) p. 395. b) p. 389.

13. Schwartz, William A. et al. *The Nuclear Seduction* (1990).
a) p. 225. b) quoted on p. 137. c) p. 138. d) p. 64.

14. Blechman, Barry M. and Kaplan, Stephen S. *Force without War* (1978), pp. 48, 51.

15. Joseph J. Romm. In: Tsipis, Kosta et al. (eds). *Arms Control Verification* (1986), p. 37.

16. Dillon, G. M. *Defence Policy Making* (1988), p. 66.

17. Chaliand, Gerard. *Report from Afghanistan* (1982), pp. 7-8.

18. I cannot document this statement in this book. It is distilled from documents of the State Department, from the writings of many former State Department officials, and from the writings of a large random sample of Western scholars. Interested readers can simply study in detail American relations with *any* poor country and judge for themselves. Alternatively, they can begin with the following factual accounts. Greece: Wittner, Lawrence, S. *American Intervention in Greece; 1943-1949* (1982); Stavrianos, L. S. *Greece: American Dilemma and Opportunity* (1952). Vietnam: The best study I have come across is Bernard Brodie's brief account in his *War and Politics* (1973). Other accounts of this tragedy can be found in: Karnow, Stanley. *Vietnam: A History* (1983); Lederer, William, J. *Our Own Worst Enemy* (1968).

19. Whetten, Nathan L. *Guatemala: The Land and the People* (1961).
a) p. 211. b) p. 86. c) p. 160.

20. Fried, Jonathan L. et al. (eds). *Guatemala in Rebellion* (1983).
a) p. 104. b) p. 43.

21. Immerman, Richard H. *The CIA in Guatemala* (1982).
a) p. 24. b) p. 44. c) pp. 49-50. d) p. 86. e) p. 5. f) pp. 171-172.
g) Daniel Graham, quoted on p. 186.

22. Findling, John E. *Close Neighbors, Distant Friends* (1987).
a) p. 92. b) p. 90. c) p. 109. d) p. 112. e) p. 180. f) p. 178.
23. Blasier, Cole. *The Hovering Giant: U.S. Responses to Revolutionary Change in Latin America* (1976).
a) p. 55. b) p. 154. c) pp. 59-60. d) pp. 62-63. e) p. 158 (quoting a Soviet publication).
24. Grieb, Kenneth J. *Guatemalan Caudillo, the Regime of Jorge Ubico* (1979), pp. 7, 8, 248-250.
25. It should come to us as no great surprise that in 1954, when the oligarchs regained power, they decreed the burning of Victor Hugo's *Les Miserables* on the ground of subversiveness. What is surprising, however, is that they left intact the Bible, which is, after all, far more subversive. See for example the laws in the Old Testament regarding debtors (*Leviticus* 25: 39-43) and gleaning (*Leviticus* 19:9-10), or Jesus' strong egalitarian sentiments (Matthew 19:21-24).
26. John Weeks in: Di Palma, Giuseppe and Whitehead, Laurence (eds). *The Central American Impasse* (1986).
a) p. 114. b) p. 123. c) p. 117. d) p. 126.
27. Schlesinger, Stephen and Kinzer, Stephen. *Bitter Fruit* (1982), p. 181.
28. Alan Riding, quoted in: *The Bulletin of the Atomic Scientists*, October 1983, p. 12.
29. Organization of American States. *Report on the Situation of Human Rights in the Republic of Guatemala* (1983).
a) p. 1. b) p. 41. c) p. 69.
30. Excerpted from letters of Stuart Gold and Marc Grant to the *New York Times*, November 30, 1990, p. A14
31. *Natural History*, November 1990, p. 35.
32. Wilkie, James W. and Lowey, James (eds). *Statistical Abstracts of Latin America*, 1987, vol. 25.
33. Chomsky, Noam. *Necessary Illusions* (1989), p. 268.
34. Organization of American States. *The Situation of Human Rights in Cuba, Seventh Report* (1983).
a) p. 181. b) p. 182.
35. Menon, Rajan and Nelson, Daniel N. (eds). *Limits to Soviet Power* (1989), p. 193.
36. Lederer, William, J. *Our Own Worst Enemy* (1968), pp. 66-67.
37. Ramazani, Rouhollah K. *The United States and Iran* (1982), pp. 69-70.
38. Bialer, Seweryn. *The Soviet Paradox* (1986), p. 278.

Chapter 9: ROOTS OF COLLECTIVE MISBEHAVIOR

1. Quoted in: *The Metro Times* (Detroit), July 13-19, 1988, p. 11.
2. Myrdal, Alva. *The Game of Disarmament* (1982 Pantheon Books revised edition), pp. xv, xvi.
3. This passage is taken from a 1776 letter by Adam Smith to William Strahan, recounting a conversation with David Hume seventeen days before

Hume's death. See: Hume, David. *Essays: Moral, Political and Literary* (an 1898 reprinting, edited by Green, T. H. and Grose, T. H.).

4. Djilas, Milovan. *The New Class* (1957), p. 56.

5. T. R. Malthus, 1798, cited in: Meek, Ronald L. *Marx and Engels on Malthus* (1953), p. 15.

6. Dubos, R. *Man Adapting* (1965), p. 359.

7. Richard Peto in: Peto, R. and Schneiderman, M. (eds). *Quantification of Occupational Cancer* (1981), p. xiv.

8. Herbert York (*Race to Oblivion*, 1970, p. 235), a former Director of Defense Research and Engineering in the Department of Defense, provides extensive documentation for his assertion that "when the principal programs or activities of . . . [defense-related] organizations are threatened, they react as if endowed with the instincts of living beings."

According to historian Richard J. Barnet (*Roots of War*, 1972, p. 137), the decisions made by the men who define the national interest "can be understood only by relating them to the struggles of bureaucratic politics. Bureaucracies respond to their own inner logic and to their own laws. Bureaucracies lose touch with the original purposes for which they are founded, and bureaucratic momentum often carries men far beyond the point to which they originally intend to go." See also: Capra, Fritjof. *The Turning Point* (1982), pp. 221-222. Jacobsen, Carl G. *The Nuclear Era* (1982), p. 118.

9. Yarmolinsky, Adam and Foster, Gregory D. *Paradoxes of Power* (1983).

   a) p. 31. b) p. 44. c) p. 39.

10. Quoted in: Gelb, Leslie H. with Betts, Richard K. *The Irony of Vietnam: The System Worked* (1979), p. 310.

11. Fallows, James. *National Defense* (1981), pp. 76-77.

12. Brodie, Bernard. *War and Politics* (1973), pp. 481-483.

On the question of brilliance, another analyst observes: "I was struck by how little 'edge' most of the generals seemed to have to their characters, how bland most of them seemed, not only in comparison with the captains and colonels beneath them, but also compared to successful men and women in other fields." (Fallows, James. *National Defense*, 1981, p. 122).

13. Smith, Hedrick. *The Power Game* (1988).

   a) p. 196. b) p. 156. c) p. 155. d) Lloyd Cutler on p. 253. e) pp. 188-189.

14. Egginton, J. *The Poisoning of Michigan* (1980).

15. Congress of the United States, Office of Technology Assessment. *Technologies and Management Strategies for Hazardous Waste Control* (1983), p. 6.

16. Miller, G. Tyler, Jr. *Living in the Environment*, (1987; 5th edition), p. 503.

17. *Newsweek*, July 11, 1988, p. 22.

18. *Detroit Free Press*, May 10, 1990, p. 12A.

19. This is a widely shared view. For instance, according to a Justice Department study, nearly three out of four *retired* corporate executives believe that government regulations of industry are necessary (cited in *Common Cause Magazine*, May/June 1983, p. 8).

20. Parkinson, C. Northcote. *Parkinson's Law* (from Preface to the 1957 edition).

21. Collingridge, David. *The Social Control of Technology* (1980).
a) pp. 16-17. b) pp. 12, 183.

22. Popper, Karl. *The Open Society and its Enemies*, vol. 2. *Hegel and Marx*, (1966; 5th edition).
a) Arthur Schopenhauer, quoted in Chap. 12, I, p. 33.

23. Robert Cahn and Patricia L. Cahn. In: United States Council on Environmental Quality and the Department of State. *The Global 2000 Report to the President of the U.S.* (1980), vol. II, p. 685.

24. Quarles, John. *Cleaning Up America: An Insider's View of the Environmental Protection Agency* (1976), excerpted from pp. xv, xvi, 174, 242, 243.

25. *Public Citizen.*
a) Fall 1983, p. 6. b) Spring 1984, p. 6.

26. Malbin, Michael J. (ed). *Money and Politics in the United States* (1984).
a) David Adamany, p. 105. b) Gary C. Jacobson, p. 65.

27. Adams, Gordon. *The Politics of Defense Contracting* (1982).
a) quoted on p. 112. b) p. 77. c) p. 24.

28. Cox, Arthur M. *Russian Roulette* (1982), pp. 63-64.

29. Senators Barry Goldwater and John Stennis, quoted in: *The Wall Street Journal*, July 18, 1986, p. 1.

30. Richard Reeves in: *Detroit Free Press*, March 22, 1990, p. 11A.

31. *The Sunday Oregonian* (November 27, 1983), p. A16.

32. Greene, Robert W. *The Sting Man: Inside Abscam* (1981), p. 6.

33. James P. Gannon. *The Detroit News*, November 16, 1990, pp. 1A, 6A.

34. Adamany, David W. and Agree, George E. *Political Money* (1975), pp. x, 7, 42.

35. David Cortwright in a letter to *Sane* supporters.

36. Huxley, Aldous. *Brave New World Revisited* (1958).
a) pp. 54-55. b) quoted on p. 32. c) pp. 33-35. d) p. 107.

37. *Newsweek*, September 12, 1988, pp. 22-23.

38. Steinbeck, John. *Cannery Row* (1945), Chapter XXIII.

39. From James Barton Adams' poem: "Bill's in Trouble."

40. *Statistical Abstracts of the United States* (1987; 107th edition).

41. Paraphrased in Thucydides, *The Peloponnesian War*, bk. II, 39. The translation is Karl R. Popper's (*The Open Society and its Enemies*).

42. Albert Einstein (1948), quoted in: Nathan, Otto and Norden, Heinz (eds). *Einstein on Peace* (1960), p. 502.

43. Frankland, Mark. *Khrushchev* (1967), pp. 159-160.

44. William Dorman and an anonymous co-author, quoted in: Rubin, Barry. *Paved With Good Intentions* (1980), p. 339.

45. Lederer, William, J. *Our Own Worst Enemy* (1968), p. 86.

46. Bagdikian, Ben H. *The Media Monopoly* (1987; second edition).
a) pp. 169-173. b) p. xvi. c) p. 4.

47. *Life on the Mississippi*, Chapter XIV.

48. Like so many other uncomfortable truths about our ailing democracy, my portrayal of the media is "controversial." See, for example, S. Robert Lichter and Stanley Rothman in: Pfaltzgraff, Robert L., Jr. and Ra'anan, Uri

(eds). *National Security Policy* (1984), pp. 265-282. See also: Bozell, L. Brent, III and Baker, Brent H. (eds). *And That's the Way It Is(n't)* (1990).

But I shall not tire the reader with the media's countless apologists. Laying their various claims to rest would, for one thing, require a whole book. There is in fact an organization—*Fair*—dedicated to Fairness and Accuracy in Reporting. See, for instance, its January/February 1988 newsletter, *Extra*, regarding the *New York Times'* coverage of Central America.

The debate between the media's defenders and critics provides just one more illustration of our old ugly friend, the phony controversy. Long ago, my students taught me a valuable lesson: a shift in one's way of viewing the world is rarely achieved through abstract logical refutations; besides intelligence and openmindedness, the key requirement is familiarity with a few representative episodes which cannot possibly be reconciled with textbook myths. So, instead of armchair discussions of intellectually dishonest apologetics, let me mention a small fraction of the distortional episodes which came to my attention during the *single* week I was revising this chapter:

I. A study by John D. H. Downing, Chairman of the Communication Department, Hunter College, reports parallels between Soviet press coverage of the Afghanistan War and American mainstream press coverage of the Civil War in El Salvador. "Neither superpower's media may be said to offer a remotely satisfactory account of these Third World wars in which they are deeply embroiled" (*Chronicle of Higher Education*, July 27, 1988, p. A7).

II. Fact #1: General Electric manufactures nuclear reactors. Fact #2: General Electric acquired National Broadcasting Corporation (NBC) in 1986. Prediction: NBC's coverage of nuclear power will be even more biased than is generally the case in the U.S. media. Test #1: you might wish to monitor future NBC's coverage of the nuclear power controversy. Test #2: a retrospective analysis of any previous coverage. Here you can begin with an NBC program about France's secretive, government-owned, nuclear power industry (*Detroit Metro Times*, July 13-19, 1988, pp. 10-13). Note that the issue is not the desirability of nuclear power, but the inevitable praise this NBC program lavished on the French massive project. NBC's one-sided coverage is evident, for instance, not only from the divergence between this program and the views of vehement opponents of nuclear energy, but from the sharp contrast between this program and such balanced academic reviews as *Global 2000 Report to the President of the U.S.* or most introductory ecology texts (e.g., Miller, G. Tyler Jr. *Living in the Environment*, 6th edition; 1990). An update: Despite growing signs that nuclear power is the "largest managerial disaster in U.S. business history" (Miller, p. 404), for NBC, nuclear power remains "a long-time solution to the energy problem" (*Extra*, November/December 1990, p. 7).

Many more representative episodes, and an unanswerable indictment of the U.S. mainstream media, can be found in: Parenti, Michael. *Inventing Reality* (1986). Herman, Edward S. and Chomsky, Noam. *Manufacturing Consent* (1988). Chomsky, Noam. *Necessary Illusions* (1989). Lee, Martin A. and Solomon, Norman. *Unreliable Sources* (1990).

49. Fulbright, J. W. *The Pentagon Propaganda Machine* (1970).

a) pp. 45-46. In 1986, the number of veterans still stood at some 28 million (*Statistical Abstracts of the United States*, 1988; 108th edition, p. 327).

b) p. 12.

50. Brown, Harold. *Thinking about National Security* (1983), p. 60.

51. *Public Papers of the Presidents of the United States.* Dwight D. Eisenhower, 1960-61, pp. 1038-1039.

52. Edward Thompson in: Barnaby, Frank and Thomas, Geoffrey. (eds). *The Nuclear Arms Race—Control or Catastrophe?* (1982), p. 68.

53. Marc Pilisuk in: *The Bulletin of the Atomic Scientists*, November 1982, p. 16.

54. O'Keefe, Bernard J. *Nuclear Hostages* (1983), pp. 228-229.

55. Lars-Erik Nelson in: *Detroit Free Press*, March 2, 1990, p. 9A.

56. *Nature* (1983), vol. 302, pp. 558, 560A.

57. Quoted in Galbraith, John K. (1983) *The Anatomy of Power*, p. 24.

58. Chomsky, Noam. *Towards a New Cold War* (1982), pp. 67, 80, 81.

59. Bury, J. B. *A History of Greece* (1900), IX, 5, p. 366.

60. Quoted in: Farley, Christopher and Hodgson, David (compilers). *The Life of Bertrand Russell* (1972), p. 31.

61. Shure, Gerald H. et al. *Journal of Conflict Resolution*, vol. 9, no. 1, March 1965, pp. 106-117.

62. Unfortunately, owing to this social pressure, this study fails to distinguish the relative contributions of conformity and callousness.

63. See his essay "An outline of intellectual rubbish." In: Egner, Robert E. and Dennon, Lester E. (eds). *The Basic Writings of Bertrand Russell* (1961), p. 87.

64. Steinbeck, John. *The Winter of Our Discontent* (1961), p. 115.

65. Darley, John M. et al. *Psychology* (1988; 4th edition), p. 166.

66. Festinger, Leon et al. *When Prophecy Fails* (1956).

67. At this writing, the exact date is still uncertain. The view which I shall (somewhat arbitrarily) assume to be true, is that the U.S. conducted its first H-bomb test in February of 1954 and that the USSR conducted its first test in November of 1955 (Holloway, David. *The Soviet Union and the Arms Race*, 1983, p. 24). A conflicting opinion can be found in Medvedev, Zhores A. *Soviet Science* (1978), pp. 52, 147. According to Medvedev, "the explosion of a thermonuclear device of military design took place in the USSR on September 12, 1953, about six months earlier than in the United States (March, 1954)."

68. Ernest Partridge, in: Kunkel, Joseph C. and Klein, Kenneth H. *Issues in War and Peace* (1989), p. 88.

69. Bundy, McGeorge. *Danger and Survival* (1988), p. 76.

70. George W. Ball in: Miller, William Green. (ed.) *Toward a More Civil Society?* (1989), pp. 247-248.

71. Gorbachev, Mikhail S. *Toward a Better World* (1987), pp. 18-19.

72. Kuhn, Thomas S. *The Structure of Scientific Revolutions* (1970; 2nd edition). Many other examples of conceptual conservatism in science can be found in: Asimov, Isaac. *Asimov's New Guide to Science* (1984).

73. De Kruif, Paul. *Men Against Death* (1932), chap. 1.

74. Nissani, M. and Hoefler-Nissani, D. M. 1992, *Cognition & Instruction*, Vol. 9, #2.

75. Nissani, M. *Psychological Reports*, 1989, vol. 65, pp. 19-24.

76. Asch, Solomon E. *Psychological Monographs*, 1956, vol. 70, no. 9.

77. Dillon, G. M. (ed). *Defence Policy Making* (1988) p. 76.

78. Milgram, Stanley. *Obedience to Authority* (1974), p. 123.

79. I cannot go here into the underlying causes of conformity and obedience. For my part, I am convinced that the contribution of conceptual conservatism in both cases has been underrated (see Nissani, M. *American Psychologist*, vol. 45, pp. 1384-1385, 1990). But regardless of causes, the laboratory and real life evidence for conformity and obedience seem strong enough to justify their inclusion in the text.

80. Bauman, Zygmunt. *Modernity and the Holocaust* (1989), pp. 152, 122.

81. Lisa Peattie in: *The Bulletin of the Atomic Scientists*, March 1984, p. 34.

82. Solzhenitsyn, Alexander I. *The Gulag Archipelago* (1974), vol. I.
    a) pp. 173-174. b) p. 298.

83. Quoted in: Ferrell, Robert H. *American Diplomacy* (1975; third edition), p. 501.

Chapter 10: A SURGICAL REFORM STRATEGY

1. The words are Pierre Bezukhov's, *War and Peace*'s hero.

2. Iskander, Fazil. *The Goatibex Constellation* (translated into English in 1975 by Helen Burlingame), p. 43.

3. From his poem "Do Not Go Gently into that Good Night."

4. Vonnegut, Kurt Jr. *Cat's Cradle*, Chapter 110.

5. Alva Myrdal quoted in: Stockholm International Peace Research Institute. *World Armaments and Disarmament: SIPRI Yearbook* (1986), p. v.

6. Frank Barnaby. In: Barnaby, Frank and Thomas, Geoffrey (eds). *The Nuclear Arms Race—Control or Catastrophe?* (1982), p. 35.

7. Quarles, John. *Cleaning Up America: An Insider's View of the Environmental Protection Agency* (1976), pp. 174, 242.

8. For example, Jeremy J. Stone (in: Forsberg, Randall et al. *Seeds of Promise* (1983), p. vi) puts it thus: "Only an outraged and vigilant public can secure meaningful arms control. . . . Conversely, when the public is not up in arms, even constructive treaties like the SALT II treaty have trouble securing Congressional passage."

9. Like so many other ills, the typical specific reformer's narrow vision and optimism could be traced in part to lack of information, which, in this case, included lack of familiarity with the history of early struggles. I know many dedicated and sincere peace activists, for example, but have yet to meet one who actually read Lawrence S. Wittner's excellent history (1933-1983) of the American peace movement (*Rebels Against War*, Revised Edition, 1984).

10. Quoted in: Bonhoeffer, Dietrich. *The Cost of Discipleship* (1963; translated from the German by R. H. Fuller, second edition), p. 22.

11. Kennedy, John F. *Profiles in Courage* (1956), Chap. 1.

12. Hubert Humphrey quoted in: Adamany, David W. and Agree, George E. *Political Money* (1975), p. 8.

INDEX

A number alone stands for a page number. The combination number-slash-*n*-number stands for page number/*note* number. For instance, the entry "Acheson, D." can be found on p. 171; while the entry "Adams, G." begins on p. 305, *Notes and References* section, *note* 27.